Shall We Dance
Rediscovering Christ-Centered Standards

A Project Affirmation
Publication coordinated with

Hancock Center for
Youth Ministry at
La Sierra University

North American Division
Joint Boards of Education

La Sierra University Press

Piece of the Pie Ministries

Shall We Dance

Rediscovering Christ-Centered Standards

Edited by
Steve Case

Foreword by
V. Bailey Gillespie

Contributors

Steve Case
Vladimir Corea
Fred Crowell
Delwin Finch
Bill Knott
Esther Ramharacksingh Knott
Stephen Chavez
Dick Duerksen
Steve Daily
Willie Oliver
Timothy Gillespie
V. Bailey Gillespie
Amber Murphy
Noelene Pang
Caleb Rosado
Gary Russell
Celeste Ryan
Sharon Sheppard
Stuart Tyner
Adrian Westney

LA SIERRA
UNIVERSITY PRESS

Project Affirmation Series Editor:
V. Bailey Gillespie

Copy Editing: Sharon Churches
Cover Design: V. Bailey Gillespie
Book Design: Stuart Tyner
Manuscript Editor: Stuart Tyner

Copyright ©1996 by La Sierra University Press/North American Division of Seventh-day Adventists—Joint Boards of Education/John Hancock Center for Youth Ministry at La Sierra University and Steve Case

Cataloging-in-Publication Data
    Shall We Dance : Rediscovering Christ-Centered Standards / edited by Steve Case ; foreword by V. Bailey Gillespie.
        p. em.

    ISBN 0-944450-26-1

I. Amusements—Religious aspects—Christianity.
II. Standards, Religious. 1. Case, Steve. 2. Gillespie, V. Bailey (Virgil Bailey)
BV4587.S   9081172

Printed in the USA

LA SIERRA
UNIVERSITY PRESS
Riverside, CA 92515

Contents

Contents

Contents

Dedication

This book is dedicated to the many
youth leaders who grapple with these
issues as they lead their young people to Jesus.

May your tribe increase!

Foreword

V. Bailey Gillespie

It is just simply assumed that Christians have high and definite standards which govern their behavior. In a larger sense, most would argue that unless Christians have high standards, they have not fully grasped the nature of the responsibility inherent in the Gospel message. And it is not uncommon to see churches testing the validity of the power of the message of Christ by asking the question, "What are you doing with your life?" Because it is logical to assume that when one encounters the saving message of Jesus, one's life has to change. Adventists join the church in baptism agreeing with official statements of belief. Standards are not omitted.

This books recognizes that any behavior must be a product of a close Christ-centered relationship.

9

How do you establish clear, concise, detailed biblical standards as a Christian? This book, *Shall We Dance* clarifies the content of standards for young Christians and hints at the process whereby these standards—based on spiritual values— become motivators for their behavior.

[1]Charles M. Shelton, *Adolescent Spirituality: Pastoral Ministry for High School and College Youth* (New York: Crossroad, 1983), 61.

Young people, on the other hand, see at work in the church another set of standards. The inconsistency between the ideal and the actual practice is often dramatic. When youth encounter Jesus' call to "come, follow me," they encounter one of the cornerstones of adolescent spirituality. They believe that the radical change Jesus suggests will make them *be* different and act in a new way. Often in this quest they encounter "degrees" of commitment and behavior from their role models—pastors, teachers, other youth, parents, and friends. What seemed like such a clear call somehow clouds. Their behavior often drifts back to the median of their peers or family. Discouragement sets in, and some long for consistency or clarification. Often rejection or a creeping apathy toward lifestyle choices becomes their norm.

How do you establish clear, concise, detailed biblical standards as a Christian? This book, *Shall We Dance,* clarifies the content of standards for young Christians and hints at the process whereby these standards—based on spiritual values—become motivators for their behavior.

But this book is not written for youth alone. Adults will benefit from its counsel. Adolescents vary in their own understanding and reasoning about personal standards and values. The youth's developmental level influences how he or she perceives personal problems and life situations. Charles Shelton says, "It is helpful for the adults to be able to understand how an adolescent reasons about life dilemmas and moral problems."[1] So this book spends time not only talking about the biblical content and philosophical reasons to hold high standards as a Christian, it focuses on the process of developing and understanding one's own personal value system.

This books recognizes that any behavior must be a product of a close Christ-centered relationship—a relationship that focuses on the powerful life-changing grace of God and one that recognizes the significant individual character of the faith experience itself.

In this regard, standards oftentimes do not seem as set as many would like. In the massive research project for Seventh-day Adventist youth called *Valuegenesis* (a part of the Project Affirmation process in the North American Division) one thing that stands out is that Adventists focus on behavior so much that the power of the impact of the Gospel is often lost. Youth see behavior so central to the Adventist message that they have failed to recognize that behavior must flow naturally from a close, personal, life-giving relationship with the Lord of the universe—their personal friend Jesus Christ.

Roger L. Dudley, reporting on *Valuegenesis* warns us, "Make no mistake. How we handle church standards is the crucial issue in the determination of whether or not we will retain the rising generations in the church. Acceptance of Adventist standards was the second most important variable in the entire study in predicting whether or not the students intended to remain as Adventists by age 40 and the most important in predicting denominational loyalty."[1] He

This books recognizes that any behavior must be a product of a close Christ-centered relationship

[1] Roger L. Dudley with V. Bailey Gillespie, *Valuegenesis: Faith in the Balance* (Riverside, CA: La Sierra University Press, 1992), 147.

goes on to claim that "Rules and standards are the 'stickiest' point in the whole youth value arena, or, as I like to suggest, it is the 'hinge of retention.'"[1]

What Does the Research Tell Us?

Some have suggested that the massive research project that explored 15,500 youth in Adventist schools attempts to do away with standards. As the research base grows with additional churches, schools, and youth groups completing the Short Form of *Valuegenesis*, additional thousands seem to feel the same way as the primary sample. This shallow criticism shows how difficult it is to clarify the portrait of Adventist youth to the church at large and to open up this topic for mature discussion. If anything is clear after looking at the discussion which is evoked by research on standards, it is that *the process by which we understand and communicate Adventist standards must be reordered.* We somehow have failed to put Christ at the center of our standards. In His place we have placed historical precedence, "we've always done it that way" mentality, alongside "you're tearing down the pillars" rhetoric. Instead, we must look at what youth are saying about the centrality of behavior in their religious experience. Just obeying without any reason simply won't cut it with this generation of young Christians anymore.

Valuegenesis research points out some problems with an approach to religious life that is solely focused on

[1] *Ibid.*

> We somehow have failed to put Christ at the center of our standards. In His place we have placed historical precedence, "we've always done it that way" mentality, alongside "you're tearing down the pillars" rhetoric.

behavioral issues: (1) When behavior becomes central, the message of Jesus is lost; (2) If behavior is central and we note that some standards start to shift due to cultural reasons or clarification of biblical principles, there is a tendency to judge the complete message as meaningless; (3) If we have made behavioral standards the test of orthodoxy, we apply a subjective criterion that can be interpreted personally by whoever is in authority. In addition, when behavioral standards are the most talked about issues in a church, we just never have time to balance behavioral discussions with deep thoughtful reflection on the power of the grace of God at work in creation.

Most youth accept some church standards and seem to reject other ones. This points to the confusion about standards that youth face. While visiting one group of students at a Christian high school during focus groups, the students shared some amazing attitudes about church standards and their view of what constitutes an Adventist Christian. We had just concluded a discussion about theater attendance. Upon learning that all fourteen in the group attended movies regularly, with the exception of one young woman who admitted she watched almost everything on video at home because her parents did not like her going to the actual theater, the discussion veered to a dialogue about how to witness as a Christian. One young person shared how at school sporting events with other high school students the opportunity often came where they could share their belief system. We probed how one would do

Valuegenesis **research points out some problems with an approach to religious life that is solely focused on behavioral issues.**

• **When behavior becomes central, the message of Jesus is lost;**

• **If behavior is central and we note that some standards start to shift due to cultural reasons or clarification of biblical principles, there is a tendency to judge the complete message as meaningless;**

• **If we have made behavioral standards the test of orthodoxy, we apply a subjective criteria that can be interpreted personally by whoever is in authority.**

Now this generation wants biblical, Christ-centered answers and needs to see how mature Christians decide what is right and wrong. It is our intention that *Shall We Dance* will promote this quest.

Other publications in this series of titles include:

Valuegenesis :
Faith in the Balance,
by Roger Dudley with
V. Bailey Gillespie

Project Affirmation:
Teaching Values
by Doris and Roland Larson

Project Affirmation:
Perspectives on Values,
Edited by V. Bailey Gillespie

Call 1-800-785-HCYM to order your copies

that, and the answers were revealing of what may be typical of Adventist youth today: "I tell them about Adventists," the youth said.

"What do you tell them?" we queried.

"We tell them that Adventists have high standards. And we usually say that Adventists, for example, don't go to movies!"

Obviously this group of youth was working with a unique view of Adventism, especially since they had just revealed they regularly attended the movies. They were operating with a different definition. This definition was not based in reality, but in a historic position that even their parents did not adhere to, according to the focus group discussion.

The conclusion of pointing out the conflict in reasoning moved the discussion to the need of a clear and detailed process which would clarify the reasons for viewing and for not viewing. This book recognizes this tension. We have been told, traditionally, Adventists behave a certain way. But now, this generation wants biblical, Christ-centered answers and needs to see how mature Christians decide what is right and wrong. It is our intention that *Shall We Dance* will promote this quest.

V. Bailey Gillespie
Hancock Center for Youth Ministry

Introduction

Steve Case

This book is *not* an official statement of the Seventh-day Adventist Church regarding standards and values.

Rather it is an invitation to open discussion concerning lifestyle issues. Hopefully even better biblical principles will become the bedrock for our distinctive lifestyle as we move from the peripheral, but ever-present issues to the weightier matters of living the Christian life.

You'll find the authors inviting you to discover the principles for Christian behavior in the Scriptures and to examine where you stand on each issue, even if that means asking questions about previously held positions.

The chapters in this book can be utilized as openings for profitable discussions. This will require an openness to

This book is *not* an official statement of the Seventh-day Adventist Church regarding standards and values.

15

Please accept this as an invitation for a personal evaluation of where you stand on these issues, especially if you haven't examined your perspectives recently.

other people's views, a tolerance for divergent understandings, and a personal commitment to apply the principles to all aspects of one's life. For those who take this seriously, beware! This easily could result in a much more stringent lifestyle than the subcultural norm.

But this doesn't mean that the resulting opinions should be used to tell others what to do. Don't let your lifestyle become the norm for others. Gently probe others to identify the principles by which they live their Adventist Christianity; and be ready to share yours, always open to fresh applications to your current life.

Each section of the book has several chapters related to a given lifestyle issue. One chapter identifies biblical principles and the location of most principles in Scripture. Another chapter reveals how an individual has dealt with the issue on a personal basis. Some chapters present one person's understanding of a Christ-centered perspective on the topic.

The diversity inherent in this approach is intended to be helpful in reaching a greater number of people, depending on which point of reference they are most open to at the time of their reading. Don't expect uniformity with the variety of writers who comprise this team! Hopefully, by coming to a clearer consensus on the principles of Adventist living while providing and protecting personal applications of those principles—we will be able to move on to the bigger issues of Christianity, and Adventism in particular.

Special People

I'd like to thank Greg Madson, a seminary student and my graduate assistant at the Youth Resource Center at Andrews University, who was my personal sounding board on these issues during the mid to late 80s at Andrews University. The various writers included are people I admire for their courage and ability to articulate their understanding on some potentially volatile topics.

Another note of thanks goes to the many people who purchased this book before it was printed. As deadline after deadline passed, they kept hoping that it would really come to fruition one day. Thank you for your patience. I'm hopeful the wait has been worth the product you now have.

And "Thank You" to the Hancock Center for Youth Ministry, La Sierra University Press, and the daring leadership, insights, and suggestions from Bailey Gillespie and Stuart Tyner. These two individuals were able to recruit writers and secure several chapters that would otherwise be missing from this book. Stuart Tyner deserves a special thanks in reworking chapters and editing manuscripts to reflect the best style and tone. Sharon Churches, the University Press copy editor has my heartfelt thanks, too. The book has taken a very different shape and is much more "user friendly" due to their input. And thanks for the gentle nudges to stay with this project!

When work on this started nearly a decade ago, there was a certain amount of fear that the book would be

This book is full of user friendly information about lifestyle issues

The purpose is to live for Jesus by identifying and then living by Christ-centered, biblical principles.

divisive if used by the church. That would certainly run counter to its purpose of inviting people to live for Jesus by identifying and then living by Christ-centered, biblical principles when it comes to lifestyle issues.

The response to the cassette tape series *Shall We Dance*, released prior to this volume has been encouraging! Church leaders, pastors, parents, educators, and youth have taken the information as one way of becoming informed and challenged to live for Christ. This volume is much more complete. For that I'm grateful. I'm hopeful that the book will have a similar impact, sparking worthwhile discussions among groups of Adventists and motivating individuals to live for Jesus.

Steve Case
Piece of the Pie Ministries

Section 1

Thinking About Standards

*Roger L. Dudley with V. Bailey Gillespie, *Faith in the Balance (Riverside*, CA: La Sierra University Press, 1992), 549-50.

[1] Since the conception of this book, Martin Weber's two books on Adventist lifestyle issues have been published (*Adventist Hot Potatoes* [Boise, ID: Pacific Press], 1991 and *More Adventist Hot Potatoes* [Boise, ID: Pacific Press], 1992). This volume, *Shall We Dance* deals primarily with lifestyle issues not addressed in his books.

Section 1
Thinking About Standards

This book focuses on lifestyle issues and their biblical roots which help us build a Christ-centered Seventh-day Adventist lifestyle. The core of Seventh-day Adventism—it's foundation—is the Gospel of Jesus Christ. Some would question spending time on peripheral issues when the crux of Adventism is the Gospel. Perhaps this is why so little has been written about these volatile areas.[1] However, lifestyle issues need to be addressed for at least several reasons: First of all, biblical faith is living faith. It moves beyond mental assent to the way we live. How tragic it would be for us to believe the doctrines of Adventism and yet fail to see their implications or to apply them to their lives. Still others know and live the applications but have difficulty identifying the sources for their reasons for behavior.

A Parable

Once upon a time there were only two colors—black and white. The beauty of this lay in its simplicity. But as life became more complex, people learned how to mix the two colors, yielding various hues of gray. Those preferring to maintain a simple lifestyle had to choose between several alternatives. They could move to a secluded area that permitted only black and white (no gray). They could identify each hue of grey as either "more black" or "more white." Some even went so far as to rename the various hues of gray as "black" or "white," thereby denying that grey existed. In all the ruckus, some chose to ignore the entire issue. For some reason they lacked the perception of the importance of gray. Many of the young people had difficulty identifying black and white since most of their world seemed to consist of grey.

Although the topic of gray always seemed to stir a great discussion, it wasn't until people began to write about it that things really became heated. There seemed to be greater agreement when people spoke about grey, than when they wrote about it. Some wrote about *grey*, while others referred to the color *gray*. How could the trumpet give "that certain ring" when there was confusion regarding something as important as the issue itself: *gray* (or *grey*, depending on which side you would choose). This naming assisted in the clarification of this vital issue. Those for gray were labeled "conservi*als*," while those for

Others know and live the applications but have difficulty identifying the sources for their reasons for behavior.

21

grey were called *liber*atives." Each person could be labeled clearly as a conserv*ial* or a *liber*ative, depending on who did the labeling and what they meant by it.

As the sides became more clearly demarcated, not only individuals but also schools and geographical areas of the country became labeled. Leaders formed committees to ensure that the next generation would fight to the end to maintain gray (or grey, depending on which side you had chosen). It wasn't long until both sides reached for their ultimate argument: God called it gray (or grey, depending on which side you had pledged your devotion). Some threatened to possibly initiate a reformed grey denomination. Others began their desktop publishing and mass mailing to call everyone back to their true roots and calling to be gray (or grey, depending on which side you knew God was on). Still others decided gray wasn't so important and lost complete interest in even black and white.

The following generation became bored. They seemed to consider these "pillars" unimportant. A few, while reading some of the alternative meanings in the Great Dictionary discovered that gray could be grey and grey could be gray. You can imagine their surprise at finding both spellings in the same book. Hadn't their parents read the entire book? Could they be so blind as to see only one way of spelling the same thing? It was quite a discovery, but even the new generation didn't realize that they were looking at God's creation as black and white and gray/grey, while God still saw it in living color.

> **As the sides became more clearly demarcated, not only individuals but also schools and geographical areas of the country became labeled.**

22

How This All Began

With the advance of technology and the resulting age of mass communication and telecommunication, more cultures are interacting, leading to conflicts between religious and cultural mores. Such conflicts may occur as people from various religions of the world interact, whether it be through immigration or ethnocentrism. Other conflicts may come through the cultural differences between generations. By the time a consensus has been developed, it easily has been outdated.

During the mid-late 1980s, the Youth Resource Center at Andrews University conducted youth ministry training seminars across North America in which participants completed a worksheet called "Christian Freedom" (see Appendix A). On it they made decisions of "permissible" or "not permissible" regarding several issues that would be considered "gray areas" for many Adventists. At most seminars at least one person would call out, "Should I answer this for me or the way Adventists are supposed to respond?" Seminar leaders allowed either option because the purpose of the worksheet was to stimulate a realization of the tension in the area of lifestyle issues.

When the group of participants would be asked, "Do other Christians view it the same way you do?" invariably the majority would shake their heads with a hand-in-the-cookie-jar "no." In other words, the majority of seminar participants considered themselves to be different from the

With the advance of technology and the resulting age of mass communication and telecommunication, more cultures are interacting, leading to conflicts between religious and cultural mores.

"Should I answer this for me or the way Adventists are supposed to respond?"

established norm. For some reason the participants failed to realize that most of them fit into what might be the true (silent) majority, but either they had fallen prey to a vocal minority that claims to speak for the Body of believers or their perceptions of the majority are distorted.

Valuegenesis

Data from the Project Affirmation survey, *Valuegenesis*, confirm this. In the past we tended to group all lifestyle issues, such as theater attendance, rock music, alcohol, jewelry, premarital sex, caffeinated drinks, dancing, and Sabbath keeping, into one basket labeled "standards." *Valuegenesis* has shown that we can no longer do this. Through a statistical process called factor analysis, we have found that there are now three baskets for Seventh-day Adventist (lifestyle) standards. Various lifestyle issues called standards are grouped into three baskets or clusters.[1]

The first cluster could be labeled "substance abuse," for it contains standards such as illegal drugs, tobacco, beer, liquor, and wine. It's easy to see how these group together. The second cluster we'll label "Adventist lifestyle" because many of its components include uniquely Adventist standards, such as Sabbath observance, no unclean meats, sex only within marriage, and modest clothing. The third cluster has been given the label "Adventist popular culture" because many consider its elements part of the popular culture. This cluster includes standards such

[1] According to Dennis Child in *The Essentials of Factor Analysis* (London: Holt, Rinehart and Winston, 1970), 1, "Factor analysis is the orderly simplification of a number of interrelated measures." When a number of variables have a lot in common, they form a factor. In the past we thought all standards shared enough in common to form one factor. From the *Valuegenesis* study we have discovered that Seventh-day Adventist standards fall into three groups ("factors") rather than one.

as jewelry, caffeinated drinks, rock music, dancing theater attendance, wedding rings, competitive sports, and TV/videos.

Some people lament that we no longer hold to our standards. Such comments are both true and false. When viewed as three clusters of standards, we can more accurately assess what is being retained and what seems to be lost. The first cluster, "substance abuse (drugs)," still contains a very high degree of commitment by Adventist young people in their understanding of what it means to be an Adventist. In their view, Adventists don't drink, do drugs, or smoke. This doesn't mean they haven't experimented with these substances. It means their understanding of Adventism includes freedom from these substances.

The second cluster, "Adventist lifestyle," continues to hold a strong majority of Adventist young people. For example, young people might believe in the sanctity of the Sabbath and the corresponding special observance of the day, but the details of how they keep the Sabbath holy could be very different from adults, and misunderstood as a result. Still, a clear majority hold to the second cluster of standards, though not as highly as the first cluster.

A dramatic and significant decline can be seen with each of the items in the third cluster, "Adventist popular culture." The vast majority of Adventist young people do *not* hold these to be part of Adventism. When people comment that the standards are slipping, as far as the third cluster is concerned, they're gone. This doesn't mean they can't be reclaimed. It simply indicates that Adventist

Some people lament that we no longer hold to our standards. Such comments are both true and false.

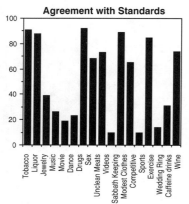

Figure 1— Youth (SDA Youth in SDA Schools Grades 6-12) Agreement with standards—from *Valuegenesis* research

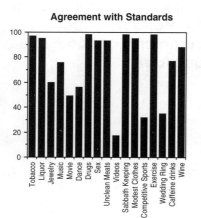

Figure 2. Agreement with Standards Parents of SDA Youth in SDA Schools grades 6-12—from *Valuegenesis* research

young people buy into the first two clusters of standards, but not the third cluster. This book deals with standards in each of the clusters.

Because the data from *Valuegenesis* provided a perspective not only from Adventist young people in grades 6-12 in North America but also parents, teachers, principals and pastors, the researchers decided to compare the lifestyle scores of these different groups. As might be expected, the greatest slippage from full agreement for each standard came from the young people rather than adults. Since there continues to be high agreement on a majority of the specific items, tracing the cumulative scores yields a chart that looks somewhat like a mountain range. The high levels of agreement form the peaks and the low levels form the valleys (see Figure 1).

We traced the same standards with parents. While their slippage wasn't as great, the contour of the agreement showed remarkable similarity with the youth. In other words, the parents scored higher but questioned the same standards as the youth (see Figure 2). The teachers showed a similar contour, with almost identical scores as the parents (see Figure 3). School principals scored slightly higher than teachers but maintained the same contour (see Figure 4). Pastors scored the highest of any group; yet they replicated the same contour, showing that they question the same standards as do the principals, the teachers, the parents, and the youth (see Figure 5). When all five groups are stacked on top of each other, the similarity in their contour and the fluctuation of agreement and disagreement with the various standards is remarkable (see Figure 6).

The question begs to be asked, "who are we fooling?" When somebody says Adventists don't go to the movies, we should correct them by informing them that they are not alone. In fact, 19 percent of Adventist young people would agree with them. But they shouldn't think or even pretend that they are speaking for most Adventists with such a statement. The fact is, most Adventists *do* go to the movies. It's time to deal with the issues rather than pretending they don't exist. And with the behavior well into habit patterns, commanding a change is more likely to exacerbate the problem than to correct it. The better approach is to begin to dialogue about these issues.

Is This Book For You?

This book isn't necessarily for everyone. Perhaps it is for you. The reader should be aware of the target groups for whom this book was written. First of all, this book is for those who work with youth who ask "Why?" to Adventist lifestyle issues. This includes youth pastors, academy and college administrators, teachers, deans, chaplains, youth leaders, parents, and others who work with youth.

This book is also for young adults, baby boomers, and others who question Adventist lifestyle issues. For example, at one Youth Resource Center seminar when participants shared the questions their youth were asking

The fact is, most Adventists *do* go to the movies. It's time to deal with the issues rather than pretending they don't exist.

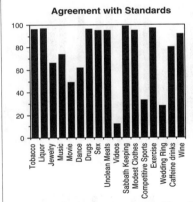

Figure 3. Agreement with Standards Parents of Teachers of SDA Youth in SDA Schools—From *Valuegenesis* research

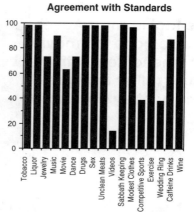

Figure 4. Principals of SDA Youth in SDA Schools

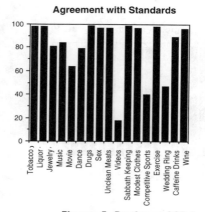

Figure 5. Pastors of SDA Youth in SDA Schools

[1] See Matthew 7.

regarding Sabbath activities, one adult demonstrated her personal interest when she queried, "Is it okay to have sexual intercourse on the Sabbath?" If her youth really were asking that question, perhaps the issue she should deal with is sexuality rather than Sabbath observance. This participant showed that many adults have an interest in the same lifestyle issues, especially if they have teenagers—a group that seems to spur such interests.

This book is for those who desire to live the Adventist Christian lifestyle. It is not written as a cop-out for those who profess Adventism while denying the lifestyle that accompanies that faith.

Finally, this book is for those who live at the level of principled, integrated lives. This corresponds to those who propose stages of moral development. One of the challenging contributions of this theory is the focus on motives rather than behavior. Christ denounced some of the piety of the religious leaders of his day because of the selfish motives for their good behavior. On the other hand, the religious leaders denounced Christ because of his law-breaking Sabbath behavior, although his motive was one of salvation for others.

While it is dangerous for humans to guess the motives of the behavior of others, it is at least equally dangerous to make value judgments on behavior alone. Some would argue that behavior and motives "aren't any of your business." (With a cursory reference to "judge not.") [1] Perhaps they aren't. But it is a thoughtful person who resists the superficial judgement of behavior without discovering the motive(s) from those involved. Too often, behavior is all that is needed to stimulate creative thought on the part of others. In this regard, 1 Samuel 16:7 (man looks on the outward appearance, but the Lord looks on the heart) could be loosely translated, "God reads the motives, but people look at the behavior—and they surely do look!"

Questions Youth Are Asking

• What difference does all this discussion about standards make?

• Wouldn't we be better off just letting people live how they want to live?

• What does the Bible say about standards?

• How come everyone seems to pick on young people? Adults are doing the same types of things in their own way, aren't they?

• My parents did the same things I do, so why don't you just leave me alone?

• How come the rules always change?

• Why doesn't the Bible plainly spell out the standards for us, like the Ten Commandments?

• Aren't things different for us compared to the first Seventh-day Adventists?

• What's the difference between going to the movies and watching something on a video?

• What are some reasons Seventh-day Adventists are concerned about behaviors and standards so much?

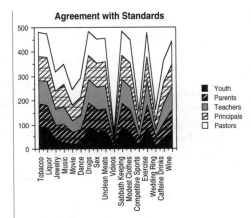

Figure 6. SDA youth in SDA Schools—Youth, Parents, Teachers, Principals, and Pastors

Some vocabulary words which will assist you in this discussion:

Faith—Faith is both an affair of the heart and a commitment of the mind. It is the way we feel about God. Faith is a gift from God, and when we receive it, it opens our life to God's guidance.

Grace Orientation—A belief that salvation is given to us only because of the goodness of Jesus, His atoning death, and the perfect life He lived on earth. It focuses completely on God's goodness in offering us this gift, which we can never earn by ourselves, and one the wonderful promises of God.

Works Orientation—A belief that salvation is given to us because we are good or have done good works. A works orientation focuses primarily on our behavior, on how we have obeyed the rules or followed the standards.

- Since everyone's doing it, doesn't that make a difference?
- Is this what is supposed to make us a "peculiar" people?
- How can we get more young people to hold to these standards?

Focusing the Discussion

The general topic of standards must be addressed to provide a background and foundation for greater understanding and discussion of individual lifestyle issues.

•"Socially Conditioned Reality." Caleb Rosado, university professor and pastor, points out how much our understanding of "truth" has been conditioned by our background and current environment. Perhaps what is most alarming is that we usually are oblivious to our "socially conditioned reality."

•"Basic Considerations." Steve Case provides terms for discussions to prevent disagreements due to the use of words. What's the difference between a principle and an application? Potential dangers also get identified to clear the way for profitable dialogue rather than polarizing arguments. (In the side-bar on this and the following page you will find the classic definitions which were used in the *Valuegenesis* book, *Faith in the Balance*. See if you agree with them).

•"Ground Rules for Discussions." Steve Case completes this introductory section by identifying four basic principles for discussing lifestyle issues. Unless you agree to abide by these, entering a lifestyle discussion simply isn't worth it.

Value—A preferred quality or action. In a general sense, it refers to what is good, desirable, and worthwhile. In a religious sense, what we value indicates what we see as being in balance with , in harmony with, and central (core) to the expressed will of God.

Principle—A fundamental guideline that flows from our values. It does not deal with specific applications ("should this dress end one or two inches above my knee?"), but with general understandings of behavior ("I choose to dress modestly.").

Standard—A practical application of a principle. A standard provides specific direction and clear goals for Christian behavior. One might say, "I think I should not lie." While "honesty" is the value, "not lying" is the standard that demonstrates the value.

Rule—A specific interpretation of a standard for a local setting. A rule is established as an aid in organizing behavior. One might say, "At this high school we have decided not to stand on the bleachers."

This book is for those who desire to live the Adventist Christian lifestyle.

[1] George A. Theodorson and Achilles G. Theodorson, *A Modern Dictionary of Sociology* (New York: Barnes & Noble Books, 1979), 295.

Socially Conditioned Reality

Caleb Rosado

All of us view the world differently, due to the cognitive process of "selective perception"—the tendency of individuals to perceive those elements of a situation which support previous expectations."[1] I remember when I bought my first Volkswagen. All of a sudden, Volkswagens started appearing out of nowhere; everywhere I turned, I saw Volkswagens. I never realized so many people owned Volkswagens. Where did all these Volkswagens come from? Nowhere. They were there all the time; I just hadn't noticed them. Prior to buying a Volkswagen, these small German cars were not part of my selectively perceived world; they were just another car on the road which I occasionally noticed. But when I finally bought one, they entered my immediate perceived reality; and suddenly, they were everywhere.

This is due to the fact that human knowledge tends to be socially conditioned. "The only knowledge that we have is a knowledge which is limited by the position which we occupy" in society.[1] In other words, "Judgments are based on experience, and experience is interpreted by each individual in terms of his [or her] own enculturation."[2] Thus, how one looks at Scripture and how one constructs an understanding of God from the facts given in the Bible "depends on the position one occupies within society. In every historical, [religious], and political contribution it is possible to determine from what vantage point the objects were observed." Why? Because "our thinking is determined by our social position," and all spiritual and "political thought is integrally bound up with social life."[3]

This is why liberals in the church tend to see things differently from conservatives. "Even in the formulation of concepts, the angle of vision is guided by the observer's interests."[4] This is one reason why administrators and theologians, teachers and students, pastors and laity, Blacks and whites, First World people and Third World people, the rich and poor, men and women, don't always see eye-to-eye in viewing the same reality. A person's "thought is directed in accordance with what a particular social group expects. Thus, out of the possible data of experience, every concept combines within itself only that which, in the light of the investigators' interests, it is essential to grasp and to

[1] Karl Mannheim, *Ideology and Utopia* (New York: Harcourt, Brace & World, Inc., 1936), 147.

[2] Melville J. Herskovits, *Cultural Relativism: Perspectives in Cultural Pluralism* (New York: Vintage Books, 1973), 15.

[3] Mannheim, 125.

[4] *Ibid.*, 273.

[1] *Ibid.*, 273-274.

[2] *Ibid.*, 274.

[3] Karl Mannheim, *From Karl Mannheim* (New York: Oxford University Press, 1971), 132.

[4] *Ibid.*

[5] *Ibid.*, 133.

[6] *Ibid.*

incorporate."[1] For this reason, "people in different social positions think differently."[2] In other words, *where you stand determines what you see!*

Styles of Thought

Now just as there are differences in "styles of living" between the rich, the middle income, and the poor, so also there are different "styles of thought"[3] which differentiate people. We tend to think in "habitual patterns of thought," which simply means "that people automatically use established patterns not merely in their overt behavior but in their thought too. In most of our intellectual responses, we are not creative but repeat certain statements, the content and form of which we have taken over from our cultural surroundings either in early childhood or in later stages of our development and which we apply automatically in appropriate situations. Thus [our thoughts] are the products of conditioning just as are our other habits."[4]

Now this is not a mechanical, morally nonresponsible development, however; for "if thought developed simply through a process of habitmaking, the same pattern would be perpetuated forever, and changes and new habits would necessarily be rare."[5] Karl Mannheim says, "A more careful observation . . . makes it clear . . . that in a differentiated and especially in a dynamic society the patterns of human thought are continually changing."[6]

Members of the various Christian denominations have been socialized within religious systems that have their own unique "styles of thought," which results in a corresponding habitual pattern of thinking. The unique Adventist style of thought, with its pattern of thinking, is a worldwide phenomenon due to the similarity of the message, the literature, the organizational structure, the preaching, and the Adventist educational system throughout the world. This is not to imply that it is all negative, for it isn't. Uniformity can be advantageous to the advancement of the cause of God. But it may also be a hindrance by failing to encourage diversity in a world of multiple options.

What Makes Us Different?

Every week millions of people throughout the world gather together to worship God in diverse settings. If we were to visit these different places of worship, we would walk away with different understandings and images of God, even within the same denomination.

Christians in Cuba, for example, have a different understanding of God than Cuban Christians in the United States. The same could be said of Jamaicans or Africans in the United States as opposed to those in their homeland. In fact, even in your own town, if you were to move from the church where you worship to other churches of your same denomination, you would discover subtle differences in the understanding of God being presented in these churches. And this does not take into consideration the way Methodists, Baptists, Christian Reform, Pentecostals, Lutherans,

If you were to move from the church where you worship to other churches of your same denomination in the same town, you would discover subtle differences in the understanding of God being presented in these churches.

Adventists, Catholics or other religious groups in town view God.

To what do we attribute these differences? In part to what was presented earlier, the fact that human knowledge tends to be socially conditioned. As was stated previously, a basic premise of the sociology of knowledge is that a people's understanding of God is shaped by those social factors that give formation to them as a people. It is out of this experience, unique to their culture (culture here understood as "shared understanding"[1]), that people begin to articulate questions about God. Herein lies the basic principle of theological and moral development: *"Judgments are based on experience, and experience is interpreted by each individual [or group] in terms of [their] own enculturation."* [2] Because human experience differs from group to group, each must readdress the question of God out of the context within which each is found. In other words, we are a product of the society in which we are socialized.

Biblical Understanding

In view of this, how are we to gain a proper understanding of the God whom we claim to worship? The answer lies in the Scriptures. But here again we have the same problem if there is any truth to the influence of society on our knowledge. For "what we see in the text, especially its implications, is what our experience, our gender, our social

[1] Howard S. Becker, "Culture: A Sociological View," in *Doing Things Together: Selected Papers* (Evanston, IL: Northwestern University Press, 1986).

[2] Herskovits, 15.

position, and our political affiliations have prepared us to see."[1] In other words, when we open the Bible, we are not just opening it *tabula rasa*—with a clean slate, a blank state of mind devoid of any outside influences. We already come to Scripture with certain preconceptions. And when we look at the text, it may tell us something today which we might not see tomorrow.

Have you ever had that experience? Have you ever marked your Bible because the text spoke to you at the moment, only to discover six months later a different message from the same text? This is why I have stopped marking my Bible; it was throwing me off. In one setting my experience was such that the text spoke to me in a certain way, but in another setting it spoke to me in another manner. I finally realized that if I leave the Bible unmarked, then every time I go to the Scriptures, I come to it fresh. As Jeremiah declares: "The steadfast love of the Lord never ceases, his mercies never come to an end; they are *new* every morning; great is thy faithfulness."[2] Yesterday's God will not do for tomorrow; we need God afresh each day.

Thus, depending on our culture and socioeconomic, political reality, we can all see different things in the Bible that speak to our unique experiences. It is thus possible for "Nicaraguan Sandinistas . . . to discover social implications in the Scriptures which we middle-class North Americans never would have dreamed of seeing."[3] And African Americans and Hispanics can come to the Bible and see

[1] John H. Elliott, *A Home for the Homeless: A Sociological Exegesis of 1 Peter, Its Situation and Strategy* (Philadelphia: Fortress Press, 1981), 12.

The influence of culture on our perceptions of God is so subtle and so much a part of our everyday existence that we often are not even aware of it.

[2] Lamentations 3:22, 23.

[3] Elliott, 12-13.

things in the text that those who are not African-American or Hispanic may not immediately see. The same can be said of women, Asians, and Third World poor in their approach to Scripture, in contrast to the traditional views by white Euro-American males.

But I Know What God Thinks About This

The influence of culture and social position upon our thinking, our perceptions of God, and our interhuman relationships are so subtle and so much a part of our everyday existence that we often are not aware of their influence and how much they impact the way we organize our lives. Ignorance of these sociocultural forces leads some to believe that the way they view God and standards for living the Christian life is a pure distillation of the divine understanding of truth for all humankind in all times and in all places. But all along, much of it has been the result of their socialization. This is not to say that God is subject to culture, for God isn't. But much of our understanding of God is.

Scripture, therefore, must be approached from the premise that we all tend to bring to it our biases and interests which we seek to protect. An imperceptive person is one who thinks that she or he comes to Scripture with clean hands and a bias-free mind. Recognizing and admitting this biased approach is a strong start towards new and honest discoveries.

Scripture must be approached from the premise that we all tend to bring to it our biases and interests which we seek to protect.

The arrogance behind such a position is staggering. Such was the position and attitude of the Pharisees. And it may well be that Jesus had this narrow, bigoted mindset in mind when He told the Pharisees, "You search the scriptures, because you think that in them you have eternal life; and it is they that bear witness to me; yet you refuse to come to me that you may have life."[1]

Instead of blindly stating, "The Bible says . . ." we would do well to first identify our personal, cultural, and denominational biases. Discussions with people who think differently than we do can be very helpful in this regard. Then both our world view and our understanding of Scripture will have a greater opportunity to expand beyond the limited parameters we formerly labeled as "truth."[2]

[1]John 5:39, 40.

[2]A portion of this chapter appears in Caleb Rosado's Book, *Women, Church, and God* (La Sierra University Press, 1991), 14-23.

Instead of blindly stating, "The Bible says . . ." we would do well to first identify our personal, cultural, and denominational biases. Discussions with people who think differently than we do can be very helpful in this regard.

Perhaps the major cause for disagreement of lifestyle issues is the confusion between *principles* and *applications* of principles.

Basic Considerations

Steve Case

Perhaps the major cause for disagreement on lifestyle issues is the confusion between *principles* and *applications* of principles. Principles are timeless and cross-cultural. What was true for one generation is just as true for the next. What is true for one group of people is equally true for another group. For example, most people in most cultures throughout the years have held modesty in high esteem. Modesty is good.

But principles are theoretical. Applications must be made for principles to be lived (operational). Applications require interpretation of principles, which may change from one generation to the next and from one culture to another. For example, let us apply the principle of mod-

40

esty. Being seen in a swimsuit by someone of the opposite sex might be considered immodest for one generation but not for another generation. Both generations might agree on the importance of the principle of modesty but disagree on the application of that principle. One culture expects females to keep their breasts covered at all times, and another culture expects females to stay topless at all times. One culture would never expose their feet in public, and yet another culture is always barefooted. Each culture is pragmatic in its standard of modesty.

Although it is possible for some applications of principles to remain the same from generation to generation or from culture to culture, we should not expect that to be the case, especially in a pluralistic society in which change seems to be the constant. When people quote, "I am the Lord, I change not,"[1] surely this should be understood as "the principles of the Lord are unchanging." Jesus himself changed applications of principles, as He did in changing the Passover for the children of Israel to the Lord's supper for Christians.[2]

Principles must be applied. The theoretical must be concrete, but should not be set in concrete. There must be flexibility in the application while agreeing on the principle. People must look for the reasons behind certain actions rather than assuming that each person's specific action's are based on the same principle. It would be far better to seek universality in principles and allow for some fluidity in specific actions.

Various generations might agree on the importance of a given principle but disagree on the application of that principle.

[1]Malachi 3:6.

[2]Matthew 26:17-30; 1 Corinthians 11: 23-26.

The identification of biblical principles for lifestyle issues has become hazy, at best, for many Adventists.

The identification of biblical principles for lifestyle issues has become hazy, at best, for many Adventists. It's almost as if several generations were taught and memorized specific applications of biblical principles without discovering the principles which are the bedrock for the applications. Those who memorize only the application lack a satisfying answer when people ask "Why?" This can lead either to defensiveness or giving up one's previously held lifestyle practice. Because times change, the application of one generation can be inadequate for succeeding generations. Fresh applications demonstrate the relevance of biblical principles.

Wanted: Quick Answers; A Correct Look

Many people want shortcut answers. Their cry is for a quick fix with ready-made applications. For example, they want to know if a certain music group, or even a specific song by the group, is acceptable. A simple yes-or-no response might be quick, but hardly leads the person to make a rational decision based upon principle. Rather, the questioner will likely compare their personal opinion with your verbalized application. As a result, it easily becomes an argument about applications rather than about principles. Those who distribute "approved lists" of musicians, movies, etc., feed the shallow demand for answers geared for immature reflectors of other people's thoughts. To allow flexibility requires a tolerance that few are willing to permit, especially in a large group setting such as an

Adventist academy or college, a congregation, or other church-related group. To allow freedom of personal application removes the uniformity that provides the false impression that we all think alike. As long as that image can be maintained, few would dare to tamper with the thoughts or motives behind the facade.

The danger lies in the tendency to do the right things for the wrong reasons. The outside might look good, while the inside is rotten. As Jesus said, "On the outside you appear good to everybody, but inside you are full of hypocrisy and sin. You make the outside of your cup look like it is spotless, but inside you are full of selfishness. If you would clean the inside of the cup first, the outside will take care of itself."[1] Unfortunately, it is quite possible to have an acceptable, even admirable appearance and still have an unclean, corrupt, or even a dead heart.

To change the focus from externals to motives behind the actions may result in variable behavior. However, it may be the only avenue by which people will begin to live what they really believe. It may be dangerous to permit, or even encourage such an approach. But isn't it more dangerous not to?

To move from principle to application requires formal operational thinking, which may begin in early adolescence. Therefore children will need applications spelled out for them. Youth and adults may need such direction, as well, if their passage through adolescence is incomplete.

As a "squeaky clean" Adventist from childhood, I have found, without exception, that once I discovered

To allow flexibility in applications requires a tolerance that few are willing to permit.

[1] Adapted from Matthew 23:25-28.

43

Youth and adults may need the same direction as children, since abstract thinking isn't guaranteed simply because a person has reached or passed through adolescence.

[1]Some would argue from a basic dualistic perspective, such as salvation being a simple yes or no choice rather than a multiple option. However, Scripture frequently incudes a perspective that demonstrates options, although it doesn't fit well into a proof-text methodology (compare Acts 4:12 with Romans 1-2).

biblical principles behind a lifestyle issue, the application was far more encompassing than the church's standards had ever been. Admittedly, I found some of the specific activities that supposedly were taboo, weren't necessarily wrong, But I found I no longer could participate in some of the activities that were "acceptable."

The chapters in this book attempt to identify biblical principles for lifestyle issues currently in question and how to apply them. It would be easier to list specific behaviors we should follow to be a member in good standing in the "club." But such an approach rejects variables such as thought, choice, maturity, values and responsibility. This is where the subjective element comes into play.

Begin with an attempt to understand the principles rather than discussing specific applications. Then, expect multiple applications rather than one simple response for all people.[1]

Source(s) of Authority

Seventh-day Adventists embrace the Bible as their official source of authority. Unofficially, some SDAs utilize a blend of the Bible and the writings of Mrs. White. Ellen White made many applications of biblical truth. A large number of Adventists have found Ellen White's applications to be helpful to them as they seek to live by the Scriptures. As could be expected, some of Ellen White's applications are not timeless, although the principles she identified are. Some people experience confusion regarding whether some portion of Ellen White's counsel is a principle or an application of a principle. Seventh-day Adventists fully support the Reformation principle of *sola scriptura*, the Bible as its own interpreter and the Bible alone as the basis of all doctrines.[1] For Adventists, the Bible stands unique and supreme as the test of Christian faith and practice.[2]

Because of the official statements that the Bible is the only source of faith and practice for Seventh-day Adventists[3] and because confusion and misuse of the writings of Ellen White detracts from the issue at hand, the Bible will be the source of authority for this book. This should not be misunderstood as a denial of the crucial role and inspiration of the writings of Ellen White for the Seventh-day Adventist Church. To deal with Ellen White's comments in these lifestyle areas would require another book. Already, George Knight's *Myths in Adventism*[4] relates to some of these issues. He, and several other historians within Adventism, are well suited to write from such a perspective.

Missing the Mark

Another danger in dealing with lifestyle issues is that the issue may replace Jesus. If this results, it's blasphemous. This book will attempt to pierce the protective hedge of inconsequential rules and get to the core of God's revelation. Is it possible we have surrounded the truth

[1] Ministerial Association, *Seventh-day Adventists Believe . . .* (Hagerstown, MD: Review and Herald Publishing Association, 1988), 227.

[2] Francis Nichol, ed., *The Seventh-day Adventist Bible Commentary*, Vol 7 (Washington, DC: Review and Herald Publishing Association, 1957), 877.

[3] Ironically, these statements are expressed best when the topic of spiritual gifts and Ellen G. White is under consideration rather than when the topic is the Bible.

[4] George Knight, *Myths in Adventism* (Washington, DC: Review and Herald Publishing), 1985.

For Adventists, the Bible stands unique and supreme as the test of Christian faith and practice.

of Jesus to the point that others can see only the lifestyle issues? By opening a discussion on these issues, we hope people will be able to dialogue on those peripheral items that may be burning issues to them, and then move on to the core of the matter: Jesus.

Ground Rules

Steve Case

Basic biblical principles are important when leading a discussion of standards and Christian values. It is equally important to understand exactly what the texts mean in order to be both relevant and appropriate. Once biblical principles are identified, apply them to your own life. Relevance is crucial. Application is impossible without thorough discussion and understanding of the whole texts. Here is where the discussion gets more interesting.

Review the following biblical principles and discussion that follows. Prepare to immerse yourself in a discussion of Christ-centered standards. Be ready to think deeply about lifestyle issues. You may want to keep some notes on your thoughts as you review these biblical concepts.

Review the following biblical principles and discussion that follows. Prepare to immerse yourself in a discussion of Christ-centered standards.

1 John 2:15-17

Do not love the world or anything in the world. If anyone loves the world, the love of the Father is not in him. For everything in the world—the cravings of sinful man, the lust of his eyes, and the boasting of what he has and does—does not come from the Father, but from the world. The world and its desires pass away, but the one who does the will of God lives forever (adapted from the NIV).

[1]See also Luke 16:13.

[2]See Joseph Aldrich "Avoiding Evil Instead of its Appearance" in *Life-Style Evangelism* (Portland, OR: Multnomah Press, 1981), 39-56.

Matthew 5

[3]Matthew 5:21.

Principle #1: The Way of God and the Way of the World Are Opposites

The first passage is 1 John 2:15-17. The purpose of sharing this text is to remind those involved in Adventist lifestyle discussions of the two opposing forces and the resulting choices: either you love the world and hate the Father, or you love the Father and hate the world.[1]

Sometimes people see how close they can get to the line of worldliness without crossing it. According to 1 John 2:15-17, it's not a matter of getting as close to the world as you want, as long as you don't cross some arbitrary line that separates the Father and the world. What is involved is two forces going opposite directions. As a Christian, one's life moves in the direction of the Father and away from worldliness. Simply avoiding the *appearance* of evil (1 Thess. 5:22, KJV) is replaced by *avoiding every kind of evil* (1 Thess. 5:22, NIV).[2]

Principle #2: The Spirit of the Law Exceeds the Letter of the Law

In the Sermon on the Mount, Jesus presented a number of pronouncements that began, "You have heard it said, but I say unto you..." For example, "You have heard that it was said to the people long ago, 'Do not murder, and anyone who murders will be subject to judgment.'"[3] Most human beings would agree with this. After all, most of us never murdered anyone. However, the very next verse states, "But I tell you that anyone who is angry with his brother will be subject to judgment."[1] That's getting rather picky and personal. Who hasn't been angry with another person? Does this mean everyone is a murderer? Yes, if viewed from a principled perspective.

Later in the same chapter we read, "You have heard that it was said, 'Do not commit adultery.'"[2] Of course adultery is not permissible. Many could claim to never have broken the seventh commandment—they have not participated in intercourse outside of marriage. "But I tell you that anyone who looks at a person lustfully has already committed adultery with that person in one's heart."[3] This is terribly extreme! What human being hasn't ever lusted after somebody else at least once in their life? Does this make everyone guilty?

Evidently being "squeaky clean" on the outside isn't enough. A person must be clean on the inside as well. As one person unwittingly said, "But if we followed this, it would affect every part of our lives." My response is, "*Exactly!*"

Principle #3: Don't Purposely Offend Others; And Quit Tripping Over Every Little Thing

For many, the stumbling-block issue provides adequate motivation to participate or refrain from a given activity.[4]

[1]Matthew 5:22.

[2]Matthew 5:27.

[3]Matthew 5:28.

"But if we followed this, it would affect every part of our lives."

**1 Corinthians 8:9-13;
Matthew 15:12-14;
1 Peter 2:6-8**

[4]A major presentation of this principle can be found in 1 Corinthians 8 (also Romans 14:13-17).

Be careful that the exercise of your freedom does not become a stumbling block to the weak. The weaker brother might be destroyed by following your enlightened actions. When you sin against your brother by wounding his weak conscience, you sin against Christ. Therefore, if what I eat causes my brother to fall into sin, I will never eat food offered to idols again, so that I will not cause him to fall. (1 Corinthians 8:9-13), adapted from the NIV.

[1] Romans 9:32-33, NIV; see also 1 Peter 2:6-8.

[2] See Matthew 15:12-14; Acts 4:1-21; Acts 5:17-42. See also George E. Rice, *Christ in Collision* (*Mountain* View, CA: Pacific Press Publishing Association), 1982.

It seems quite simple. Don't do anything that would offend a weaker brother. Is it possible to live without offending others? Aren't some people easily offended even when you may try not to offend?

Perhaps there is a flip side to the discussion. Note who wrote the "weaker brother" passages—the one who will never do anything to cause another person to stumble. It's the same person who caused riots wherever he went! At least a dozen times in the book of Acts, Paul creates major offenses against others. (See page 55 for a look at Paul's adventures in the book of Acts).

Of all the biblical writers, Paul would seem least likely to write about not offending weaker brothers. John the Beloved would be a better candidate. However, the most profound example in history of tripping over stumbling blocks is Israel itself, and note who causes it!

"All Israel stumbled over the 'stumbling stone.' As it is written, 'Now, I lay in Zion a stone that causes men to stumble and a rock that makes them fall, and the one who trusts in him will never be put to shame"[1]

Not only is it impossible to never be a stumbling block, but Jesus and his followers frequently offended others.[2] Perhaps we have become so inoffensive that we aren't even a factor in people's lives.

Who are the weaker brothers that aren't to be offended? In context it probably refers to new believers—those who lack knowledge that comes from living for some time in the Christian community. New believers may be surprised to discover that some Adventists do not spend every Sabbath in constant Bible study and meditation. Others may be disappointed because of high expectations from an Adventist institutional environment that is not always composed of loving, kind, and religious people.

Some believers are stumblers. They become offended by almost anything beyond their strictly defined limitations. They have been referred to as "professional weaker brothers"[1] who should learn to walk again so they won't continue stumbling over the "stumbling stones."

The weaker brother/stumbling block issue has two sides: one side is handle with care the freedom Christ gave you by considering a new believer's faith. The other side is to learn how to walk. Let's pick up our feet so we don't trip over minor differences in lifestyle practices.

Principle #4: Be Accepting and Tolerant, Especially To Those of Weak Faith

Finally, this book should be viewed in relationship to bigger issues. Paul wrote, "Accept him whose faith is weak, without passing judgment on disputable matters"[2] ("disputes over opinions," RSV). The context is Paul's longest treatise on righteousness by faith.[3] Therefore, because of righteousness by faith,

> I urge you, brothers, in view of God's mercy, to offer your bodies as living sacrifices, holy and pleasing to

[1] Aldrich, 46.

Romans 14:1-4

[2] Romans 14:1.

[3] Romans 1-11.

51

God—this is your spiritual act of worship. Do not conform any longer to the pattern of this world, but be transformed by the renewing of your mind. Then you will be able to test and prove what God's will is—his good, pleasing and perfect will.[1]

Paul spelled out his theology. Then he presents the implications. This is where he addresses the issue of acceptance of others when it comes to disputable matters.

Lifestyle issues in the Adventist church today are too often disputable matters. Although convictions may be strong, the fact that committed Adventists agree on basic tenets but disagree on specific applications opens the door to dispute. But such matters are not critical to Adventism, or Adventism will need to be redefined.

Consider the situation in Rome. Pagans and Jews were becoming Christians. The Essene branch of Judaism placed greater emphasis on diet than the Pharisees did. This influenced the church in Rome,[2] which created certain fast days. Because the Essene calendar differed from the official priestly calendar in Jerusalem, "One person considers one day more important than another" (the "Sabbath" is not mentioned in this context). Which days should be feast days and which days should be fast days for the Christians in Rome? The issue is a "disputable matter."[3] Paul cautions the believers not to pass judgment on each other in such areas, but to accept each other.

Adventist lifestyle issues are disputable. Rather than passing judgment on one another, be accepting. One Adventist may hold a view opposite yours. Paul calls for you

[1] Romans 12:1-2, NIV.

[2] Note Romans 14:2-3.

[3] See Raoul Dederen, "On Esteeming One Day as Better Than Another" in *Andrews University Seminary Studies, No. 9* January, 1971), 16-35.

to accept each other without passing judgment. Frankly, no issue is more important than love for one another.

This calls for serious personal reflection. As you discuss these lifestyle topics with someone who disagrees with you, if you find your love for that person diminish then it probably won't be profitable for you to continue. The writers, editor, and publisher request that you put this book down if you are unwilling to accept others without passing judgment. It's simply not worth it if it lessens our love anyone.

It's not worth it to discuss these disputable issues if it lessens our love for each other.

Suggested Additional
Resources

Aldrich, Joseph C., *Life-Style Evangelism* (Portland: Multnomah Press), 1981.

Dudley, Roger L., *The World: Love It Or Leave It?* (Boise: Pacific Press Publishing Association), 1986.

Fischer, John, *True Believers Don't Ask Why* (Minneapolis: Bethany House Publishers), 1989.

Hawley, Don, *Set Free!* (Clackamas, OR: Better Living Publishers), 1989.

Insight, special edition on "Entertainment," (November 8, 1986).

Knight, George R., *The Pharisee's Guide to Perfect Holiness* (Boise: Pacific Press Publishing Association), 1992.

Kraybill, Donald B., *The Upside-Down Kingdom* (Scottdale, PA: Herald Press), 1978.

Phillips, J. B., *Your God is Too Small* (New York: MacMillan Publishing Company), 1961.

Consider some of Paul's adventures as recorded in the book of Acts

• Acts 13:46—rejection of the Jews and going to the Gentiles
• Acts 14:11-12—people worship Paul
• Acts 14:19-20—the same people who worshipped Paul now stone him
• Acts 15:37-40—Paul disagrees so strongly with Barnabas that they part company
• Acts 16:19-24—Paul is thrown into jail
• Acts 17:5—the Jews start a riot because of Paul
• Acts 18:6—Paul shakes the dust off his feet
• Acts 19:28-34—another riot, this time in Ephesus
• Acts 21:27-36—Paul's presence incites another riot, this time in Jerusalem
• Acts 22:22-24—Paul creates another uproar
• Acts 23:3—Paul calls the high priest a whitewashed wall
• Acts 23:6-10—Paul creates pandemonium by stirring up a Pharisee-Sadducee controversy while he was on trial

Perhaps there is a flip side to the discussion. Note who wrote the "weaker brother" passages—the one who will never do anything to cause another person to stumble. It's the same person who caused riots wherever he went!

Section 2
Thinking About Dancing

Section 2
Thinking About Dancing

What's the Discussion About?

"Dancing stimulates the lust of the flesh." Perhaps this is why it is wrong, why so many concerned adults find themselves opposed to young people dancing, and why so many young people (just into puberty) seem so interested in doing it. As more than one person has said, "If you can stand before someone of the opposite sex who is gyrating like that and not be turned on, you're not spiritual—you're dead!" Those who ignore or deny the potential sexual stimulation from dancing aren't seeing the whole picture.

But those who associate all dancing with sexual stimulation and promiscuity also fail to see the whole picture.

Valuegenesis Byte

How do you feel about enforcement of standards?

- 66% Adventist rules and standards serve a useful purpose.
- 50% Non-Adventists laugh when they hear what Adventists are forbidden to do.
- 47% Some adults insist on certain rules or standards for younger Adventists that they do not observe themselves.
- 45% The feeling is conveyed in the Adventist Church that *how* one behaves is more important than *what* one believes.

"Dancing stimulates the lust of the flesh."

57

Those who associate all dancing with sexual stimulation and promiscuity fail to see the whole picture.

Even little children naturally move to music. But adolescents and dancing are associated with sex. Some adults would permit dancing with one's spouse only. Once again the issue is the sexually explosive potential and the concomitant responses to it.

Adventist Christians have so tightly married the sexuality argument to dancing, that someone (perhaps an Adventist teenager) pointed out the humor of the situation this way: "Question: Why are Adventists opposed to sex? Answer: It might lead to dancing!" While few go this far, a desire to prevent pre-marital and extramarital sex causes many to fully remove this potential avenue of temptation.

In addition to the issue of sex is the issue of music in dance. Sometimes music to dance by is questionable. Music forces two opposing viewpoints to clash. Those opposed to dancing usually oppose the music associated with it. While those who like dancing appreciate the music that serves as a catalyst for their movement.

The Background of the Discussion

In the early days of Adventism in the United States, various religious groups shunned dancing. They considered it as worldly amusement, associated with alcohol and sex. With the soon return of Jesus in mind, why would an Adventist dabble in sensuous and temporary pleasures of this world?

During the 20th century some religious groups dropped their ban on dancing while Seventh-day Adventists maintained their position against it. However, church and school groups searched for acceptable substitutes for dancing.

The grand march seemed like a reasonable event. Participants could socialize in a healthy manner without booze and under the direction of leaders. Couples could form, but they wouldn't be isolated. Physical contact rarely went beyond walking side-by-side or possibly holding someone's hand for a short while.

Roller skating provided another acceptable Saturday night activity for Seventh-day Adventists. Males and females had the opportunity to socially interact with limited physical contact. Once again, the issues of alcohol and intimacy could be controlled under the watchful eye of chaperones or sponsors. Some Adventist academies forbade hand-holding while skating. Young people invented the arm-in-arm method to "assist" those who were just learning how to skate. Of course, the entire art of balancing prevented too many romantic moments, as did sweaty bodies and foot blisters. Questionable music was no problem since adults in charge at the academy or college gym controlled the music.

More recently Adventists have developed gymnastics as an acceptable physical activity which includes routines involving "dance-like" movements. Some schools utilize gymnastic teams as recruiting groups who tour and provide Saturday night entertainment for Adventists.

Frequently these gymnasts add religious programming to their performance. Some utilize their gymnastic

Substitutes for dancing became acceptable.

skills to win the respect of a secular audience while presenting Christ as their reason for living and performing.

As Adventist colleges expand their Saturday night on-campus options, visiting artists sometimes include cultural folk dances from various countries. Adventists can *watch* but not *participate* in these "dances" because they are expressions of foreign culture. In some places in the world church folk dancing festivals have been coupled with Pathfinder events. But there doesn't seem to be a folk dance for America.

With the increased interest in exercise and aerobics, "Jazzercise" has become an acceptable activity because it provides physical exercise, no alcohol, and physical intimacy is not possible. Sometimes questionable music makes its way into the exercise room, but the idea is to get the heart beating not the hormones rushing.

Valuegenesis research indicates that dancing may very well be where going to movies was approximately ten years ago. We know youth are developing dancing habits. Many are beginning to participate, and this number is growing. It is probably safe to say that the majority of Adventist young people in North America do not consider dancing as wrong. Most will admit they've heard that Adventists don't dance, and probably most adults don't, however, a great number of youth do dance. Their choices range from under-18 clubs that do not serve alcohol to dance clubs that are little more than "meat markets" for sexual pickups.

Gymnastics provides a physical activity that is an acceptable Adventist alternative to dancing.

60

Most Adventist churches are silent about dancing. Adventist schools are required to enforce the no dance tradition but have little power for enforcement off campus. Some Adventist churches have sponsored square dances claiming they are simply doing a cultural folk dance of America.

With dancing, we seem to be moving towards integration with our culture. Is it possible that one day we will be restore dance as an act of celebration and worship?

Questions Youth Are Asking

• What's wrong with dancing? And what's wrong with the music we use?

• Why do you think everything about dancing is sexual? I'm just going to be with my friends and hang out.

• What forms of dance are acceptable? You really don't think all types of dances are wrong, do you?

• How come the church can sponsor a square dance but the school can't?

• This is just my self-expression or personal art form. What can be wrong about that?

• The Bible says that David danced, so why can't we? Was there something wrong with David's dancing?

• Can you list the major biblical reasons why dancing is or is not a good activity for Christians?

• How do you think the church is changing regarding dance?

Today the majority of Adventist young people in North America do not consider dancing as wrong.

Few have researched the Bible on dance.

Was there something wrong with David's dancing?

• What should parents tell their youth about dancing?
• What is wrong with the environment of a dance?
• Is the environment any different than riding a city bus?

Here are some other basic questions that need discussion.

• Is it fun being a Christian?
• What are the times when you have had the "most fun" and what makes times the "least fun?"
• Are some activities worse than others? Where would you put dancing? Is it a sin or not?

Focusing the Discussion

• "Shall We Dance?" Bill Knott, pastor of the Walla Walla College Church, reminisces about community dances in New England during his childhood and the struggle he faced with childhood adages which no longer matched his maturing experience. He then plunges into a Scriptural search of the subject which few before him have studied.

What is the foundation for your current views on dance? Is it primarily from tradition, personal opinion, Scripture, or elsewhere? Can you find passages in the Bible that give credence to your position?

• "Dancing With My Generation." College student Noelene Pang shares her desire to learn ballet and the conflict it imposed on the religious values of her parents. This led her to search for her own answers from the Bible.

What view of dancing did you grow up with? To what extent has it changed over the years? What caused the change? What is the best way to prepare people to make good choices when it comes to dancing? What level of maturity is needed for people to choose this on their own? Do you feel competent to make these choices yourself?

• "Dancing to the Lord." Timothy Gillespie, a young pastor and member of Generation X, provides a unique and contemporary look at basic questions about dancing which may help to open up a discussion with teenagers. He reflects on some basic considerations when thinking about this topic. He urges considering motivation, satisfaction, and insight into contemporary dance itself. He hopes pastors, teachers, parents and youth workers consider these themes which must focus any discussion about dance. These issues frame this section. You will be challenged to include them in all of your discussions with youth about this topic.

• "Dancing with a User-Friendly Concordance." Spend some time studying all the dance texts in the Bible. Use any number of versions to explore these passages. There are only 27. While your study of dance probably shouldn't be limited to "dance texts," it is a good place to start! Try to draw your own conclusions about this crucial and timely topic.

What is the foundation for your current views about dance?

What is the best way to prepare people to make good choices when it comes to dancing?

Look through the "Suggested Additional Resources" which offers a few items to start you thinking about dance. And if you have time, spend a few minutes each day watching MTV on your television. Many youth of today are spending hours each week being impacted with this media message about the nature and purpose of dance.

Shall We Dance?

Bill Knott

"Yankee Doodle Days."

The name still summons up a smile more than 25 years after I first heard it at the age of nine. Images return of mild August nights in a tiny Massachusetts town, fireworks painting the night sky and reverberating down the river valley, fiddlers sawing on well-worn instruments, the smell of warm popcorn wafting over the ballfield.

And square dancing.

Of all the features that made "Yankee Doodle Days" exciting to my brothers and me, it was the novelty of seeing brightly dressed men and women moving with such ease and style across the high school tennis court, their faces lit with laughter and enjoyment. Good little Adventists that

And what about square dancing?

we were, we knew that dancing of any kind was contrary to the will of God. Yet here were decent, wholesome people—people who ran the gas station, owned the general store, and drove truck for the town highway department—dancing, and looking none the worse for it, either.

It would have satisfied all my church school-learned prejudices if one of the square dancers, just one of them, had thrown a leering look at some passing skirt or muttered dark obscenities underneath his breath, for then their dancing would have absorbed the taint I needed it to have to keep my world view in place. Instead, I came away unsure for the first time in my life that what I had been taught was always and altogether true.

Bringing It Home

I half expected Mom and Dad to fill in all the blanks about the evils of dancing on the way home. But they were curiously quiet, choosing only to answer our questions as the headlights probed the winding, hilly road. Perhaps they sensed and welcomed the ferment that was happening in three little Adventist minds in the back seat. They certainly didn't object when we began chorusing the caller's sung instructions to the square dancers:
"First couple promenade the outside,
And Two and Three will follow;
Couple Three make an arch and Two will go through.
Now you wheel with Jane and Harry,
And you wheel with Dick and Mary,

Good little Adventists that we were, we knew that dancing of any kind was contrary to the will of God.

And when you're through, you do the dosie-do."

As children, we learned first of all a set of unexceptional rules:

"Never climb up on the hearth and play with ashes in the fireplace."

"Throwing food is always wrong."

"Breaking off Mommy's pretty flowers is bad."

Exceptional or Unexceptional?

But the first time Daddy thanked us for "helping him" clean out the fireplace, the first time we saw a comedian throw a cream pie in someone's face, the first time we watched Mommy's eyes well up with happy tears when we picked one of her flowers and handed it to her as a present, we began to doubt the rules that tolerate no exceptions. Categorical, unexceptional thinking was replaced with "exceptional" thinking, a maturing intelligence that was able to distinguish between the good and bad effects of a given behavior.

Whereas throwing potato salad at your sister during dinner was always and only wrong, good church members would line up and pay real money to throw whipped cream pies at the school board chairman during a fund-raising evening at the gym. The rule that in our earlier childhood had tolerated no exceptions was now seen to be capable of several. This was all a part of what adults meant when they talked about "growing up."

As we matured, categorical, unexceptional thinking was replaced with "exceptional" thinking.

Sociologists of religion frequently use the model of child-to-adult maturation to explain the phenomenon of change that occurs within almost all religious movements as the decades pass. Like the toddler, the early adherents of a new faith frequently adopt a set of unexceptionable rules:

"No one who plays cards will be ready for the coming of Jesus."

"Entering a theater is wrong."

"Dancing is a pastime of the devil."

Behavioral rules adopted by the movement at this stage are relatively few and starkly uncompromising. It is often asserted that "no genuine believer" will *believe* otherwise or *practice* otherwise. The simple, categorical clarity of this step attracts converts who long for black-and-white solutions to intractable problems, who seek the discipline of following externally imposed commands. Appeals to Biblical authority are often narrowly based, avoiding equally inspired material that would soften or moderate the rules:

But with increasing age comes the inevitable exceptions to the rules: (1) "What if I use playing cards but never gamble with them?" (2) "Is it still wrong to enter a theater when the evangelist holds a big crusade there?" (3) "Isn't there a difference between square dancing and night club dancing?" In each of these cases (and many others could be cited) the categorical rule has shown itself capable of reasonable exception.

Early adherents of a new faith frequently adopt a set of unexceptionable rules.

68

Biblical Principles

Because we Adventists recite no creed, we bear the burden not only of citing "particular" or "distinctive" truths, but also of conveying the whole message of what the Bible says upon a given topic. For instance, we must not hide from people that Scripture is not universally condemnatory toward decorative jewelry.[1] It's certainly more uncomfortable to go about our task this way, but anything like integrity demands it.

Principle #1: Dance is a Component of Divine Worship

When we study Scripture we find that what it says about dance and dancing is not only *not* condemnatory, but in some cases positively prescriptive:

> "Praise him with trumpet sound;
>   praise him with lute and harp!
> Praise him with timbrel and dance;
>   praise him with strings and pipe!"[2]

A half hour with a good concordance leaves the lingering impression that there is more to a truly Biblical perspective on dance than has previously met our Adventist eyes. Of some 27 references to dance (dance, danced, dances, dancing) in the Scriptures, only four occur in a

Appeals to Biblical authority are often narrowly based, avoiding equally inspired material that would soften or moderate the rules.

[1] See the section "Thinking About Jewelry" later in this volume.

2 Samuel 6:14; 1 Chronicles 15:29; Psalm 149:3; Psalm 150:4.

[2] Psalm 150:3,4.

[1]Exodus 32:19; Matthew 14:6; Mark 6:22; 1 Corinthians 10:7-8.

clearly negative context,[1] and even these references nowhere describe dancing as the object of God's displeasure. Other business—the worship of a golden calf, the execution of John the Baptist—makes the scene unholy. The dance is incidental and is not determinatively evil.

Principle #2: Dance is an Appropriate Expression of Community Joy

Judges 11:34; 1 Samuel 18:6; Matthew 11:17; Luke 7:32; Luke 15:25.

We must also tell them that what the Bible says about dance and dancing is not only *not* condemnatory, but in some cases positively prescriptive.

By contrast, fully 16 of the 27 references are uniformly positive about the experience of dance, both as a component of divine worship and an appropriate expression of community joy. Jeremiah pictures God as saying to his people,

[2]Jeremiah 31:4.

"Again I will build you, and you shall be built,
O virgin Israel!
Again you shall adorn yourselves with timbrels,
and shall go forth in the dance of the merrymakers."[2]

[3]2 Samuel 6:14.

[4]Exodus 15:20.

Scriptures seem to know of no distinction between "sacred" and "secular" dance. The "dance of the merrymakers" is as fully capable of receiving God's approval as the dance that David does before the Lord.[3] Communal, festive dancing receives the same positive association as the dance in which Miriam and the women of Israel celebrate God's decisive victory at the Red Sea.[4]

Did Jesus Dance?

Indeed, though the gospel writers make no specific mention of it, it is no mere "argument from silence" to suggest that Jesus very likely participated in the festive dancing at the wedding of Cana. Jewish weddings of the first century, and each century since, routinely included communal dancing as an expression of the joy of the family and friends in the creation of a new home.[1] To have attended the wedding but absented himself from the communal dancing would have been inconsistent with his intention by attending in the first place. Inconsistent or unusual behavior is what requires comment, not routine behavior. If Jesus had sought to make a point in contrast to the accepted practice of his times regarding dancing, he certainly would have done it, for we never find him reluctant to do so elsewhere.

Nothing less than a thorough transformation of our Victorian "man of sorrows" will allow the average SDA to tolerate the image of Jesus dancing at a wedding or elsewhere. Indeed, a 1989 survey of one group of Adventist ministers[2] found fully 75 percent believing that Jesus didn't participate in the social dances of his day, even where they otherwise disagreed with certain aspects of the church's stance on dance.

Though significant majorities of Adventist academy and college students sampled in the same survey[3] indicated their belief that most forms of dancing are suitable, 53

[1]Hayam Halevy Donim, *To Be a Jew* (New York: Basic Books, Inc., 1972), 289.

What becomes painfully apparent is that many Adventists have a primary problem with the humanity of Jesus.

[2]Warren Ruf, "Adventists and Dancing: Watching Your Steps," (Unpublished paper, Andrews University, 1989), 27.

[3]*Ibid.*, 28.

It disturbs us deeply to imagine that the Lord whom we most frequently picture in an agony of prayer in Gethsemane might have known the simple fun of a dance with his friends.

We do not know what to do with a fresh-faced carpenter who found joy in His feet as well as His mouth.

percent said "No" when asked if they believed Jesus participated in the social dances of his time.

What becomes painfully apparent through such surveys is that many Adventists have a primary problem with the humanity of Jesus. Could that dignified, white-robed figure that is fixed in our minds from Harry Anderson's paintings have known the taste of sweat or the pleasure of a midnight swim in the Sea of Galilee? It disturbs us deeply to imagine that the Lord whom we most frequently picture in an agony of prayer in Gethsemane might have known the simple fun of a dance with his friends.

Like dull disciples, we continue to see only those aspects of his personality and mission that conform to our already established ways of seeing. We miss His wit, His warm humor, His holy slyness in conversing with His foes, for like the image of Jesus dancing, these notions run against the grain of pietist tradition. We want a Jesus pale and drawn, beaten down with bearing sin. We do not know what to do with a fresh-faced carpenter who found joy in His feet as well as His mouth.

Erring On the "Safe" Side

Five generations of Adventists have grown to maturity with lingering suspicion that there is really only one answer—a negative one—to that oft-repeated question of Victorian religious sensibility "What would Jesus do?" He has become for a great many believers a Lord of negations, defined primarily by all the questionable practices we believe he wouldn't engage in if he lived in the here and now. We have congratulated ourselves that if we are in error, at least we have come down on the side of caution. It should also be abundantly clear to thinking Adventists that we have also come down on the side of joylessness and passivity, and that these qualities have nothing "Christlike" about them.

What emerges from even a brief survey of the Biblical references to dance is the healthy conclusion that dancing is neither categorically good nor categorically evil, any more than sex, food, or entertainment is evil in a fallen world. Dance has about it qualities that may uplift and ennoble; it may also have qualities that destroy or debase. What should matter most to the maturing Christian is the content and the character of the dance that beckons him.

Principle #3: Dance Should Praise No Other god but God/ Yahweh/the LORD

Principle #4: Dance Should Not Promote Inappropriate Sexual Arousal

Principle #5: Appropriate Dance is Dance in Which God is Invited as a Witness and Participant

We have come down on the side of joylessness and passivity, and these qualities have nothing "Christlike" about them.

Exodus 32:19.

1 Corinthians 10:7-8; Matthew 14:6 and Numbers 25:3 by Implication 1 Corinthians 10:31; Romans 14:23b.

73

Certain types of dance may still be identified as always and invariably wrong: (1) the dance in praise of any other god than the Lord; (2) the dance which promotes inappropriate sexual arousal; (3) the dance which cannot invite God as witness and participant.

These three principles don't leave believers with a hopelessly relativistic model for deciding whether or not a given dance is appropriate for an Adventist Christian. Certain types of dance may still be identified as always and invariably wrong: (1) the dance in praise of any other god than the Lord; (2) the dance which promotes inappropriate sexual arousal; (3) the dance which cannot invite God as witness and participant.

By these three broad but simple criteria, a large percentage of the dancing that is practiced in high school gyms, concerts, night clubs and televised dance parties falls short of the Christian standards. The specious reasoning, best exemplified in the 1980s' movie "Footloose" that equates the lustful gyrations of adolescents with David's dance before the Lord will succeed only where there is shallow Biblical understanding and immature faith. It seems inconceivable that any serious Christian would try to build a spiritual defense for these kinds of dances.

Redeeming Dance

Having said that, there remains a task for Christians who take their Bibles seriously to reclaim for believers those kinds of dances which pass the above criteria. Christian responsibility in a fallen world isn't simply to avoid those categories of behavior (sex, food, entertainment, dance, etc.) in which the devil has been successful in deceiving many, for this leads to nothing but the delusions of asceticism. Adventists must actively redeem for godliness the holy joys and proper enjoyments of experience in the world in the name of the One who called them "good" from the start, including the experience of dance.

One place to start is for Adventist parents and youth leaders to teach a renewed appreciation for the importance of the physical body in worship. For decades we have left the impression that God wishes only to meet our minds in worship, or perhaps our "hearts" as the organ plays "Just As I Am." But our feet and hands, our torsos, our legs and arms might just as well stayed home. Youth must instead be taught that God invites the wholeness of the person to come before Him in worship, and that the whole person, including the feet and hands, may properly be called upon in the act of worshipping Him. In reality, it may necessitate that young people take the lead, since many adults, in the name of conscience, have destroyed their ability to move purposefully in worship to God.

As challenging as it is to our notions of respectability and decorum, it seems evident that Adventists should give new thought and study to the inclusion of dance as part of the worship of God, at least in selected communities and on special occasions. To "praise Him with the timbrel and dance" does not simply mean to move as we will and assume that He will make sense of it. Believers must ensure that every component of worship—music, praise, prayer, testimony, dance—has the clear intention to bring honor and glory to God, and exists not just as a vehicle for restless members to "express themselves."

It seems inconceivable that any serious Christian would try to build a spiritual defense for these kinds of dance.

Adventists must actively redeem for godliness the holy joys and proper enjoyments of sensual experience in the world, including the experience of dance.

Many adults, in the name of conscience, have killed their ability to move purposefully in worship to God.

Scripture makes it clear that God is honored through worshipful dance. It remains to be seen if Adventist believers will have the courage and maturity to explore how dance may again be included as part of the community's celebration of God.

Parents and youth leaders must focus attention on those kinds of dance that appropriately express community joy and festivity. There is encouraging evidence of changing attitudes within the church, even among groups often thought to be unflinchingly conservative.

What Some People Think

[1]Ruf, 27.

A 1989 survey[1] discovered that 70 percent of the Adventist ministers surveyed believed that folk dancing (square dancing, clogging, etc.) is "not a sin." However, an almost identical number (67 percent) said they wouldn't participate in it. Aerobic dance (defined by the survey to include "Jazzercize") wasn't deemed sinful by 63 percent of the ministers, and ballet was held harmless by 53 percent. Dances that presuppose a specific environment, including ballroom (waltz, tango, fox trot), country-western (two-step) and disco/night club dancing were deemed wrong by sizable majorities.

[2]*Ibid.*, 28.

The parallel survey of Adventist academy and college students[2] found strong support for all of the above forms except disco/night club dancing which suggests a different basis for evaluating whether a given dance could be appropriate. Only the "trendiest" of the dance options was deemed unsuitable by the youth surveyed. Older, more established forms of dance, including ballet, ballroom, country-western, and folk dancing appear to have been judged innocuous.

When two such historically diverse groups as Adventist ministers and Adventist youth can agree on the acceptability of certain dances (such as folk dances, marches, round dances, and square dances) it seems high time to rethink and reformulate the church's official statements about dancing.

The above statements are cited, not to suggest the church's position on dance should be determined only by survey or vote, but as evidence that any standard developed by the church ought to reflect a solid consensus of what "good and regular" members believe Scripture to be teaching on that topic.

How Far Do We Go?

Lastly, Adventists must remain open to the possibility that even certain forms of two-by-two dancing (waltz, polka, etc.) could be appropriate for certain situations and events. How many Adventist couples who might never walk on a dance floor nonetheless express their affection and intimacy in moonlight waltzes in their living rooms? Is there anything materially different about that waltz if it occurs with the other family members or friends present?

It remains to be seen if Adventist believers will have the courage and maturity to explore how dance may again be included as part of the community's celebration of God.

Is the time right to re-think and reformulate the church's official statements about dancing?

[1]Ellen White, *The Great Controversy* (Mountain View, CA: Pacific Press Publishing Association, 1971), 566.

Could two-by-two dances in which persons dance only with their spouses also be appropriate, whether in home gatherings or large settings?

These and other questions will seek answers as Adventists more openly explore the world of dance. In so doing, we will no doubt feel as clumsy as we individually did in our physical adolescence. But the process holds healthy promise of reclaiming for believers joys God never intended we should live without.

And when we stand outside the New Jerusalem, drawn up in what Ellen White delights to call a "a hollow square,"[1] let's leave it to those who cannot tolerate the idea now to observe that it looks for all the world like the beginning of the start of a dance.

Dancing With My Generation

Noelene Pang

Valuegenesis Byte

"Quite strictly enforced" and "very strictly enforced."

- 46% The "no dancing" standard is enforced in your home.

- 78% The "no dancing" standard is enforced in my church.

- 61% The "no dancing" standard is enforced in my school.

"Except for a few top substance-abuse issues, the church enforces the standards more strictly than the family does." *

*Roger L. Dudley with V. Bailey Gillespie, *Valuegenesis: Faith in the Balance* (Riverside, CA: La Sierra University Press, 1992), 157-58.

"Adventists Don't Dance."

Pink ruffly tutus and pink leather toe shoes swirled through my four-year-old head the day my parents promised me ballet lessons. Or was it really a promise? In my excitement, my glassy young eyes overlooked the concern that creased their foreheads, and my ears blocked out the hesitation in their voices. The splendor of being a ballerina lay just beyond tomorrow, and my mind was busy picking out a pink outfit.

Not knowing how to tell me that Adventists aren't allowed to dance, my parents dodged the issue for a couple of days. When my patient waiting turned into impatient prodding, they bluntly broke the news to me.

"You can't take ballet lessons because Seventh-day Adventists don't dance."

"Why?"

"They just don't."

"But why?"

"Don't ask questions!"

End of discussion.

I felt done in. Why didn't they tell me in the first place? Did they even know why Adventists don't dance?

Getting to the "Bottom Line"

Years later I asked them the same question. And I received the same dead-end answers, except they were a bit longer this time, as were my questions.

"Adventists don't dance!"

"Why? People danced in Bible times!"

"But it was different then."

"How? People danced to express their feelings, like joy and gratitude. Music and dancing were a part of their regular celebrations. Can't people dance to express their emotions today?"

"They had folk dances."

"Isn't ballet a type of folk dance? It's an art form, as full of rhythm, culture, discipline, and structure as any other folk dance. It seems like you've lumped ballet into the "All dancing is bad" category. How long have you believed that dancing is wrong for Adventists?"

"For as long as we can remember. Our Bible teachers told us dancing was wrong."

I received the same dead-end answers.

"And you never questioned them?"

"No."

Finally I had reached the "bottom line" for why dancing was wrong from my parents' point of view: Because
some Bible teacher said so. I felt angry that a Bible teacher
I'd never known successfully prevented my potential career with the New York Ballet Company.

Then and Now

I couldn't really blame them for not giving much
thought to the topic of dancing. While they were growing
up, getting food on the table and paying for an education
absorbed all the energy they had. Who could afford the
time or energy to dance? In this setting, a word from a
trusted Bible teacher was all they needed on the subject.

So how does this relate to my generation? Most young
people nowadays aren't afraid to question traditions or
"what some Bible teacher said." Young people want to be
part of the evaluating process to make their religion their
own. Who wants it handed down like a dusty heirloom? For
religion to be active in our lives, we must constantly
reevaluate it. Questions must receive welcomed consideration instead of defensive posturing. Rules need logical
reasons for support. So how does the issue of dancing fit
into this picture?

Who wants it handed down like a dusty heir-loom? For religion to be active in our lives, we must constantly revalu-ate it.

81

Check the Bible

The Bible has quite a few references to dancing. The Psalmist encourages us to praise God with dancing, singing, and musical instruments.[1] The Israelites danced with joy and praise to God after safely crossing the Red Sea.[2]

But the Israelites didn't always honor God with their dancing. While Moses was detained on Mount Sinai, they danced and worshipped a golden calf.[3] We also note that in Biblical times dancing served as a form of entertainment, such as when the daughter of Herodius danced for Herod and his dinner guests.[4]

As can be seen from these texts, people in Biblical times danced for a variety of reasons. The same is true today. People dance because of their cultural traditions: as an art form, to entertain, and as a social pastime. Although the motivations for dancing vary in purpose and intent, one cannot deny the distinctive beauty in the marriage of music and movement. God and His people were sensitive to this beauty and thus strongly recommended it for expressive worship.[5]

Can't Stop Moving

The harmony that exists between music and movement reveals itself in day-to-day living. Consider a figure skater's beauty of form, poise, and athletic ability when the skater "feels" the music and responds to it. Most of us have caught ourselves unconsciously tapping our foot or fingers

[1] Psalm 149:3; Psalm 150:3-5.

[2] Exodus 15:20.

[3] Exodus 32:19.

[4] Mark 6:22.

To express themselves poets choose words, musicians choose instruments, and dancers choose movement.

[5] See Psalm 30:11; 2 Samuel 6:14 and Ecclesiastes 3:4.

to music. Moving to music comes naturally for many and it's a physical manifestation of how a person feels when emotionally stirred by music. To express themselves, poets choose words, musicians choose instruments, and dancers choose movement.

As an expression of our emotions, dancing is like art and music. It can be as structured as a Bach concerto (such as ballroom dancing, jazz, ballet, square dancing and folk dancing). Or it can be as spontaneous and creative as a jazz band's jam session or a concert pianist's own medley (like recreational dancing, funk, and hip-hop).

Even within the strict meter of Bach's music, there is ample room for individual interpretation. When expressed in a different context, dance can take on a different meaning. An individual's intentions and emotions determine the nature of the music as well as the nature of the dancing.

Intentionality

Behavior can be judged as morally right or wrong based upon a person's intentions. Dance is not inherently evil. But it can be associated with evil if it invites immoral behavior. Dancing often gets a "bad rap" because recreational dancing often is associated with nightclubs, bars, and rowdy parties where drinking, smoking, and perhaps sex and drugs are present.

But that brings up the issue of intentions once again. Is your purpose to have a "good time" with friends no

When expressed in a different context, dance can take on a different meaning. An individual's intentions and emotions determine the nature of the music as well as the nature of the dancing.

Do you need to be in a group of supportive people who will strengthen your resolve in issues that might get challenged?

matter what they decide is a "good time"? Are you the type of person who stands strong no matter who's present? Or do you need to be in a group of supportive people who will strengthen your resolve in issues that might get challenged?

The example of Jesus beckons us to focus on people and their salvation. With the Incarnation, Jesus modeled going *to* the people. He didn't seem very concerned about others' prejudice about his social interactions.[1] A person's ability to be a light in a dark place or to be snuffed out depends on that person's temperament, spiritual maturity, and response to the grace and call of God.

[1]See Matthew 11:18-19.

What About You?

When it comes to dancing, what are your intentions for your behavior? Dancing seems to be one of the natural avenues for expressing emotions. While we shouldn't be surprised that the Devil has led people to misuse this gift, we shouldn't automatically eliminate it just because *some* people misuse it.

How and where a person chooses to dance or how dancing is interpreted depends on one's values and experiences. Unfortunately, Adventists have lumped all dancing into the "sins of the flesh" category in an effort to steer clear of potential evil. What are your other places of contact with these "evil people" for whom Christ died?

Learning how to make choices in the area of dancing will equip young people in other areas of life too.

Perhaps it's just easier to condemn all dancing rather than sift through what, when, and where our participation might be appropriate. The fact is, learning how to make choices in the area of dancing will equip young people to make decisions in other areas of life too. The family and the church have an immense responsibility to instill solid values into their youth. The youth, however, are morally responsible for evaluating and choosing which values will guide their future.

The family and the church have an immense responsibility to instill solid values into their youth.

*Roger L. Dudley with V. Bailey Gillespie, *Valuegenesis: Faith in the Balance* (Riverside, CA: La Sierra University Press, 1992), 162.

Dancing has gone though the same kind of change. When someone uses the term "dance" we are not quite sure just what is meant.

Dancing to the Lord

Timothy Gillespie

Much has changed in the last 20 years. The technological age has arrived. People don't go out anymore. You can sit at your desk and surf through the Internet or World Wide Web and have access to almost any product within imagination. These changes have impacted the youth culture. When your family computer crashes, it is not unheard of in this day and age to have parents ask their children to fix it.

This changing age impacts everything in our culture. The changes have become so dramatic most of our staid categories and definitions must be revised. The term "movies" must now include video and television, while the term competition must go beyond sports and invade the academic arena. Dancing has gone through the same kind of change. When someone uses the term "dance" we are not quite sure just what is meant.

Today, you would have a tough time making any sense to a youth if you told him or her that, "Christians shouldn't do the funky chicken or the twist." These types of dance have long been outdated by a youth culture that seeks innovative and new alternative outlets for their energy and enthusiasm. The types of dance older adults think of when they refer to dancing (such as the "Fox Trot" or "Tango"), are now only seen in television movies or promoted in professional competitions. These were the dances condemned by religious leaders of a previous generation and associated with dance halls and smoke-filled rooms. And the arguments that were used to keep youth from falling into the "pit of sin" may make little sense today.

When we talk with youth under the age of eighteen about dance, we need to explain what it is that we mean. For example, few fifteen-year-olds will be tempted to go to dance clubs of today. However, dancing *is* taking place at parties and concerts. The *Valuegenesis* research project which continues to reflect on the faith life of youth and young adults in the church, recognizes that many more youth are participating in dancing than among older generations. Some have suggested that dancing is today where moviegoing was ten years ago. If this is the case, we need relevant and persuasive arguments if dance is negative for faith life.

If parents, youth leaders, pastors, and teachers are to provide help or guidance to youth today, they must first of

Today, you would have a tough time making any sense to a youth if you told him or her that, "Christians shouldn't do the funky chicken or the twist."

all be relevant and attempt to understand the culture that permeates the youth of today in regards to dancing.

Contemporary Forms

In most of the United States dancing has taken on a new look. In some locations line dancing to country music may be in vogue, but with the youth culture today what is more likely to occur is described by such terms as "moshing" or "slamming." Other youth are involved in a more "hip-hop" style, which makes more sense to them. These styles of dance most Christians don't understand or may have never seen. But the MTV generation has seen them, watched them, and probably tried one form or another.

Some who attend concerts have had the chance to "mosh" or "slam" while working their way up close to see the band. All around are people being thrown into the air and into each other. To call this "dancing" is to stretch the term a bit, but nevertheless, youth express themselves in what seems to be an aggressive, angry, or exciting outburst of energy. This is one style of contemporary dance.

This type of "dancing" appeals to many youth. Most concert attendees are between 16 and 18 years of age, and 23-year-olds often feel like an alien generation at such fests. It is not uncommon to see at such concerts masses of bodies swirling with an occasional body flying above the rest carried along the hands of the masses. How does a Christian make sense of these forms of dance? What can be said that might frame a discussion about contemporary dance?

In most of the United States, dancing has taken on a new look.

In some locations line dancing to country music may be in vogue, but with the youth culture today what is more likely to occur are described by terms such as "moshing" or "slamming."

88

Times Don't Really Change

When I was growing up in the mid-80s, break dancing was popular. Everyday during recess my friends and I would hang out by the concrete steps and try out our new moves. We thought that we were "cool." We were getting our exercise for the day. We talked break dancing and shared moves and became preoccupied with this form of expression.

I look back on that now and laugh. But I am hard pressed to say there was anything substantially "wrong" with it. It was a form of expression everyone was trying, the moves were complex, it was a "solo" activity, and we were proud of what we had learned. No moral value was attached to it when I was doing it, at least not by those who participated. Today, "rap-dancing" is an evolution of that early style of movement.

Now older, I realize break dancing was more a form of exercise. It was a type of dance generally unaccepted by the large religious culture I was a part of. As this craze died, so did my involvement in it. But at the time it was important to be "part of the group" or "leader of the group" so I got involved. It was crucial to my junior high school identity. Much of today's dance is simply that—an expression of one's identity.

However, it is a shame that many don't find their identity in Christ but in forms of contemporary culture that reflect secular values. The fact that youth seek personal identity shows the need to express oneself is natural. It will continue even when the dominate culture, Christian

How does a Christian make sense out of these forms of dance? What can be said that might frame a discussion about contemporary dance?

Much of today's dance is simply that—an expression of one's identity. However, it is a shame that many don't find their identity in Christ but in forms of contemporary culture that reflect secular values.

or secular, attempts to challenge that behavior. Identity issues must be considered when approaching the topic of dance, since expression of oneself often can be seen in outward activity and involvement.

Inconsistencies Cause Concern

Obviously, some unique forms of dance are now more accepted. Jazzercise seems better than doing a choreographed routine to Snoop Dogg's new hit. And if you have watched some of the exercise programs on television, they often mimic dance moves and help us keep fit. If done in the privacy of one's home, such dances serve a useful purpose. This inconsistency does not help us confront the decision to dance or not to dance. Why is folk dancing in some countries viewed as acceptable, while in other places it is considered suspect? Youth have a hard time with the inconsistencies in some adults basic argument against their behavior. If you hunt far enough, you can find inconsistencies in the behaviors of various cultures throughout history.

In reality, the issue of dancing is more basic. When one tries to detach the morality from the discussion, questions emerge that bring us back to the basic issues in this discussion. Here is a list of questions for any thoughtful discussion about dancing when understanding and growth are the goal.

1. Why do you move the way you do in dance? (What is your motivation for the movement?)

2. What do you want to get out of the movement? What is your satisfaction in the dancing?

> **Youth have a hard time with the inconsistencies in some adults basic argument against their behavior. If you hunt far enough, you can find inconsistencies in the behaviors of various cultures throughout history.**

3. Where is the activity taking place?

Motivation

Trying to understand our own motivation is difficult. We often don't know why we do what we do. As we mature, we become more reflective of why we do things. But young people, who generally are pragmatic in their decision making, seldom understand their motives or even think about them at all. When you ask teenagers why they dance, they simply say, "its fun!" Seldom does the answer get more profound. That is why the question of motivation is so central to discussions of dancing. Be reflective and ask this simple question: "What motivates you to dance?" Sort through the motivations, trying to understand which motives are self-serving and which motives stretch us to higher goals. Reach. Stretch. Grow. Expand. Sort. Knowing our motives moves us closer to responsibility for our own actions. We all know we can use more responsibility!

Satisfaction

What do you want to get out of the movement of dance? Does your involvement in this activity help you become more like Christ? This is an often-asked question, but central to the discussion, nevertheless. Are you deriving satisfaction because of the sexual movements? Are you satisfied with yourself as you see the person you are becoming because of your actions? Do you like the changes you are

Here is a list of questions that must be understood in any thoughtful discussion about dancing where understanding and growth are the goal.

• What is your motivation for moving your body the way you are?

• What do you want to get out of the movement? What is the satisfaction in the activity?

• Where is the dancing taking place?

91

making in your life? If you can say decidedly "yes," then move ahead securely with your activity. If you don't like the person you are becoming or you find your friends influence you to do things you know to be morally unfit for a young Christian, change your behavior.

The Spirit of the Place

A college president occasionally asked us if we understood the "spirit of the place" in regards to our own university. The spirit of a place is difficult to identify and yet is somewhat tangible if you take a closer look. Where are you going to dance? Is it in a club? In a room with your friends? At Woodstock II with 200,000 people slipping and sliding around in the mud? Are drinks being served? Are people participating in activities that don't benefit anyone? The place *is* important because we are influenced by our environment. That is why interior decorators do important work: to make us feel differently about our environment. When we walk into a Cathedral, we immediately know we are in a "different" kind of place. The same is true on a golf course or in a football stadium. Environment impacts us either negatively or positively. Be circumspect where you go. Don't go anywhere you feel uncomfortable. Trust your values.

Ask Yourself

The answers to these questions will affect our decision-making process. To be relevant to the youth we teach,

Be reflective when you think about going out to dance and ask this simple question, "what motivates you to go?"

either as minister or as parent, look at their music. We may say what we do or do not like about the music to identify the positive and negative messages or behaviors that are influenced by the music. Be aware of the "idols" behind the music, as well as the message that the music is sending. Too often we condemn music with a beat. Let's remember that even King David danced before the Lord. The centrality of God, the excitement of the occasion, and probably the beat of the oriental music caused him to be expressive in dance. Every music has beat or rhythm which humans respond to. Movement alone is not bad. The question is, "How do I control it?" How do I decide what I want to do?

Dancing is obviously different than it used to be. I would venture to say many times you can't tell what it is. Is it aerobicizing or just a goofy walk across the campus on a given day. Things change, times change, and we should deal with that change positively as Christians. That does not mean ignore the essential issues that face youth today. Motivation is a major factor, so is presentation.

Those who did the "butterfly" made pretty suggestive moves with their bodies, but this dance, outdated today, confronted youth of that generation with the same basic questions: "What is our motivation? What makes us satisfied? And, what is the environment like?

In all things we should connect with our beliefs. Many youth attend Christian concerts where people do a modified mosh and sway or dance to music dedicated to God. Obviously, motivation has something to do with acceptance of this action. The more I think about dancing the

Ask, are you deriving satisfaction because of the sexual movements?

Are you satisfied with yourself as you see the kind of person you are becoming because of your actions?

Do you like the changes you are making in your life?

To be relevant to youth we teach, minister or parent, we need to be aware of the nature of their music.

Dancing is obviously different than it used to be. I would venture to say that a lot of times you can't even tell what is dancing. Is it aerobicizing, or even just a goofy walk across the campus on any given day.

more I recognize that movement is not inherently evil any more than donuts are inherently evil. It is what we do with our thoughts, our motives, our leisure that makes a difference in our conduct.

Can we praise the Lord though our movements? Of course. We can dance to the Lord like David, reflecting an outburst of excitement for the glory of God; or we can introspectively turn that excitement inward, reflecting on ourselves and our selfish desires.

Let's discover what we are trying to do with our life. Once we understand our ultimate link with Christ, we can then understand how to make decisions motivated by the grace of God rather than ourselves. Until then simply telling people not to dance will fail and the Adventist church, already seen by many youth as coercive, restrictive, and judgmental, will have been confirmed as such to many youth.

Open up this discussion with young people. Find time to approach them where they are. Think about how they approach this topic and begin to clarify the real issues in this question of dance. The discussion *is* the important thing. The conclusions may or may not be what you had expected. Christian youth are notoriously conservative and often more so than their parents during times of growth. You may find that after you spend the necessary time to explore this lifestyle practice, your teens may agree with a more traditional understanding. If not, you will still be closer to them for having been involved in their thinking and clarification than ever before. The dialogue you begin is crucial.

Learn that the discussion must be open and reflective of the issues. Don't forget that even the tone of your voice communicates a message as you share concerns with youth. And, by all means, don't forget that the Bible does seem to approve something an awful lot like dancing as an expression of the overpowering love of God in the lives of those who participated in the opening of the temple of God in Jerusalem. Then think about the first time you will meet Jesus in heaven. How will you feel? Won't you want to rejoice with your whole being? I think so.

Shall we dance? Definitely! Dance to the music, rhythm, and rhyme provided by the Maker of all things.

*Roger L. Dudley with V. Bailey Gillespie, *Valuegenesis: Faith in the Balance* (Riverside, CA: La Sierra University Press, 1992), 152-53.

Dancing With A
User-Friendly Concordance

Steve Case

Can you imagine trying to undertake a study of dancing by searching through a concordance? Exhaustive concordances can easily seem too tiresome to open.

It's quite simple, really, since the forms of the word (dance, dances, danced, dancing) occur a grand total of 27 times in the entire Bible.

So instead of using a concordance for weight lifting, take some time to focus on the following 27 verses from Scripture (King James Version). You may prefer to use your own Bible to better grasp the context of these usages. Use a notebook or scrap paper, or the space provided in this book for your note taking. This can be done alone or with a group.

A Few Steps in the Process

Before you consider what God revealed in Scripture, jot down what you think you will find in the Bible.

Next, identify your personal views. These might be similar to or different from what you expect to find in the Bible. In other words, What is your personal bias regarding the topic of dancing?

Now you're ready for prayer. Pray for an open mind and fresh perspective as you open God's word.

Do not be defensive if the Bible reveals something different from your personal views. It may not support your prejudices. What an opportunity for transformation!

Now you're ready to look at the words. Here they are as they appear in the Bible, in the context in which they are used. (For example, the references in Judges 21 won't make much sense unless you read the whole chapter along with chapter 20.)

What themes weave through the passages? Consider not only the words but the concepts the words embody.

Dance

1. **Judges 21:21** - And see, and, behold, if the daughters of Shiloh come out to **dance** in dances, then come ye out of the vineyards, and catch you every man his wife of the daughters of Shiloh, and go to the land of Benjamin.

2. **Job 21:11** - They send forth their little ones like a flock, and their children **dance**.

What do you think the Bible says about dancing?

My personal views about dancing.

What themes have you seen in these Bible texts about dance?

3. **Psalm 149:3** - Let them praise his name in the **dance**; let them sing praises unto him with the timbrel and harp.

4. **Psalm 150:4** - Praise him with the timbrel and **dance**; praise him with stringed instruments and organs.

5. **Ecclesiastes 3:4** - A time to weep, and a time to laugh; a time to mourn, and a time to **dance**.

6. **Isaiah 13:21** - But wild beasts of the desert shall lie there; and their houses shall be full of doleful creatures; and owls shall dwell there, and satyrs shall **dance** there.

7. **Jeremiah 31:13** - Then shall the virgin rejoin in the **dance**, both young men and old together: for I will turn their mourning into joy, and will comfort them, and make them rejoice from their sorrow.

8. **Lamentations 5:15** - The joy of our heart is ceased; our **dance** is turned into mourning.

Dances

9. **Exodus 15:20** - And Miriam the prophetess, the sister of Aaron, took a timbrel in her hand; and all the women went out after her with timbrels and with **dances**.

10. **Judges 11:34** - And Jephthah came to Mizpeh unto his house, and, behold, his daughter came out to meet him with timbrels and with **dances**: and she was his only child; beside her he had neither son nor daughter.

11. **Judges 21:21** - And see, and, behold, if the daughters of Shiloh come out to dance in **dances**, then come ye

out of the vineyards, and catch you every man his wife of the daughters of Shiloh, and go to the land of Benjamin.

12. **1 Samuel 21:11** - And the servants of Achish said unto him, "Is not this David the king of the land? Did they not sing one to another of him in **dances**, saying, 'Saul hath slain his thousands, and David his ten thousands?'"

13. **1 Samuel 29:5** - Is not this David, of whom they sang one to another in **dances**, saying, "Saul slew his thousands, and David his ten thousands?"

14. **Jeremiah 31:4** - Again I will build thee, and thou shalt be built, O virgin of Israel: thou shalt again be adorned with thy tabrets, and shalt go forth in the **dances** of them that make merry.

Danced

15. **Judges 21:23** - And the children of Benjamin did so, and took them wives, according to their number, of them that **danced**, whom they caught: and they went and returned unto their inheritance, and repaired the cities, and dwelt in them.

16. **2 Samuel 6:14** - And David **danced** before the LORD with all his might; and David was girded with a linen ephod.

17. **Matthew 11:17** - And saying, "We have piped unto you, and ye have not **danced**; we have mourned unto you, and ye have not lamented.

18. **Matthew 14:6** - But when Herod's birthday was kept, the daughter of Herodias **danced** before them, and pleased Herod.

The Bible has many texts that explore the concept of dance.

19. **Mark 6:22** - And when the daughter of the said Herodias came in, and **danced**, and pleased Herod and them that sat with him, the king said unto the damsel, "Ask of me whatsoever thou wilt, and I will give it thee."

20. **Luke 7:32** - They are like unto children sitting in the marketplace, and calling one to another, and saying, "We have piped unto you, and ye have not **danced**; we have mourned to you, and ye have not wept."

Dancing

21. **Exodus 32:19** - And it came to pass, as soon as he came nigh unto the camp, that he saw the calf, and the **dancing**: and Moses' anger waxed hot, and he cast the tables out of his hands, and brake them beneath the mount.

22. **1 Samuel 18:6** - And it came to pass as they came, when David was returning from the slaughter of the Philistine, that the women came out of all cities of Israel, singing and **dancing**, to meet king Saul, with tabrets, with joy, and with instruments of music.

23. **1 Samuel 30:16** - And when he had brought him down, behold, they were spread abroad upon all the earth, eating and drinking, and **dancing**, because of all the great spoil that they had taken out of the land of the Philistines, and out of the land of Judah.

24. **2 Samuel 6:16** - And as the ark of the LORD came into the city of David, Michal, Saul's daughter looked through a window, and saw King David leaping and **dancing** before the LORD; and she despised him in her

What does it mean to "dance before the Lord?"

heart.

25. **1 Chronicles 15:29** - And it came to pass, as the ark of the covenant of the LORD came to the city of David, that Michal, the daughter of Saul, looking out at a window saw King David **dancing** and playing: and she despised him in her heart.

26. **Psalm 30:11** - Thou hast turned for me my mourning into **dancing**: thou hast put off my sackcloth, and girded me with gladness.

27. **Luke 15:25** - Now his elder son was in the field: and as he came and drew nigh to the house, he heard music and **dancing**.

Your Discoveries

Now that you are familiar with "dance" verses in the Bible, here are a few questions based on your study.

• What themes took shape over the various passages? And which themes are primary? Which ones are secondary?

• Review the principles Bill Knott cited earlier. Compare your discoveries with the biblical principles he identified. How are yours similar? How are they different?

• What biblical principles, even though they might not actually have the word "dance" in them, should also be considered when it comes to dancing?

• How could we dance before the LORD today? What type of dance would it be? Why do people dance nowadays?

- Is dancing "for community joy" acceptable for Seventh-day Adventists?
- Will you or won't you dance? Why or why not?

Suggested Additional
Resources

Adams, Doug, *Congregational Dancing in Christian Worship* (Austin, TX: The Sharing Company), 1971.

Fischer, John, *Real Christians Don't Dance* (Minneapolis: Bethany House Publishers), 1988.

Fisher, Constance, *Dancing the Old Testament: Christian Celebrations of Israelite Heritage for Worship and Education* (Austin, TX: The Sharing Company), 1980.

Litherland, Janet, *Let's Move* (Colorado Springs, CO: Meriwether Publishing), 1979.

Litherland, Janet, *Let's Move Again!* (Colorado Springs, CO: Meriwether Publishing), 1980.

Taylor, Margaret Fisk, *A Time to Dance: Symbolic Movement in Worship*, rev. (Austin, TX: The Sharing Company), 1981.

R. Ver Eecke, R., and Gagne, R., and Kane, T., *Introducing Dance in Christian Worship* (Austin, TX: The Sharing Company), 1984.

Section 3
Thinking About Music

Section 3
Thinking About Music

Just for a moment, think about one of your all-time favorite songs. Perhaps it's a special hymn from your childhood church; one you sang loudly, standing next to your mother, as she looked down at you and smiled with pride.

Perhaps it's a piano piece you practiced over and over again for that big recital; one you can still play by heart.

Perhaps it's a popular love-song that became meaningful to you in your first big romance. You still know every word.

Or perhaps the majestic music to which you marched into the church the day of your wedding.

Think about that favorite song of yours for a moment.

Think about one of your all-time favorite songs

Mentally listen to the music. Sing the words to yourself, play the piece in your mind, or hum it out loud. Reexperience the precious moments you associate with that favorite song. Recall the joy, the warm feelings.

Now for the shocking and rude truth: somewhere in this world there's somebody who thinks your favorite song is absolutely awful. Worse yet, there's a good likelihood that we could find someone out there who thinks your favorite song, even your favorite religious song, came straight from the devil.

How could people be so wrong? What is it about music that causes so much controversy? How can such an incredibly wonderful accompaniment to our lives evoke such conflict?

What's the Discussion About?

Music is intensely personal. The never-ending argument over music is perpetually fueled by the subjective nature of music appreciation. All of us are critics. We like the music we like. And we don't care much for anybody else's musical tastes.

Musical interest begins in childhood and is influenced by our cultural background, the songs we enjoyed as kids, and the music preferred by our parents.

Aaron Goldberg had a violin in his hands almost from the time he could walk. The adults in his life were the best music teachers in New York City. His uniform was a

Music is intensely personal. The never-ending argument over music is perpetually fueled by the subjective nature of music appreciation.

tuxedo and his social life a continual round of classical concerts and recitals.

Jeremiah McCoy also grew up with a violin. In his home town in a backwoods hollow of the Appalachians, everybody called it a fiddle. The mountain music he played would have seemed out of place in Lincoln Center. But it sounded just right coming from the squeaky old rocking chair on his front porch.

Lynwood laPierre learned how to play the trumpet by imitating the sounds he heard the old men play every night at Preservation Hall in New Orleans.

Loretta Trumble grew up listening to the country music stations in Nashville. She played the steel guitar in church while her sisters sang from their hearts, "Jeesus is maah Saeevyoor, Aah shall not be mooved."

Carol Kolwinski still gets tears in her eyes when she hears an accordion playing the polkas she knew as a child in her Polish neighborhood in Chicago.

Eloy Ramirez brightens up when he gets within a block of a band of strolling mariachis.

The cultural principle is obvious: We appreciate the songs we've learned to appreciate. But there are some who feel compelled to put a *spiritual* value on our musical *preferences*: my choice indicates a higher spiritual plane than your choice, they tell us; slow is more religious than fast; country is spiritually preferable to jazz, easy-listening is better than country, classical is the most religious of all!

We must be careful not to confuse spirituality with style or cultural conditioning. As Christians, we certainly

We appreciate the songs we've learned to appreciate.

107

apply high spiritual standards to all our activities, including our music. But we must also be quick to be tolerant in situations where the issue is merely one of differing musical tastes. Let's not create unnecessary conflict.

The Background of the Discussion

Youthful innovations and contemporary directions in music have been questioned by many in the older generations, including music which we now we venerate as classical. The clash over music repeats generation after generation.

Some religious leaders in the early Middle Ages considered Gregorian chants unfit for use in worship because they sounded too much like the popular secular songs of the day.

The church members of Arnstadt complained that their teenage organist mixed strange tones into his music. The teenager's name was Johann Sebastian Bach.

Older musicians criticized a youthful Beethoven for the revolutionary sympathies of his music, for his moody themes, and for his attention to the money-making part of his business.

Debussy's early romantic harmonies and dance rhythms annoyed his teachers at the Paris Conservatoire.

Aaron Copeland was told his music was too loud. Following the premier performance of one of his symphonies, the disapproving conductor turned to the audience

The conflict must be settled over and over again by each new generation.

108

and said, "If a young man at the age of twenty-three can write a symphony like that, in five years he will be *ready to commit murder!*"

The complaints sound like they could have been voiced today. They will still sound current years and years from now.

While the clash between musical values is not exclusively a generational one, it is where most of the shouting is heard. The resulting conflict, as ancient as Jubal and as contemporary as tomorrow's latest release, must be settled over and over again by each generation through the application of timeless principles to current situations.

Questions Youth Are Asking

• Since our grandparents thought our parents' music was bad, why should we be concerned if our parents don't care for our music?

• Shouldn't I decide what I listen to on the basis of the words, not the music?

• Do adults object to contemporary Christian music because it is *contemporary* or because they don't think it is Christian?

• The music doesn't affect me; but even if it did, what's wrong with getting a little excited?

• What is wrong with music with a beat? Didn't even classical music in its day field criticism because of its contemporary beat?

Focusing the Discussion

• "The Power of Music." Musician and songbook editor Stuart Tyner identifies the physical and emotional components of music—their elements and insights—from a number of people within the music industry.

Read some of the quotations to start a discussion regarding the power of music. Ask people how they use music in their lives and what impact it makes on them. Ask about the use of music in commercials or in setting the mood for a particular scene in a movie. How is music utilized at church, and how effective is it there? Why?

• In "Between Rock and a Hard Place" Stuart Tyner continues his examination of the music controversy by providing steps for engaging in worthwhile music discussions, especially with those whose musical tastes differ from your own.

Follow the steps outlined in the chapter. When it comes to "becoming informed," what are your sources? How current are they? Do you lean towards advocating your personal position by clearly articulating it? Or do you lean more towards assisting others to clarify their own position? Stuart then presents four biblical principles to evaluate music.

• "Have You Heard This One?" Adrian Westney challenges listeners with some pointed questions regard-

> Follow the steps outlined in the chapter. When it comes to "becoming informed," what are your sources? How current are they? Do you lean more towards advocating your personal position by clearly articulating it? Or do you lean more towards assisting others to clarify their own position?

ing the music they listen to, as well as the music they don't listen to, for whatever reason.

Adapt the suggested activities to your current situation. Use them as a starting point for developing your own materials for a worthwhile lab and discussion on this topic. And don't limit the discussion to your personal bias. If possible, team up with another dedicated Christian whose personal taste in music differs from your own. Be sure to have the right equipment to play music. Talking about music is tame compared to actually having music to listen to so you can demonstrate its power!

• "Suggested Additional Resources" identifies helpful materials to deepen your background on this topic. Be sure to add your own resources which includes musical selections from your music library, along with selections from a person with a different point of view.

How do you use music in your own life? What impact does music make on you?

Unless we are intentional about our music, we surrender the power of this influence to someone else's intention.

The Power of Music

Stuart Tyner

Music causes controversy because it is such a powerful influence in our lives. Music can be a soothing friend or a frightening foe; an effective ally or a formidable enemy. It can boldly demand our attention or insidiously manipulate our moods. We can actively choose from a dazzling array of styles and content, but we can also become so needy that we listen to whatever happens to be available. And in a religious setting, the power of music is obvious. Evangelists, pastors, teachers, and most religious persons have experienced the uplifting power of spiritual song.

Unless we are intentional about our music, we surrender the power of this influence to someone else's intention.

112

Let's focus on two aspects of this influential power of music—the physical power and the emotional power.

The Physical Power

British pastor and educator John Peck calls our attention to the powerful physical nature of music. "Music is profoundly physical," Peck says. It "acts at the point at which our minds interface with our bodies."[1]

This physical effect often is dramatic. Research indicates that slow baroque music, played softly, "tends to slow the body processes of pulse and respiration and helps in lowering blood pressure and decreasing the flow of stress hormones."[2]

The physical power can have a significant effect on learning. One small parochial elementary school in the South Bronx gives the credit for their scholastic excellence to their intensive music emphasis. "When you have music, you learn to focus," reports one of St. Augustine's students. "It teaches you to concentrate in the rest of your studies."

Music's physical power also has a negative side. The potentially hazardous volume achieved during most rock concerts has been discussed widely. Humorist Garrison Keillor graphically describes such sound as being so loud it "can re-part your hair, take the skin off your face, and wipe out blemishes."[3]

Stereo earphones blasting away for hours may be a greater threat than concerts. Hearing loss among rock

[1] John Peck, "An Englishman Comments on the Revolution," *Cornerstone*, 14:77.

[2] Vicki A. Moss and Judith A. Webster, "To Your Health," *Nation's Business*, (May, 1986).

[3] Garrison Keillor, "Mammoth Concert Tickets," *Gospel Birds and Other Stories of Lake Wobegon*, (St. Paul, MN: Minnesota Public Radio, 1985).

That intentional sexual impact becomes a problem for Christians whenever the music invites us to abandon our values.

[1] V. Bailey Gillespie, "I Love Rock 'n' Roll," *Insight*, (August 29, 1987).

[2] "Little Red Corvette," *Rolling Stone*, (September 8, 1988).

musicians has led to the establishment of an organization in San Francisco named HEAR (Hearing Education Awareness for Rockers) to alert performers, technicians and concert-hall staffers to the perils of loud music.

Other elements of music go straight for the heart. "The pounding of the amplified bass," recalls one writer of the physical effect of his first rock concert, "was just a little faster than a heartbeat. I could feel my pulse racing to catch up with the driving rhythm as the lead singer slid to the floor and screamed into the mic."[1]

Neither can we ignore the ability of music's physical power to arouse our sexual feelings. From classical pieces (Ravel's "Bolero" is an obvious and frequently cited example) to the teasing tunes of the 50s to today's most blatant songs, the sexual power of both lyrics and music has been well understood by composers and performers. A *Rolling Stone* review noted, "The sexual motif is reinforced by the song's rhythmic structure, which builds from a mellow, pulsing synthesizer opening, then chugs into a power-driven sing-along chorus."[2] That intentional sexual impact becomes a problem for Christians whenever the music invites us to abandon our values and take part in the excitement of the moment, regardless of what the spiritual consequences may be.

And it's not just conservative Christians who recognize what can happen. Pablo Guzman put it this way, "Sweat flies off foreheads, hair whips around faces, clothes stick to bodies: the dancers are lost in a whirl of exotic movement. This is the music of the night. All school-week cares and workaday worries have been abandoned. The moment is everything—and it screams Release!"[1]

"Lust has a good beat, and you can dance to it," writes Eve Zibart in an almost biblical *Washington Post* review of a new rock band. "Even when the lyrics refer to shame or . . . guilt, the music is far more persuasive: urgent, sensual, unsated and unapologetic. The flesh is willing, and the conscience is weak."[2]

The problem is not always stated so delicately. The vocalist for American rock group Black 'n' Blue crudely describes the raw sexual atmosphere of a recording session for one of their albums. "The boys found themselves in a constant state of arousal," admits the singer. "And they weren't the only ones. The girls who showed up this time weren't just there to listen to music, believe me! They were like cats in heat—and so were we."[3]

It's obvious why Vicki Moss and Judith Webster, two registered nurses talking about music and health, advise choosing your music as carefully as you would choose a healthy diet

The Emotional Power

But the physical power of music (the interface of mind and body) plays second fiddle to the emotional power (the intersection of sound and soul). Jon Pareles wrote, "Pop's real value isn't informational, of course—it's emotional. What I've got rattling around between the ears is an

[1] Pablo Guzman, "Rhythm is Gonna Get You," *Seventeen*, (August, 1988).

[2] Eve Zibart, "Guilt-ed Palaces of Sin," *Washington Post*, (July 29, 1988).

[3] Hank Peters, "Heating It Up, "*Hit Parader*," (October, 1988).

[1]Jon Pareles, "Lyrics to Live—and Love—By," *Mademoiselle*, (November, 1986).
[2]Noel Becchetti, "A Word From the Editor," *Youthworker*, (Summer, 1988).

[3]Adrian Westney, "Music and Emotion," *Message*, (January-February, 1987).

[5]Gil Schwartz, "They're Playing Our Song," *Seventeen*, (July, 1986).

[5]John Leland, "Rap and Race," *Newsweek* (June 29, 1992).

encyclopedia of moods, conveyed both lyrically and musically."[1] Noel Becchetti adds, "Music isn't an intellectual medium. It's an emotional one that penetrates our deepest reaches and inevitably evokes a response."[3]

Adventist musician Adrian Westney agrees. "Music can make you want to laugh or cry. It can cause you to feel energetic or lazy, relaxed or disturbed, delightfully crazy and outgoing or frightfully sane and alone. Even holy or sinful."[3]

Much of this emotional power comes from the fact that music so often deals with relationships. In a *Seventeen* article, "They're Playing Our Song," Gil Schwartz gives advice on finding "that very special song that's just right for the two of you." Schwartz tells about the emotional power of one such song from his own experience. "It seemed to thaw some of the natural frost that clings to all new relationships," he recalls. "After a while, just hearing its first notes made me feel sort of warm inside."[4]

It is in this emotional arena that pop music often comes under its most severe criticism. In the most serious accusations, rock or rap have been credited with promoting extreme violence. "Pop music," charges *Newsweek*, "has become our most pointed metaphor for volatile racial polorization."[5] Heavy-metal band and performers have actually been sued by parents who claim the rock music "mesmerized" their children, convincing them to attempt suicide and propelling them into acts of horrible violence.

Many other parents, feeling their families are less threatened by the influence of the radical elements of contemporary music, are nonetheless convinced that rock undermines Christian values—especially when the music is coupled with video images like MTV with its millions of viewers each week. Those feelings seem to be supported by research conducted in Ohio that indicates MTV directly affects the attitudes of teenagers on questions such as violence and premarital sex. More adolescents tended to agree with the use of violence and with premarital sex after viewing the MTV videos than before viewing them.[1]

One article gives a hint as to why MTV might have such an effect. In "The Video Vice," author Jim Farber quotes Jeff Feldman, Ph. D., about the escapism of today's music. "By watching, you can relatively quickly and easily escape from the world of parents, school, and authority. And the world you'll escape to is a lot more fun. Here everything is geared toward fantasy. No one ever dies. There are no consequences for any action."[2]

To Rock Or Not To Rock

The elements that make music so controversial also make it necessary for us as Christians to thoughtfully consider the role we allow music to play in our lives. Twenty years ago we would have called the music of most young people "rock music." Not surprisingly, it was the most controversial style. Today even "rock music" has a number of variations (hard, soft, heavy metal, punk, thrash, rap, alternative, etc.).

[1]David Lynn and Jay Voigt, "And Neither is MTV," *Youthworker*, (Fall, 1987).

[2]Jim Farber, "The Video Vice," *Seventeen*, (August, 1988).

The elements that make music so controversial also make it necessary for us to thoughtfully consider its place in our lives

God created music; but He didn't compose any top-40 tunes.

How do we deal with rock? Should we take the view that nothing's wrong with it? Is it merely a harmless youthful style? Or should we come down much harder on rock? Is it unquestionably a Satanic influence? These two opposite views demand our attention.

Nothing's Wrong With Rock

One approach to rock music begins with the acceptance of all musical styles as harmless and neutral. Not surprisingly, this view is often held by those involved in some aspect of the music industry, including the contemporary Christian music portion (like producers, promoters, performers, and retailers). Without calling into question anyone's commitment to a certain style of musical ministry, it is nonetheless fair to examine the two main premises of this approach.

God Created All Music. The first premise goes like this: since all things were created by God and for God (Col. 1:16) and since everything God created is good (1 Tim. 4:4), music, including rock music, cannot be considered evil.

The mistake this assumption makes is in an overly ambitious application of the phrase "all things." Yes, God created music. But He did not compose any top-40 tunes. God created laughter. But if someone turns an ethnic slur or a vulgarity into a comedy routine, Christians can't laugh and dismiss it by saying, "God created all things." God created sexuality. But if someone perverts sexuality, we

118

can't take part and excuse our actions by saying, "All things which God created are good."

Music is an incredible gift from our heavenly father. But, as with all His gifts, He has not dictated our use of the gift. If we choose to distort music—if, for example, we direct it toward self-worship instead of praise, or we promote discord instead of harmony, or we accentuate feeling in place of faith—then our music ceases to be heavenly. It is the distortion of the gift, not the gift itself, that causes problems.

Of course, we don't have to be rock 'n' roll devil-worshippers, actual Satanist, for that distortion to occur. "The essence of Satanism is selfishness," observes David Hart, rock music seminar presenter. Whatever proceeds from selfishness comes from Satan, whether the music is rock or gospel, country or classical.

Only Words Can Be Evil. The second premise of a no-questions-asked acceptance of all music is that only the lyrics of the performers can make music evil. The music itself—the melody, harmonies, rhythms, and dynamics—is a neutral element and therefore cannot be considered evil.

The thought that music is neutral certainly is foreign to composers. Listen to multi-Grammy award winner Paul Simon: "For me, music takes precedence over lyrics . . . I tried to write lyrics that fit the mood of the tracks. If the song felt like a love song, I wrote a love song. If it felt more powerful and had stronger overtones, I wrote something more serious."[1]

[1] Paul Simon, "A Songwriter's South African Odyssey," *U.S. News and World Report*, (March 2, 1987).

[1] Helen Epstein, "Vladimir Horowitz," in *Music Talks*, (New York: McGraw Hill, Inc., 1987), 11,13.

[2] You may want to demonstrate these principles to your youth group. Play the musical scores from movie scenes that demonstrate each emotion mentioned.

When determining musical values, Christians must take into account the effect of the music itself.

It's also a foreign thought to performers of instrumental music. Instrumentalists understand that sound alone conveys great depth of feeling. "I want the public to feel what I feel," says Vladimir Horowitz, for fifty years considered one of the world's foremost pianists. "I want when I cry on the piano, or when I laugh, that the public also cries and laughs."[1]

If music is neutral, why is John Williams employed to compose musical themes for presidential candidates, network news programs, Olympic ceremonies, and epic movies? And why do evangelists choose certain music to play quietly during an altar call? It is *not* because music is neutral. In film, why is the musical background so vastly different for a comedy sequence in a Disney cartoon, a love scene in a romantic drama, the triumphal moment in a science fiction epic, and the fearful pursuit of a crazed fan in a horror movie?[2] And why is it that you don't hear classical music or gospel songs coming from pornographic theaters or bars with live sex shows? It is precisely because music is *not* neutral. The music itself, quite apart from the lyrics, conveys emotion and produces response. When determining musical values, Christians must take into account the effect of the music itself.

Rock Bashing

The opposite approach to rock is equally irrational. It tends to classify all rock music, secular rock and Christian rock alike, as an evil force, concocted by self-serving, drug-crazed, sexually promiscuous anarchists for the explicit purpose of destroying the morality of teenagers.

This harsh view of rock has been preached for years. In the 60s, good Christian kids were told not to listen to the Beatles, even to their appearance on the Ed Sullivan Show. In the 70s, *Rock 'n' Roll: The Devil's Diversion*, by Bob Larson, made an impact on the lives of many young Christians, frequently leading to bonfires fueled by rock albums. More recently, the alarm has been sounded in such works as *Set the Trumpet to Thy Mouth* by David Wilkerson; *The Devil's Disciples* by Jeff Godwin; *Religious Rock 'n' Roll: A Wolf in Sheep's Clothing* by a pre-scandalized Jimmy Swaggart; and *What the Bible has to Say about Contemporary Christian Music: Ten Scriptural Reasons Why the "Rock Beat" is Evil in Any Form* by Bill Gothard[1]

One must be aware that most such books contain more than their share of embarrassingly false information about secular artists, and often are filled with wild conjecture, weak biblical scholarship, and poor historical research. In addition, these authors frequently descend to a childish level of name-calling and *National Enquirer*-style allegations. Even more revolting, the authors generally seek to place their opinions beyond questioning by using a God-hath-shown-me approach.

These ugly broadsides come in a variety of forms. Some follow Godwin's pitiful character assassination: John Lennon was a "violent, antisocial, thieving street

[1]Al Menconi has responded to each of Gothard's propositions in *Dear Mr. Gothard: A Common Sense Response to Bill Gothard's Criticisms of Today's Christian Music*, which is available from Al Menconi Ministries, P.O. Box 5008, San Marcos, CA 92069-3621; telephone (619) 591-4696.

121

[1]Jeff Godwin, *The Devil's Disciples: The Truth About Rock*, (Chick, 1985).

[2]David Wilkerson, *Set the Trumpet to Thy Mouth*, (World Challenge, 1985).

[3]Jimmy Swaggart, *Religious Rock 'n' Roll: A Wolf in Sheep's Clothing*, 42.

[4]Bill Gothard, *What the Bible has to say about Contemporary Christian Music: Ten Scriptural Reasons Why the "Rock Beat" is Evil in Any Form* (Oak Brook, IL: Institute in Basic Youth Conflicts, 1990), 9.

[5]Allan Bloom, "Rock Music and the Mind," *Phi Delta Kappa*, (April-May, 1988).

punk thug with severe emotional disturbances and imbalances."[1]

Others are full of pious contempt, like Wilkerson's comment: "I can listen to a Christian rock artist's music and tell in the Spirit immediately what their secret lives are like."[2] And Swaggart's typically arrogant pronouncement: "I cannot possibly see how rock music, with its origins in demonic activity, can apply to the gospel of the Lord Jesus Christ."[3] And, of course, Mr. Gothard's chain-of-command fiat, "There is absolutely no way that Christians who love the 'rock beat' can deny that they love the world."[4]

Still others exaggerate to the point of being ridiculous, as in Allan Bloom's passionate, if somewhat laughable, illustration: "Picture a 13-year-old boy sitting in the living room of his family home doing his math assignment while wearing his Walkman headphones or watching MTV . . . A pubescent child whose body throbs with orgasmic rhythms; whose feelings are made articulate in hymns to the joys of onanism, of the killing of parents; whose ambition is to win fame and wealth in imitating the queen who makes the music. In short, life is made into a nonstop, commercially prepackaged masturbational fantasy."[5]

All such shallow literary scare tactics perform a huge disservice to those who genuinely are concerned about very real negative influences, potentially present in all types of musical experiences, but especially prevalent in hard rock. We have to take today's music much more

122

seriously than such puny efforts indicate. "Destructive music, as any art form, needs to be understood and interpreted. Just as pornography and hate literature must be thoroughly challenged, music deserves the same serious, critical challenge and interpretation."[1]

Such arguments are virtually worthless in establishing reasonable Christian values concerning music. Rock bashing may sell books. It may increase donations to certain narrow "ministries." It may cement the loyalties of a particular segment of the constituency. And it may even express the honest fears of sincere Christians. But it fails to offer teenagers, or others, any solid Christian principles upon which to base their standards. Such polemics convince only the already-convinced and in reality accomplish the opposite of what they are intended to do, driving away youth instead of winning them to a true, Christian perspective.

[1] Earl Palmer, "Strategy for Sanity," *Youthworker* (Summer, 1988).

"Destructive music, as any art form, needs to be understood and interpreted. Just as pornography and hate literature must be thoroughly challenged, music deserves the same serious, critical challenge and interpretation."

Between Rock and A Hard Place

Stuart Tyner

Here are the first steps to take.

Music continues to be an issue, both for young people and adults. Doing nothing about it easily can be as destructive as putting down teens and their music. If you agree that the "Anything Goes" and the "Rock Bashing" approaches fail to lead us to solid Christian principles, but you also feel the time has come to begin exploring the subject with your youth, here are the first steps to take.

Become Informed

Don't get off to a bad start by talking about rock stars who haven't had a hit song since the members of your youth group were born. This is a constantly changing scene, and, especially for this discussion, you need to be an up-to-date witness. Do some research. Think of this as a class in your youth ministry education, a class that's preparing you to effectively communicate with your youth on a vital topic. You won't like everything you hear or read, but you'll be able to use everything you discover. In fact, non-Christian musicians often make the point much better than we can.

Here are a few required resources for this class:

MTV. Spend 20 minutes a day, at different times of the day, for several days in a row before you begin your discussion. That will give you plenty of images to refer to. Another visual resource, if it's the right time of year, is the annual Grammy music awards telecast. Even though you won't like all the music, you'll get a great overall picture of the amazing variety of musical styles, including a smattering of contemporary Christian music and an introduction to the most popular performers of the year just past.

Radio Programs. Take a quick survey in your youth group. Ask them what radio station they believe most teenagers in your city listen to. Then tune in to that station for a few minutes a day for a week. To get updated on contemporary Christian music, see if you can find a youthful Christian music station on your radio.

Music Magazines. One particularly informative magazine, especially the charts on the back page and the personality capsules toward the front, is *Rolling Stone*. Some teen monthlies, like *Seventeen* or *Sassy* might surprise you by

In fact, non-Christian musicians often make the point much better than we can.

some of the pictures and the occasionally frank discussions, but keep reading. Take in an artist's profile and study the lyrics to current hits. The advertisements can also be pretty revealing. The contemporary Christian music scene is well represented in *CCM* (*C*ontemporary *C*hristian *M*usic).

Christian Youth Magazines. You'll find well-written articles, as well as reviews of current music and recommended resources in such magazines as *Group*, *Youthworker* and *Youthworker Update*. Al Menconi Ministries publishes *Media Update* as well as other inexpensive resources on music topics.

Now you're better informed. You know who today's stars are. You're aware of the hit songs. You're in touch with the issues involved. Now you're ready to take the next step in exploring this topic with your kids.

Don't Impose Your Judgment

You've probably already made up your mind. But don't force others to agree with you; don't impose your judgment. Young people are examining options, not taking every word from an adult as gospel truth. Teens want to be able to discuss the issues, filing away items of special interest as they continue the process of determining what is true. If you go to your youth group with ready-made answers, with decisions already reached on their behalf, you'll miss a wonderful opportunity to guide them in a

Now you're ready to take the next step in exploring this topic with your kids.

Teens want to be able to discuss the issues, filing away items of special interest as they continue the process of determining what is true.

most valuable lesson—learning how to make informed decisions.

Allowing them to have their opinions is not the same as agreeing with what they decide. Author Steve Lawhead puts it this way, "Just because you are withholding judgment does not mean you are automatically condoning the evil lifestyles of rock musicians (and many are reprehensible) or anything else. It simply means you are creating an atmosphere where people are enabled to think for themselves."[1]

"Our task is not to enforce our opinions or tastes on our kids," adds David Hart, "but to help them come to their own conclusions about the best ways to use music to grow in their faith. This can be frustrating, because they may not come to the conclusions that we hold. But in order for them to gain ownership of their faith we must teach them how to arrive at spiritual decisions, rather than making those decisions for them."[2]

Honestly Evaluate All the Factors

The third step involves some hard work. You won't be able to accomplish this step through shallow stereotyping. For example, are all heavy-metal rockers really Satanists? Does a "classical" label ensure pure subject matter? Can you understand rock only when you're high on drugs? Is everything Amy Grant sings totally acceptable?

Let's get serious. If we're going to begin evaluating the music we listen to, we're going to have to be willing to take

[1]Stephen Lawhead, "Helping Kids Think About Music," *Group* (January, 1987).

[2]David Hart, "Focus on Music," in *Youthworker*, (Fall, 1986).

127

Here are four biblical principles for Christians to evaluate music.

1 Samuel 16:7; Psalm 150; Romans 14:1-4.

it category by category, artist by artist, song by song. That's an enormous undertaking, but it goes faster than you might expect. Here are four biblical principles for Christians to evaluate music.

Principle #1: Intention

What is the purpose of the music? What response is the composer attempting to elicit? How do the performers intend for us to react? This is an area that provides both easy answers and difficult challenges.

The easy answers come in response to groups that are blatantly anti-Christian. For example, "Black Metal" music with its Satanic occult images in its staging, costumes and lyrics, leather and chains characterize the attire, plus themes of sado-masochism and female domination. Then there's "Thrash Metal" with screaming guitars and music with no effort made at harmony or melody, encouraging extreme hatred and a negative attitude toward authority. And "Alternative Rock," which *Time* magazine characterized as a "deliberately abrasive" and "defiant," a "music genre ruled by high school passions" with lyrics about "despair, lust (and) confusion." It is the "sound of homes breaking," "speaking directly to unresolved issues of abandonment and unfairness."[1]

But difficult challenges arise in relation to music openly intended to be Christian music, but which compositionally cannot be distinguished from its secular counter-

[1]Christopher John Farley, "Rock's Anxious Rebels," *Time*, October 25, 1993), 60-62, 66.

part. This category includes a wide spectrum of music, from Christian country, Christian rap, and Christian new wave through the soft-rock sounds of most of today's Christian performers to the straight Christian rock and Christian heavy metal.

Supporters of these various styles ask us to examine the goals or intentions of the groups. "The number one thing is to tell people about Jesus in a way they can relate to," testified drummer Robert Sweet of Stryper. "When I sit down to write a song," adds singer Michael Sweet, "I always pray. I don't want to sing; I don't want to write. I want God to sing and write through me and to use me as an instrument."[1] Glenn Kaiser, founder of Rez Band explains his group's mission like this: "Our calling has always been twofold: to preach the gospel to the lost and to minister a simple message of biblical discipleship to Christians . . . in the language of a particular culture."[2]

Detractors on this issue insist that, while the intentions may be sincere, the style itself is questionable. Perhaps Paul would advise us to be careful here and to separate style from spirituality. "It is not for you to judge someone else's servant," he has cautioned us. "You should never pass judgment on a brother or treat him with contempt" (Romans 14:4, 10).

"It is on the intention that all depends," observes C. S. Lewis. "We must beware of the naive idea that our music can 'please' God as it would please a cultivated human hearer. That is like thinking, under the old Law, that he

[1] Steve Rabey, *The Heart of Rock and Roll*, (Old Tappan, NJ: Flemming H. Revel Company, 1986), 64, 67.

[2] Glenn Kaiser, "Rez Sez," *Cornerstone*, (vol. 14, issue 75).

"It is on the intention that all depends."

[1] C. S. Lewis, "On Church Music," *Christian Reflections*, (Grand Rapids, MI: William B. Eerdman's Publishing Company, 1968), 98-99.

[2] Noel Paul Stookey, quoted in "Expressions," *Campus Life*, (January, 1987).

1 John 4:1-3;
Philippians 1:15-18.

Be sure to utilize these questions in evaluating a Christian concert too.

really needed the blood of bulls and goats. To which an answer came, 'Mine are the cattle upon a thousand hills,' and 'if I am hungry, I will not tell thee.' If God (in that sense) wanted music, he would not tell us. For all our offerings, whether of music or martyrdom, are like the intrinsically worthless present of a child, which a father values indeed, but values only for the intention."[1]

Noel Paul Stookey (of Peter, Paul and Mary fame) expresses the same thought like this, "God hears music from the inside out."[2] Isn't that what God had in mind when he pointed out to Samuel, "God does not see as man sees; man looks at appearances, but the Lord looks at the heart" (1 Samuel 16:7).

Principle #2: Music Creates and/or Expresses a Presence That Must Be Evaluated

The second revealing element in evaluating music is presence. Before a band begins to play, you can easily observe the particular atmosphere that animates the audience. How are the guys and girls treating each other? What statement is being made by the prevailing fashion? Does the atmosphere rely heavily on drugs and alcohol? What do the lifestyles of the performers tell you about their influence? Be sure to utilize these questions in evaluating a Christian concert too. The answers to these questions, and others like them, will help determine your involvement with the music.

130

A group's presence can also be observed in a record store. Examine album/CD covers and posters. In a now famous exchange from the September 19, 1985 Congressional hearing on rock music and lyrics, an unlikely, but nonetheless accurate, witness Twisted Sisters' Dee Snider, made the point, "As a parent myself and as a rock fan, I know that when I see an album cover with a severed goat's head in the middle of a pentagram between a woman's legs, that is not the kind of album I want my son to be listening to."[1]

Principle #3: The Lyrics Communicate a Message

What is the message of the song based on the lyrics? Is it a song about love, life, anger, sex, destruction, hope, pain, friendship, death, disappointment, joy, fatalism, eagerness, the supernatural?

What does the song say about its topic? For instance, if the topic is love, what's the message about love? Does love wait, confront, give in, forgive, give, take, use, abuse, support, demand? Is it physical, emotional, spiritual, mental, or some type of combination? Many musical releases include a printed copy of the lyrics (if you can't understand the words).

Some research indicates that kids don't know the words to their songs. Test the theory with your youth group. I'm not convinced it's accurate. Watch what hap-

[1]The hearings were urged by the Parents Music Resource Center, Arlington, Virginia, publishers of a newsletter which raises excellent questions about rock music.

Philippians 4:8.

pens when a favorite rock star gets up and yells, "Come on, sing with me," or when a hit song comes on the radio in a car full of teenagers. Most of the kids know the words, but they may not pay much attention to them. It's our responsibility to focus that attention on the message the words convey and get the kids to ask discerning questions.

The primary question, according to author Stephen Lawhead, is, "Are the words consistent with what I believe?"[1] If the words are dirty or disgusting, vulgar or violent, Satanic or suggestive, the answer is obvious—the Christian shouldn't listen to it. You won't need to preach about this. Let the words speak for themselves.

But, the other side of the coin can present us with an interesting dilemma. What if the music is Christian rock and the words are consistent with our faith? How will we react in that situation? In today's Christian music, we're likely to hear words that genuinely speak to teenage concerns, from "love to political issues and from sexual morality to suicide." It's at least a possibility that we may be led to the same conclusion reached by one father and reported by *Cornerstone*: "Of the four hundred Christian contemporary albums we have, not one song promoted sin: all are consistent with basic orthodox doctrines of Scripture, and I saw nothing but benefit in the lives of myself and my teens."[2]

[1]Stephen Lawhead, "Helping Kids Think About Music," *Group* (January, 1987).

[2]Jeff Fator, "Dad Endorses Christian Rock," *Cornerstone*, (vol. 14, issue 75).

Principle #4: Music Communicates a Message. It Affects and/or Expresses One's Mood or Feelings

1 Samuel 16:23;
2 Chronicles 20:13-22.

The final arena of musical evaluation is the most difficult one. How do we fairly evaluate all the elements of the music itself—the melodies, harmonies, rhythms and dynamics? How can we separate personal preference from spiritual effect long enough to come to an accurate decision? If the intention of the composers and musicians is honorable, if the presence is acceptable, if the words are consistent with our beliefs, can the music still render a song unacceptable to Christians?

I believe there are some cases where the answer obviously is yes. A musical style can be so closely associated with a negative influence that putting spiritual words to the obviously unspiritual music is not enough to make that music acceptable. But, exactly where to draw the line is an intensely personal decision. We can invite discussion on the topic, we can offer guidelines, we can encourage decisions. But in the end, each individual will base his or her decision on the personal impact of each piece of music.

That impact varies greatly. I heard the great American jazz musician, Duke Ellington, and his band, play sacred music in gothic Grace Cathedral in San Francisco. While I appreciated the artistry of composition and performance, the blend of the style of music and the sacred intention didn't work for me at the time.

Exactly where to draw the line is an intensely personal decision.

133

But then I listened to six young singers from Oakwood College, Take 6, in a dinner theater in Washington, DC. The room was full of noisy people. Many were eating hamburgers and drinking pitchers of beer. I didn't think the atmosphere was right for a sacred concert. But within ten seconds of the time the group began to sing, something astounding happened in the room. Every ounce of attention became riveted to the singers, to their innovative sound, and to their clear, Christian witness. I've never seen music have such a positive impact on people. The place was transformed. The moment was sacred.

I've never seen music have such a positive impact on people. The moment was sacred.

Many Christian youth today find that impact in complex, classical music, expertly performed in elegant surroundings. Many have felt the impact through today's heartwarming choruses of praise, complete with motions we used to consider juvenile. Some have experienced the impact through the loud, rhythmic demands of rock. Many more are learning the wider joys of an eclectic musical taste, accepting the impact of a variety of styles on a variety of moods and needs.

Each of us must give our own answer to the question of the music itself. If its physical and emotional impact is in harmony with the spiritual song I want to sing, then I can judge it to be acceptable. If that impact battles against my spiritual sense, then I must conclude that the music is wrong for me.

Concentrate on the Spiritual Dimension. Above all, we must remember that music, as all influences in our lives, has an impact on our Christian experience. As we make decisions on this subject, let's resolve to concentrate on the spiritual dimension of the topic and not to argue about musical styles and personal preferences.

The conversation between Alice and the Cheshire cat makes the point we must realize as we discuss the value of music:

"Would you tell me, please, which way I ought to go from here?"

"That depends a good deal on where you want to get to," said the cat.

"I don't much care where," said Alice.

"Then it doesn't matter which way you go," said the cat.[1]

Music does impact our Christian experience.

[1] Lewis Carroll, *Alice's Adventures in Wonderland*, (New York: Bantam Books, 1981), 46.

Our minds can be trained to respond to various types of music.

Have You Heard This One?

Adrian Westney

This chapter contains several activities for your use in studying, experimenting, and/or discussing music.

Your Musical Background

Our minds can be trained to respond to various types of music. On Sunday mornings when you were young, you might have had the experience of awakening to the music of Beethoven or Brahms or a popular hit tune being piped through your home. Now, whenever you hear one of those pieces, you immediately feel as you did on those Sunday mornings, completely relaxed and carefree, or excited and adventuresome. You may even recall the aroma of break-fast too. It all comes back.

Or maybe there were special music records or tapes your family played as background music on Friday nights. When you hear those arrangements, especially when they are by the same artist(s), your mind goes back to falling asleep with the family all at home, a good meal in your tummy, and cleanliness from your Sabbath bath.

After pushing the radio button, you find yourself halfway through a song you heard at a concert. You remember the artist, where you were sitting, what you had to go through to even get a ticket, the way the crowd responded to the concert, and how you became part of the crowd that night.

Perhaps you used to sing a particular hymn every week at church when you were a child. A few years later, after having not attended church for some time, you hear that same hymn on the radio while searching for a station. You remember and begin to feel homesick for church.

The church choir begins their special music for the church service, and as soon as the pianist strikes the first chord, you recognize the song and this arrangement from your academy days when you sang in the choir. Your mind drifts back to those days, including choir tours and class-mates and good times.

These are partially fictional accounts. What are your musical memories? What does it take to activate them? What are the positive and negative associations you've

What comes to mind when you hear a familiar song?

137

What are the positive and negative associations you've made with music based on your background?

made with music based on your background? What different styles do you appreciate today? What styles do you listen to on a regular basis? Why?

Experiment On Yourself

Make time to try some of the following exercises on yourself:

You feel down and rejected because of something someone said to you. Recall a tune associated with a happy time of your life, and even if you don't feel like it, sing the song (or listen to it).

You have a speech or presentation to make to a large group, and you feel nervous and unsure of yourself. Find a piece of music you consider to be triumphant and sing it or listen to it.

You need to pray and meditate, but you aren't in the mood. Recall a prayer song or a meditative tune and use it to put yourself in the mood to pray.

Take note of how a particular piece of music makes you feel when you listen to it. Tuck the emotional response into your memory, and then play the song again when you want to express or create a similar emotion.

List the songs that make you feel happy. Which ones make you feel energetic? Which songs help you relax? To what extent do you use music to shape or alter your moods/emotions?

Listening Through the Years

Have a panel discussion for youth Sabbath School. The topic is music, and panel members should be the age of the youths' parents and/or grandparents. Spend the first third of your time having panel members share what they remember about the popular music of their teen years and how their parents related to the teen music and musicians. What type of church music do they remember from the same time period? Note potential generational differences.

Spend the second third of your time having panel members share their observations, interests, and concerns regarding the music (and musicians) popular to teens today. They should also comment on the similarities and differences between the music of their day and the pop music of today. Encourage the youth to listen carefully and be prepared to ask questions later in the program based on what has been presented.

The final portion of the panel discussion can be spent fielding questions from the youth for the adults to answer.

A logical follow-up program would be for the youth to be part of a panel discussion for the adult Sabbath School the following week. They can present what they learned from the adults the previous week, what their own views are regarding the topic of music (including church music), how they determine what is "good" music, what they listen to (and why), followed by a period for the adults to ask the panel members questions based on what they've heard.

Have adults share what they remember about the popular music of their teen years.

139

The Experiential Music Survey

Perhaps the most common approach to "discussing" music is to play a few songs (or portions of songs) and let that elicit debate. It's not difficult since music is so emotive. Debate can be almost guaranteed when people argue using their heads (cognitive) to discuss something (music) which primarily affects their hearts (affective).

Some leaders select a variety of tunes and play them to demonstrate the breadth of musical styles available. Virtually all styles can be found in contemporary Christian music too. Other leaders invite participants to bring their own selections of music for the group to experience and analyze. This participatory method might get people more involved and be relevant in terms of the songs they actually listen to at the time. However, you might need a backup in case people don't bring their songs or you might have to do some editing rather than trying to listen to 15 five-minute songs. Sometimes you need only a 30- to 60- second cut from a song to capture the essence of it.

Playing a variety of tunes can easily demonstrate that music reaches our emotions. Put together a string of musical exerpts. After each song, have the participants circle the word on the musical continuum from worship, devotional, neutral, worldly, blasphemous—(See sidebar) that best describes how the song makes them feel. (They can add other words if needed.) Then have them write why the song makes them feel that way.

Virtually all styles of music can be found in contemporary Christian music.

Music Continuum

Worship, Devotional, Neutral, Worldly, Blasphemous

After all the songs have been played, you'll be ready for a discussion on how music affects us. Note the similarities and differences within your group, sometimes on the same song and sometimes on a different song from the same artist.

Suggested Additional
Resources

CCM (Contemporary Christian Music) published monthly.

The Door (El Cajon, CA: Youth Specialties), music issue, July-August, 1991.

GLAD, "Variations On A Hymn" on *No Less Than All* (on compact disc, cassette tape, and even on album), Benson, 1983 and 1988.

Insight/Out (Hagerstown, MD: Review and Herald Publishing Association), contemporary Christian music issue, February, 1992.

Key, Dana, D*on't Stop the Music* (Grand Rapids, MI: Zondervan), 1989.

Media Update, a bimonthly newsletter edited by Al Menconi (P. O. Box 5008, San Marcos, CA 92069-1050).

Menconi, Al, T*oday's Music: A Window to Your Child's Soul* (Elgin, IL: David C. Cook Publishing Company), 1990.

Miller, Steve, T*he Contemporary Christian Music Debate* (Wheaton, IL: Tyndale House Publishers), 1993.

Peters, Dan, Peters, Steve, and Merrill, Cher, *What About Christian Rock?* (Minneapolis: Bethany House Publishers), 1986.

Music is powerful because it taps into our emotions.

Section 4
Thinking About Sexuality

Section 4

Thinking About Sexuality

What's the Discussion About?

S-E-X. It's okay. You don't have to spell it. You can say the word, and you can bet that teens are saying it too, perhaps like you did when you were their age. Not only is it on the minds of most youth, but some indeed are practicing it. Maybe it's time adults started talking about it more as well.

The Background of the Discussion

What is it like to be a young person today and discover your sexuality? Rumor has it that some of our parents

*Roger L. Dudley with V. Bailey Gillespie, *Valuegenesis: Faith in the Balance* (La Sierra University Press, 1992), 261.

Maybe it's time adults started talking about it more as well.

didn't hold hands until they were engaged and didn't kiss until the minister said, "You may kiss the bride." Many of today's youth have intercourse outside of marriage, and some live together without even considering marriage. Christian youth are not immune to the behavior patterns of their unchurched peers. As Tony Campolo noted during the past decade:

> The general estimate of high school teenagers in the 1980s is that 43 percent of the girls and 47 percent of the boys experience sexual intercourse prior to graduation... It is also interesting to note that while religious orientation influences the sexual behavior of young people, it does not make the enormous difference that you in youth ministry might expect. In studies made among those students in church-related colleges who consider themselves "very religious," it has been discovered that 31 percent of the girls and 39 percent of the boys have experienced sexual intercourse by the time of graduation from high school.[1]

Campolo shared further that of the kids who reported they had not had sexual intercourse during their high school years, almost one-third fell into the category of "technical virgins," a term attributed to those who experience intensive petting to the point of orgasm without having intercourse.[2]

Although data from the *Valuegenesis* research was more favorable than the public school data, it's far from the ideal we promote as we understand Scripture. Twenty-seven percent of Adventist 11th and 12th graders in SDA

[1]Tony Campolo, "Christian Ethics In The Sexual Wilderness" in *Youthworker,* Vol.1, No. IV. (El Cajon, CA: Youth Specialties, Winter, 1985), 13.

[2] *Ibid.*

academies in North America report they are no longer virgins. Mainstream Protestant youth reported 33 percent had experienced intercourse before high school graduation.[1]

Neither the rules from the Dark Ages nor the trends of the current age offer much help. Pretending that sex doesn't exist is naive and a denial of the potencies and problems of sex among teens. Young people, including Christian youth, want to know how sex fits into their lives now.

The term "sex" formerly was an abbreviated way of referring to sexuality, but eventually it lost its full meaning and came to represent only the act of intercourse (e.g., "They had sex" means "They had intercourse"). The common question teens ask in this area is, "How far can I go?" not "Is it okay to have intercourse?" They are discovering their own sexuality and know it is much more than a penis entering a vagina.

We aren't merely dealing with genitals. We are body-persons—male and female—relating to each other. "Our humanness and sexuality reflect the reality that we are not self-contained units, capable of existing in a vacuum. We are by our created nature compelled into relationships."[2] Relationships involve touching, caring, trusting, listening, needing, embracing, and loving. We are created in God's image, but it is only as we relate to one another in loving relationships (not only marriage) that God's image is realized. God created us with these needs. We cannot separate our sexuality from our spirituality.

[1] Roger Dudley, *Valuegenesis: Faith in the Balance* (Riverside, CA: La Sierra University Press, 1992), 50.

[2] Terry Hershey, *Clear-Headed Choices in a Sexually Confused World* (Loveland, CO: Group Books, 1988), 90.

Alberta Mazat wrote:

> Sometimes we get the impression that God made male and female parts, but people found out what to do with them all by themselves—and that it must have surprised God to see how pleasurable it is!...It is difficult for many people to perceive sexuality and holiness as being compatible."[1]

[1]Alberta Mazat, *That Friday in Eden* (Mountain View, CA: Pacific Press Publishing Association, 1981), 16.

Have you ever wondered what God told Adam and Eve about their sexuality? He did say, "Be fruitful and multiply," but certainly he said much more that isn't recorded in Scripture. Without the visual aids of television, movies, sexually explicit pictures and endless locker room banter, God's version of sexuality must have been awesome.

Our youth don't have that privilege. We live in a culture preoccupied with sex. Advertisers use it to sell cars, perfume, clothes, toothpaste and copy machines. People can even read about it as they wait in the checkout line to pay for their groceries. It would be ridiculous to assume that youth are unaware of sex. Not only do they experience a rush of sexual hormones, they live in a sex-saturated society.

Sexuality is a journey, not a destination. Teens in your group are at different stages in their journey. Some have reached puberty while others might be late bloomers. They are curious and are making choices about their sexuality. Consider several of the current options. A person can choose to wait until marriage to experience intercourse. With modern contraception one might have sex within marriage and still have a low risk of pregnancy. You can marry; you can have children or not have them; you can divorce and remarry; you can live with someone who is or is not a lover; you can live alone, with or without a lover; you can be gay or straight; you can even remain married and live separately.[1]

Christian youth are looking to the Bible for answers as well. "How far can I go?" Their natural curiosity leads them to search for answers. Does the Bible provide answers?

Other than warning against intercourse outside of marriage, the Bible says little. There is no mention of how far to go or whether petting is right or wrong. That's not surprising. In Bible times, couples hardly saw each other before marriage. They certainly didn't get much opportunity to touch each other's bodies. Nor does the Bible mention holding hands, kissing, hugging, French kissing or caressing.[2] The Biblical principle of sexual purity is clear; the details—applications to the principle—as with all standards have to be hammered out individually. In discussions about sex, teens are asking explicit questions.

Questions Youth Are Asking

- How far is too far?
- If the other person consents, what's wrong with it?
- Is oral sex okay?
- Is masturbation okay?
- Isn't the idea of no sex outside of marriage out of date?

[1]Susan Littwin, *The Postponed Generation* (New York: Morrow, 1987), 215.

Sexuality is a journey, not a destination.

[2]Nancy Van Pelt, *The Complete Courtship* (Washington, DC: Southern Publishing Association, 1982), 102.

What's a more current understanding?
- How can it be wrong when it feels so right?
- What if I don't want to stop?
- Can I be forgiven if I have sex, even if I think it's wrong?
- What if I never get married? Am I supposed to not have sex my whole life?
- Does it make a difference if I really love the person?

Focusing the Discussion

In a church setting we typically hear things from a male perspective. When it comes to sexuality, obviously this is not a complete representation. But rather than presenting a "He Said, She Said" debate, consider the following material and have a discussion with a group of males and females—the picture you get of God from this discussion will be a more balanced view. This discussion of sexuality provides material for your discussions with teens.

Note the six biblical principles.

•"If You Really Love Me." Pastor Esther Ramharacksingh Knott wrote this chapter while she was single. Note the six biblical principles (each of them reduced to one word that begins with the letter "C") derived from 1 Thessalonians 4. You'll also find a helpful selection of quotations from a variety of authors.

What is your personal view of sexuality? What do you think the Bible says about it? What strategies have you found helpful to maintain a principle of sex within marriage?

• "Freedom." Sharon Sheppard provides two examples of people who had sex outside of marriage and the resulting stress. She then lists a number of freedoms experienced by people who save sex for marriage.

What are the benefits of having sex before marriage? What are the benefits of only having sex within marriage? Do you know someone who had an unwanted pregnancy? What did they do about it? In what ways do males demonstrate responsibility or irresponsibility in the area of sexuality and unwanted pregnancies?

• "The Purity Challenge." Pastor Vladimir Corea, who works with Jim Burns, author of "How to Handle Your Hormones," gives both males and females a challenge for sexual purity.

Have you ever accepted challenges like this before? If so, how many? Have you accepted other sexual challenges, such as, How many people will you have sex with this school year? or Which one of us will have sex with our boy/ girlfriend? Are purity challenges realistic? Are they worthwhile?

In what ways do males demonstrate responsibility or irresponsibility in the area of sexuality and unwanted pregnancies?

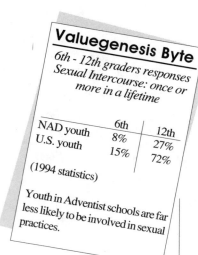

Valuegenesis Byte

6th - 12th graders responses
Sexual Intercourse: once or
more in a lifetime

	6th	12th
NAD youth	8%	27%
U.S. youth	15%	72%

(1994 statistics)

Youth in Adventist schools are far less likely to be involved in sexual practices.

Maybe it's time adults started to talk about sex more often.

If You Really Love Me

Esther Ramharacksingh Knott

If you want to get the attention of teens, just begin to talk about SEX. It is always sure to get everyone's attention. It is high time we began to talk about it in a responsible way. Teens are ready to talk.

Many of us would like God to give our youth the "Ten Commandments of Affection." They might read: "Thou shalt not kiss for more than five seconds" or "Kissing shall be done on a well-lighted porch before 9:30 p.m."

The Bible doesn't say anything about these specifically, but God has not left us in the dark on such an important subject. His Word gives us principles which govern our relationships with others. Let's look at some of these principles and make some applications.

Even though most agree that the Bible condemns sexual intercourse outside of marriage, some simply consider that passe for today. Nancy Van Pelt covers this subject in detail:

> In the New Testament the word *fornication* refers to sexual immorality in general (John 8:41; Acts 15:20-29; 21:25; Romans 1:29; 1 Corinthians 6:13,18; 2 Corinthians 12:21; Ephesians 5:3). Two passages (Matthew 5:32; 19:9) use fornication as a synonym for adultery. In four passages both adultery and fornication are used together, indicating a definite distinction between the two words (Matthew 15:19; Mark 7:21; 1 Corinthians 6:9; Galations 5:19). Two references refer to voluntary sexual intercourse between unmarried people or between an unmarried person and a married person (1 Corinthians 6:2; 1 Thessalonians 4:3-5). In 1 Corinthians 5:1, Paul applies the word *fornication* to an incestuous relationship.
>
> In the final analysis, then, 37 out of 39 biblical passages exclude premarital sexual intercourse from God's plan for men and women. The two exceptions are where fornication is used as a synonym for adultery. God asks His children to confine sexual intercourse to marriage.[1]

According to Scripture, sexual intercourse outside of a marriage relationship is wrong. This includes a NO to premarital sex. The question still remains, "So, how far *can* I go?"

The Bible in 1 Thessalonians 4:2-8 and other references, presents six broad principles to respond to this.

[1] Nancy Van Pelt, *The Complete Courtship* (Washington, DC: Southern Publishing Association, 1982), 102-103.

151

You will remember the instructions we gave you then in the name of the Lord Jesus. God's plan is to make you holy, and that means a clean cut with sexual immorality. Every one of you should learn to control his body, keeping it pure and treating it with respect, and never regarding it as an instrument for self-gratification, as do pagans with no knowledge of God. You cannot break this rule without in some way cheating your fellow men. And you must remember that God will punish all who offend in this matter, and we have warned you how we have seen this work out in our experience of life. The calling of God is not to impurity but to the most thorough purity, and anyone who makes light of the matter is not making light of a man's ruling but of God's command. It is not for nothing that the Spirit God gives us is called the *Holy Spirit.*[1]

[1] *The New Testament in Modern English,* rev., translated by J. B. Phillips (New York: Macmillian Publishing Company, 1972), 450.

When Scripture talks about avoiding sexual immorality, it's talking about not only intercourse outside of marriage, but it's warning us to avoid any sexual involvement where the degree of commitment doesn't measure up to the degree of intimacy. In this passage we discover the six principles of commitment, control, contrast, consideration, consequences, and capability.

Principle #1: Commitment

"God's plan is to make you holy, and that entails first of all a clean cut with sexual immorality." 1 Thessalonians 4:3. Our sexuality needs to be viewed in the context of our relationship with and commitment to God.

Paul entreats the Thessalonians to remember that he speaks in the name of the Lord Jesus, the one to whom they have made a commitment. "Paul tells these new Christians, whose former sexual standards had been very lax, that a Christian's sexual life must come under Christ's lordship, and that sex is an important matter that must be viewed in the context of our relationship with God."[1]

Paul's teachings are with the view that we want to learn to please God. These ethics are not motivated by fear of pregnancy, sexually transmitted diseases or AIDS, but rather by the fact that God calls us to be pure. It is his will and this is how you can be pure.

Principle #2: Control

"Every one of you should learn to control his body, keeping it pure and treating it with respect, and never regarding it as an instrument for self-gratification." 1 Thessalonians 4:4. We are to control our bodies in ways that are honorable. Our actions must reflect our level of commitment to the person.

In order to understand why self-control is mentioned in the context of sexual behavior, consider the following terms in Barry St. Clair's and Bill Jones' book *Sex: Desiring the Best*.

"Necking" Touching each other from the neck up.
"Petting" Touching each other from the neck down.

God desires to make each of us clean, pure, and whole.

[1] Letha Dawson Scanzoni, *Sex is a Parent Affair* (New York: Bantam Books, 1982), 70.

153

Petting has many different expressions:

- Hugging so that your hands caress your partner's back and sides.
- Touching breasts and groin through or under clothing.
- Laying down together or on top of each other.
- Touching sexual organs in order to reach orgasm.[1]

[1]Barry St. Clair and Bill Jones, *Sex: Desiring the Best* (San Bernardino, CA: Here's Life Publishers, Inc., 1987), 73-74.

The above actions feel good. They express intimacy and don't cause pregnancy. So is petting okay? Can we do this and remain in control? Some may say, "We're going to pet, and nothing more." That may sound good, but once your body gets going, your emotional and physical desires tend to overrule rational decisions.

A prime example of this is a couple at a boarding academy. They were saying good-bye to each other in a car in plain view of the dean's window. What started out as a farewell kiss turned into passionate kissing, heavy petting, and inappropriate fondling. All this in broad daylight, in front of the dean's apartment. When questioned later, their only response was, "We never intended to go that far."

It's like racing down a highway at 85 miles per hour and suddenly shifting into reverse. The car can't change gears that fast. And so it is with sexual motors once they're running. "Aroused sexual feelings respond reluctantly, if at all, to intelligence, reason, logic, ironclad decision, previously determined guidelines, or anything else short of sexual release."[1]

[1]Van Pelt, 106.

Petting is designed by God to end in intercourse. Some will respond that they don't actually have intercourse. "Petting to a climax without having intercourse, and calling yourself a 'technical virgin,' seems to miss the point God is making. I think God is not as concerned over a punctured or unpunctured membrane as he is over the total intimacy, the nakedness—both physically and mentally—that sex represents."[1] When our actions no longer reflect our level of commitment, we are not in control.

Principle #3: Contrast

"Every one of you should learn to control his body, keeping it pure and treating it with respect, and never regarding it as an instrument for self-gratification, as do pagans with no knowledge of God." 1 Thessalonians 4:4-5. Don't copy the world. Our actions are in contrast to those who have no knowledge of God. So it's not surprising that Paul contrasts the Christian's sexual behavior with that of the "pagans with no knowledge of God." If you are to look at the media today, you wouldn't be too far off in deciding that the opposite of what you see is what you should choose to do. The world has mesmerized us under its values of sexuality.

I often have found myself watching a movie on TV and without thinking have found myself wanting the plot to follow a course that I know is against my ethic of sexuality. It seems so natural to have the couple end up in bed together. That is what those "with no knowledge of God"

[1] Les John Christie, *Dating & Waiting: A Christian View of Love, Sex, and Dating* (Cincinnati: Standard Publishing, 1983), 60.

155

Aroused sexual feelings respond reluctantly, if at all, to intelligence, reason, logic.

are teaching us. Do we applaud when someone is victorious in saying "No" to the partner they very much would like to spend the night with? Do we applaud when a woman says "No" to a man, even though her husband is out of town and she knows he is being unfaithful at that very moment?

The world sees no reason not to gratify sexual urges and appetites in any way one pleases. Christians are different in this regard. Paul warns against becoming victims of lust, which is the world's contrast for love. We often are confused as to what the difference is. A former campus chaplain of mine helped clear the fuzzy lines for me when he said, "Love can always wait to give; lust can't wait to get."

Principle #4: Consideration

"You cannot break this rule without in some way cheating your fellow men." 1 Thessalonians 4:6. Christians keep the rights and well-being of others in mind. As God's people, we are reminded to consider others who may be hurt if we were to pursue a course of selfish gratification. One teenage girl said, " I feel like having sex would be like committing adultery in advance. I would be unfaithful and would be hurting the man I'll someday marry. I want to keep myself for him."[1] A Christian does not have the right to use somebody for his or her own sexual gratification.

Martin Buber, a Jewish existentialist philosopher, categorized interpersonal relationships into two types: He

[1]Scanzoni, 71.

believes that each person can have either an "I-It" relationship or an "I-Thou" relationship with another person. An "I-It" relationship is one in which the other person is treated as an object or a thing. In an "I-Thou" relationship the first person endeavors to empathize with the other person—the subject. There is an attempt to emotionally "enter into" who the other person is, to experience reality from the other person's subjective stance, to feel the other person's feelings as the encounter occurs. Buber claims that in every human encounter, there is the possibility for the discerning spiritual person to encounter God.[1]

Campolo applied this philosophy to the dating scene.

> Such a theology of personhood has tremendous implications for sexual interaction. If the "other person" in a romantic relationship is viewed as a mystical incarnation of God, then there will be reverence and respect in what is said and done. Exploitation of that person for the purpose of sexual gratification will be out of the question. All that the first person does with or to the other will be for the purpose of lifting up and enhancing the other. Anything that would cheapen or diminish the dignity and worth of the other must be shunned. Sexual interaction suddenly possesses a sacred dimension which prescribes how persons should relate to each other.[2]

Why do we often speak of "using" someone as an "It" when we speak of various forms of sexuality outside of marriage? Our level of commitment needs to equal or surpass our level of physical intimacy. Unless we express

If you consider the sexuality portrayed by the media today, you wouldn't be too far off in deciding that the opposite of what you see is what you should choose to do.

[1]Campolo, 16.

[2]*Ibid.*

157

Our level of commitment needs to equal or surpass our level of physical intimacy.

[1]Mazat, 107.

our sexual behaviors in a context of commitment, the behaviors will have little meaning compared to what was originally designed. Without trust and fidelity there is no way two people will develop a growing relationship. Caring about the other person will lead us to consider what effect our actions have on them. What are we telling them? Alberta Mazat challenges us to think, "What does the action indicate—this kiss, this caress, this hug? What happens to the emotional and physical system when it is experienced? What would be the result of carrying on further, right now, with these feelings?"[1]

In thinking of others, consider the following insights from St. Clair and Jones. When you get involved intimately with someone in intensive kissing, is that all you want to do, or do you want to do more? Intense kissing poses practical problems.

1. It leads to other things. Your body is designed so that when it reaches one stage it naturally wants to go to the next. It's hard to stop.

2. It intensifies the relationship. Your feelings for each other are heightened and the physical attraction is strong; so your relationship seems to be more serious than it really is. You find yourself wanting to get together with the other person more often, not because you have a solid basis for a relationship but because it felt so good to kiss that you want to do it again.

3. It lies to the other person. Your body says that you care deeply for the other person. If you care so deeply, why is it that you're kissing someone different every month?

4. It stifles your relationship. When the physical becomes the most important aspect of your relationship, then making-out takes the place of communication. The relationship stops growing.[1]

Determine what a kiss means to you. Realize that a kiss starts physical contact. Let a kiss reveal your heart, not your hormones. Don't cheat or exploit your dating partner.

Principle #5: Consequences

"You cannot break this rule without in some way cheating your fellow men. And you must remember that God will punish all who offend in this matter, and we have warned you how we have seen this work out in our experience of life." 1 Thessalonians 4:6. God will allow the consequences of selfish and uncommitted sex to take their natural course. We have been conned into believing that our bodies can be detached from our emotions. When we fall for this lie, there will always be consequences to deal with. Chap Clark explained it like this:

> When Paul says that God will punish all who offend in this matter he means at the very least that the Lord will allow the consequences of selfish and uncommitted sex to take their natural course. What the Creator is *not* doing is trying to spoil our fun. He's warning us of the awful results of not believing him when he tells us that he created sex as a gift to be used only within the context of a committed relationship. He wants the best for us; and when we hurt and abuse each other through selfishness and lack of self-control, his heart aches for us.[2]

[1]St. Clair and Jones, 76-77.

If you care so deeply, why is it that you're kissing someone different every month?

[2]Chap Clark, *Next Time I Fall in Love* (El Cajon, CA: Youth Specialties, 1987), 69.

Josh McDowell recorded some negative consequences kids came up with themselves, such as premarital sex can make future courtship much more difficult, sexually transmitted diseases are dangerous, it hurts one's walk with God and it causes self-esteem to go down. It breaks down communication in a relationship and also makes it more difficult to break up with someone. The desire for sex rather than love becomes predominant. Premarital sex often leads to extramarital sex, plus there's the fear of sexual comparison once a person is married. There's a higher divorce rate among those who had premarital sex. It gives way to misleading feelings. In short, premarital sex can lead to bad consequences for the entire society.[2]

Positive consequences of waiting included the sense that waiting allows freedom to develop strong friendships, unwanted pregnancies and abortions are then prevented, waiting brings true fulfillment on the wedding night and in marriage, it produces dignity and shows your marriage partner how much you love him or her. It brings maturity and real freedom. Waiting keeps respect for each other.[3]

While we continue to uphold the ideal, we also must be equipped to address the youth who comes to us and says, "I've already gone too far with my boy/girlfriend and I don't feel right. Does that mean I'm doomed?"

Alberta Mazat has responded:

> Well that is the bad news, and here is the good news. Praise God, you can be a new person in Christ Jesus with new desires, new values, and a new beginning.

[2]Josh McDowell, *What I Wish My Parents Knew About My Sexuality* (San Bernardino, CA: Here's Life Publishers, 1987), 171-193.

We have been conned into believing that our bodies can be detached from our emotions.

The same God that forgives us for not correctly demonstrating his love offers his robe of righteousness to cancel this impurity. "Spiritual revirgination" is what Christ offers to people who have erred in this respect.[1]

Mike Jones has added, "God's willingness to forgive and his ability to heal know no limit. But at the same time, there is no evading the results of promiscuity." He continued:

> The innocent joy of discovering the dimensions of their sexuality can never be fully shared between a husband and a wife if they have entered into casual relationships previously. Those tender experiences of ultimate vulnerability, which are God's unique gift to marriage, are closed off. Any marriage suffers by their loss.[2]

In a very real sense, there's never another first time.

Principle #6: Capability

"The calling of God is not to impurity but to the most thorough purity, and anyone who makes light of the matter is not making light of a man's ruling but of God's command. It is not for nothing that the Spirit God gives us is called the *Holy* Spirit." 1 Thessalonians 4:7-8. God's principles are extremely high, which makes it seemingly obvious that humans need the power of the Holy Spirit to have the strength to develop and express one's sexuality according to those principles.

[1] Mazat, 109.

[2] Michael A. Jones, *Help for Young Christians* (Washington DC: Review and Herald Publishing Association, 1977), 80.

Can anyone really live by these principles in a sexually confused world? The answer is "Yes" because, according to Paul, God bestows on us the strength to resist temptation and to live our sexuality according to his principles. *The Living Bible* paraphrases Philippians 2:13 in this way: "God is at work within you, helping you want to obey him, and then helping you do what he wants."

We often pray, "Lead us not into temptation." To pray this sincerely includes taking responsibility to not even get into highly tempting sexual situations. Certain times make people more vulnerable than at other times when it's easy to ignore one's limits, such as:

After 11 p.m.

After an emotional event (like a fight with your parents or each other, your team loses or wins a big game, you get a bad grade, etc.).

After special occasions (banquet, birthday, homecoming) spending time with friends who have lower standards.

At certain places (alone in the car, in the bedroom).

While dressed sexily (tight sweaters or T-shirts, tight jeans, low-cut and loose dresses).

After going certain places (sexy movie, wild party)

After praying late and alone.[1]

Sometimes we get so hung up on the physical aspects of dating that we forget what dating is all about. Dating is a prelude to the final selection of a life partner. It's a phase

[1] St. Clair and Jones, 80-81.

through which youth journey, and a very vital one at that. They gain experience in many aspects of living. They come to know other people, sample temperaments, pinpoint personality types, and begin to understand basic character types. Throughout the experience of dating, people come to know other people on a deeper level of understanding.[1] Young people need to cultivate ways of demonstrating their fondness for one another beyond only physical expressions.

One must decide coolly and logically, well in advance, what to do about kissing, necking, petting and intercourse. No one can provide a checklist of dos and don'ts which is appropriate under all circumstances. A fleeting touch can be as provocative as a caress. A bear hug can be less erotic than reaching for a hand.

Some suggest that a person write out the types of physical expression they feel would be okay to express at different stages of their relationship based on the commitment each stage represented. These can be discussed with one's dating partner. Isn't it ironic that a person might not feel comfortable *talking* to their date about this, yet feel comfortable enough to *engage* in other levels of intimacy with that person?

Although it might be awkward to discuss at first, most adolescents are more open to such conversations than previous generations were. It used to be understood that going on a date would *not* end in sex. Today the opposite is too often true. Therefore, a person *must* communicate

[1]John F. Knight, *What a Young Man Should Know About Sex* (Mountain View, CA: Pacific Press Publishing Association, 1977), 71.

God's principles are extremely high. Isn't it obvious that we need the power of the Holy Spirit to live this way?

their personal standard rather than assume the norm is acceptable.

As love develops, it needs avenues for expression. Leaders are wise to enlarge their young people's repertoire of expressing feelings to include methods of communication beyond physical intimacy. For example, giving a gift, including something personal like composing a poem or song, baking a cake or other treat. Sending flowers, candy, even a card, especially one that's homemade, provides avenues of expression. Publicly and privately complimenting a person says a great deal. Going out of one's way to do something the other person really enjoys sends a message too. Simply carrying on a conversation which goes to deeper levels, including feelings, communicates love and care.

But nonphysical expression does not replace the need for touch. We all have skin hunger, although some seem to need heavier doses than others. The key is to spread out touching so it's not focused on only one person. Group activities like the human knot, group hugs, cinnamon rolls, hug tag, pull apart, etc., provide lots of touching to fill skin-hunger needs rather than zeroing in on one person.

Even service activities that include contact with others, such as visiting retirement homes, hospitals, children's centers, and big brother/sister programs give young people a chance to touch in nonsexual ways. The Youth-to-Youth program actually teaches participants a variety of ways to hug in a friendly manner. It's a skill we all benefit from.

God looked at what he had made and said, "It is good." He made our bodies to be "user friendly."

God looked at what he had made and said, "It is good." He made our bodies to be "user friendly." He designed us to live according to his principles of sexuality. Instead of fighting our sexuality, the task before us is to make moral choices that lead to health instead of disease, to freedom instead of bondage, to wholeness instead of brokenness—in essence—to choose life instead of death.

God wants us to be complete. He wants us to carve out our sexual ethics in the presence of a loving and holy God who seeks health, not a distant deity who demands that his people maintain a list of rules and regulations. In reality, we are searching to find the fullness of the Creator's dream for us. We want to express our humanity and sexuality within a healing context; and we want to do this with dignity, health, and integrity.[1]

And God said, "It is good." This body—our body—with all its drives, needs, desires, urges, appetites, passions contradictions and emotions—is good! Our body is not a problem to be solved but a mystery and a gift to be celebrated.[2]

[1]Hershey, 13-14.

[2]*Ibid.*, 96.

Our body is not a problem to be solved but a mystery and a gift to be celebrated.

Valuegenesis Byte

Extramarital sexual experiences

Two-thirds of Adventist students in grades 6 - 12 agree with Adventist standards on sexual morality., but nearly a fifth (18%) disagreed on this item and another (14%) were not sure. Surrounded by a culture saturated with the "sexual revolution," Adventist youth may be slipping from the church's traditional vision of sexual purity.*

*Roger L. Dudley with V. Bailey Gillespie, *Valuegenesis: Faith in the Balance* (La Sierra University Press, 1992), 49.

[1] Not her real name.

"My parents said they'd kick me out of the house if I ever got pregnant."

Freedom

Sharon Sheppard

"I just can't be pregnant!" exclaimed 16-year-old Heidi.[1] Her long, slender fingers twisted a soggy Kleenex as we waited for the results of her pregnancy test. I thought of how many times I'd heard that from girls at the crisis center where I counsel.

Heidi could have passed for a model—tall, slim and blonde. Her troubled blue eyes misted over and stared at the wall. In a barely audible monotone she revealed, "My parents said they'd kick me out of the house if I ever got pregnant."

Together we watched as a minus sign formed on the test card. Both of us sighed with relief. She *wasn't* pregnant.

166

Another Saga

"We went all the way just once," said Gretchen,[1] a wistful elementary education major, "but because of it, I've lost him." Again, we held our breath as we waited for the plus or minus sign that could change her life.

"We'd been working up to it for a long time," she admitted tearfully. "I'm not very proud of our sexual experimentation, but always before, we stopped short of intercourse." She sighed, then continued. "We're both Christians, and I feel so guilty. I'd love to get back together, but he says our sexual relationship is messing up his spiritual life, so we have to stop dating. And maybe he's right."

Gretchen paused and stared at the floor. "I . . . just . . . wish . . . we'd never let ourselves get carried away in the first place." A slender minus sign emerged, and both of us exhaled, relieved that she, too, had "lucked out."

Not Always the Same Story

Unfortunately, not everybody is as "lucky" as Heidi and Gretchen. Last year more than a million teens got pregnant. You could easily get the idea that *everybody's* "doing it." But one study showed that of unmarried teens between the ages of 15 and 19, 40 percent of the guys and 47 percent of the girls are *not* sexually active. And of those who are, you can bet that a lot of them (many who show up in my office) wish they weren't sexually active. They're grappling with anxiety, remorse, and depression.

[1] Not her real name, either.

I'd love to get back together, but he says our sexual relationship is messing up his spiritual life.

167

In a culture in which virginity is generally not accorded a high value, condoms and the Pill are available on many high school campuses, and sex looks so gloriously romantic on TV, why wait?

One author gives this as a reason:

> For me, kissing expresses love as well as any action short of intercourse can. Anytime I've gotten beyond kissing, I've ended up feeling hot and frustrated. I've felt as though I'd started something that I couldn't finish. And torn between the purely sexual desire to go on, and my own responsibility to hold back, I wasn't thinking much about love. At that point it was sex, and the girl could have been any girl. Ending an evening feeling sweaty and unfulfilled is not my picture of the ideal. What good did it do?*

Real Freedom

Waiting until marriage for sexual intercourse gives you freedoms most sexually active teens don't have.

Freedom from worries about pregnancy. Getting pregnant outside of marriage leaves you with some pretty limited options—all of them unpleasant.

Marrying in haste. A staggering percentage of these "forced" marriages fail.

Having an abortion. Abortion often leaves deep emotional scars, including guilt and loss. It sometimes causes infertility or hinders a woman from carrying a baby to term later on when she really wants to have a child.

*Source unknown

In a culture in which virginity is generally not accorded a high value, condoms and the Pill are available on many high school campuses, and sex looks so gloriously romantic on TV, why wait?

Raising a child alone. Eight out of ten teenage mothers become high school dropouts, leaving them with few practical skills. Many teenage fathers also drop out of school, which limits their careers and earning potential—often for life.

Placing the child for adoption. Even though this is sometimes the best option, it often carries heartache and a permanent sense of loss.

Freedom from the dangers of sexually transmitted diseases. Two and a half million teens contracted a sexually transmitted disease (STD) last year. All of the diseases can be uncomfortable, some of them are incurable, and the current fear-instiller, AIDS, is fatal. Because some of the viruses can lie dormant for a long time, whenever you have intercourse you are, in effect, having sex with everyone your partner has had sex with, and you're exposed to anything any of them might be carrying.

Freedom from guilt and anxiety. Sexual activity outside of marriage tends to cause anxiety and a loss of self-esteem—What if my parents find out? What if I get a bad reputation? What if I get pregnant? Am I a bad person? During the past few decades, the number of adolescents admitted to hospitals for depression has tripled. Many experts believe that some of this is related to emotional problems stemming from premature sexual activity.

Freedom from damaged relationships. Many couples believe intercourse will improve their relationship and make it more secure. In reality, teens like Gretchen sometimes discover that once that line has been crossed, the

Whenever you have intercourse, you are, in effect, having sex with everyone your partner has had sex with.

other person loses interest and respect, even though he or she may have been the one who pressed for sex in the first place.

Freedom from knowing you've hurt God. The Bible has some pretty pointed things to say about sex outside of marriage, like "Flee from sexual immorality"[1] and "It is God's will that you should be sanctified; that you should avoid sexual immorality; that each of you should learn to control his own body in a way that is holy and honorable, not in passionate lust like the heathen, who do not know God."[2]

What Do You Really Want?

One young person put it this way:

> Premarital sex gave me fear as a gift . . . and shame to wear as a garment. It stole my peace of mind and robbed me of hope in a bright future. Sex smashed my concentration in class to smithereens; my desire for church activities was ground to a pulp. It made crumbs of the trust I had known in Christ . . . and in men and women. Premarital sex gave me a jagged tear in my heart that even now, seven years later, is still healing.[3]

Nobody ever said it would be easy. But waiting for sex until marriage is one of the smartest things you can do. It leaves your self-respect intact. It allows you to develop a wider circle of friends. It keeps your options open so you can make choices about your future that might not be available if you become entangled in a sexual relationship.

[1] 1 Corinthians 6:18 (NIV).

[2] 1 Thessalonians 4:3-5 (NIV).

Premarital sex gave me fear as a gift . . . and shame to wear as a garment.

[3] Josh McDowell and Dick Day *Why Wait?* (San Bernardino, CA: Here's Life Publishers, 1988), 15.

And when you're willing to wait, when sexual intercourse is experienced within the framework of marriage, you'll know the fulfillment of "maximum sex." I promise you, you'll be glad you saved it all, just as God intended!

I promise you, you'll be glad you saved it all, just as God intended!

The Purity Challenge

Vladimir Corea

40 percent of 14-year-old girls will be pregnant once before they turn 20 (if present trends continue).

Consider these facts:

- 12 million teens are sexually active.
- 8 out of 10 boys and 7 out of 10 girls report having had sex while in high school.
- 40 percent of 14-year-old girls will be pregnant once before they turn 20 (if present trends continue).
- By the age of 20, 81 percent of unmarried males and 67 percent of unmarried females have had sex.
- 50 percent of all sexually active 19-year-old males had their first sexual experience between the ages of 11 and 13.

When it comes to sex, teens and adults are constantly bombarded with mixed messages. Parents tell teens, "Don't

172

do it." Churches tell teens and singles, "Don't do it because it's a sin. Schools tell kids, "This is how you do it, here's what you need, and here are the techniques." Peers tell kids (even if it's not true), "I do it all the time." The result is a great deal of confusion.

Here Are Some Practical Guidelines

Recognize our cultural influence. When you view TV, listen to music, and watch movies, know that our society is "sex crazy" and will use sex to sell anything from soap to cars to clothes to tequila. Recognize that advertisers are using your senses to sell you stuff, attempting to bypass your decision-making process. Today's Christian teens will have to go against the grain of popular culture if they choose a Christ-centered, pure lifestyle. Expect it to be a challenge—living for Jesus is; but it's also worth it!

Set sexual standards before you go on a date. Talk about sexual standards with your date before you go out. It's next to impossible to use reason and logic in the "heat of the moment" when the hormones are going 1,000 miles per hour. Plan dates that will be fun and enjoyable while avoiding the types of dates that end up "parking" or inside an empty house. Think ahead. Pray about your temptation. Be prepared to break up if necessary. You'll need lots of support from God and friends who are also committed to not having sex outside marriage.

Today's Christian teens will have to go against the grain of popular culture if they choose a Christ-centered, pure lifestyle.

You'll need lots of support from God and friends who are also committed to not having sex outside marriage.

[1] 1 Corinthians 6:19-20 (NIV).

Take a Personal Purity Challenge

A commitment to sexual purity will be one of the most important decisions of your life, so important that it will affect your married life and perhaps even make the difference between ending up as a divorce statistic or staying married. It can even help you make sure that AIDS will not cause your death—it's that important!

Consider what the Bible says.

Do you know that your body is a temple of the Holy Spirit, who is in you, whom you have received from God? You are not your own; you were bought with a price. Therefore honor God with your body.[1]

The question is, So what? What does this have to do with my sexuality?

Think about this. How many people have you met who waited until marriage to have sex and regretted it? On the other hand, you can find hundreds of people who wish with all their hearts that they would have waited. They are now plagued by all kinds of hang-ups and carry what therapists and marriage counselors call "baggage." The survival of their marriages depends on their being able to successfully get rid of this baggage. Marriage has plenty of challenges already; why add disadvantages before you find the person you will call your husband or wife?

Would you consider making a commitment to God to stay sexually pure right here and right now? Believe me, you will not regret it!

What if You Already Went Past the Point of No Feturn?

Chances are, some teens reading this are no longer virgins. I have good news for you, in fact, very good news! It's possible to have your virginity restored in God's eyes!

Sound farfetched? It's not! This is what God says to you in Isaiah: *"I will remember your sins no more."*[1] That's right, if you ask God for forgiveness, He will forgive you and forever forget your sins.

You can also make a commitment to staying sexually pure from now on. And something else, if you've made this commitment, please tell your youth pastor or leader, tell him or her that you will be looking for support. In fact, make sure your friends know about it. It (and they) can help you with your commitment.

Congratulations! God loves you. He died for you. You're special, and don't you ever forget that!

Would you consider making a commitment to God to stay sexually pure?

[1] Isaiah 43:25.

175

Suggested Additional Resources

Burns, Jim, *Handling Your Hormones* (Laguna Hills, CA: Merit Books), 1984.

Clark, Chap, *Next Time I Fall in Love* (El Cajon, CA: Youth Specialties), 1987.

Fields, Doug and Temple, Todd (3-book series) *Creative Dating, More Creative Dating, Creative Times With Friends* (Nashville: Oliver-Nelson Books), 1988.

Foster, Richard J., *Money, Sex and Power* (San Francisco: Harper and Row), 1985.

Joy, Donald M., *Bonding: Relationships in the Image of God* (Waco, TX: Word Books), 1985.

Mazat, Alberta, *That Friday in Eden* (Boise, ID: Pacific Press Publishing Association), 1981.

McDowell, Josh and Dick Day, *Why Wait?* (San Bernardino, CA: Here's Life Publishers), 1987.

Miles, Herbert J., *Singles, Sex and Marriage* (Waco, TX: Word Books), 1983.

Smedes, Lewis B., *Sex for Christians* (Grand Rapids, MI: Eerdmans Publishing Company), 1976.

Talley, Jim and Reed, Bobbie, *Too Close Too Soon* (Nashville: Thomas Nelson Publishers), 1982.

Trobisch, Walter, *I Married You* (San Francisco: Harper and Row), 1971.

Van Pelt, Nancy, *The Complete Courtship* (Washington DC: Southern Publishing Association), 1982.

Section 5

Thinking About Jewelry

There was a time in Adventist church history, and not all that long ago, when you never saw jewelry in an Adventist church.

Section 5
Thinking About Jewelry

What's the Discussion About?

There was a time in Adventist church history, and not all that long ago, when you never saw jewelry in an Adventist church. Adventist members just didn't wear jewelry; it was part of the definition of who we were. New members were asked to remove their jewelry, even their wedding rings, before they were baptized. The same prohibition was a part of the official school rules at virtually every Adventist school—elementary schools, academies and colleges alike. Wearing any piece of jewelry was tantamount to *rebellion against the church* and was generally cause for dismissal.

In more recent years, however, we have been cautioned against making superficial issues a priority, and jewelry has been labeled as one of the "superficials." *Valuegenesis* research revealed that many of the young people who attend our schools and are members of our churches feel that our emphasis on standards, such as the no jewelry position, has crowded out the church's preaching of Jesus.[1] What is more, research indicates that enforcement of jewelry standards and the like can have a positive effect on faith development *in a loving home*. When such enforcement takes place *in a school or church setting*, it has a negative impact on both maturity of faith and denominational loyalty.

Today some church members are uncomfortable sitting in church next to someone wearing jewelry, not even knowing if that person is a member or not. Others see nonjudgmental acceptance as a sign of real progress in the church. Some colleges and academies in the North American Division have dropped the jewelry prohibition from their student handbooks, finding it more profitable to concentrate on the school's spiritual atmosphere and activities than to function as "jewelry police."

The Background of the Discussion

Virtually all Adventists agree with the following statement of Seventh-day Adventist belief:

We are called to be a godly people who think, feel, and act in harmony with the principles of heaven. For

Wearing any piece of jewelry was tantamount to rebellion *against the church.*

[1] See *Valuegenesis* research about Adventist youth and standards. Roger Dudley and V. Bailey Gillespie, *Valuegenesis: Faith in the Balance* (Riverside, CA: La Sierra University Press, 1992).

Others see such nonjudgmental acceptance as a sign of real progress in the church.

the Spirit to recreate in us the character of our Lord, we involve ourselves only in those things which will produce Christlike purity, health, and joy in our lives. This means that our amusement and entertainment should meet the highest standards of Christian taste and beauty. While recognizing cultural differences, our dress is to be simple, modest, and neat, befitting those whose true beauty does not consist of outward adornment but in the imperishable ornament of a gentle and quiet spirit.[1]

Because this is stated in the broad sweep of principles, most Adventists would wholeheartedly endorse it. The issue creates divergence, however, when we move into its interpretation for application to daily life. At this point, the focus changes for different people within Adventism.

The editors of the book *Seventh-day Adventists Believe* make their interpretation clear:

> Therefore, in view of these Scriptural teachings and principles laid out above, we believe that Christians ought not to adorn themselves with jewelry. We understand this to mean that the wearing of rings, earrings, necklaces, and bracelets, and showy tie tacks, cuff links, and pins–and any other type of jewelry that has as its main function display–is unnecessary and not in harmony with the simplicity of adornment urged by Scripture.[2]

In 1986, in response to a growing general concern in the church about jewelry, leaders from the North American Division voted on a document entitled "Jewelry–A Clarification and Appeal." They voted the following:

[1] *Seventh-day Adventists Believe* (Hagerstown, MD: Review and Herald Publishing Association, 1988), 278.

The issue creates divergence when we move into its interpretation for application to daily living.

[2] Ibid.

To affirm that the wearing of jewelry is unacceptable and is a denial of the principles enunciated in the Bible and Spirit of Prophecy concerning personal adornment...In the area of personal adornment necklaces, earrings, bracelets, rings (including engagement rings) should not be worn. Articles such as watches, brooches, cuff links, tie clasps, etc., should be chosen in harmony with the Christian principles of simplicity, modesty, and economy.[1]

Questions Youth Are Asking

• Why don't we deal with the core issues of being a Christian instead of focusing on peripheral things such as jewelry?

• Why does the jewelry issue focus on women? Aren't there adornment standards for men as well? Why don't we talk about those issues?

• No one has ever established why we have chosen to talk about some items of jewelry (such as rings and earrings and necklaces) but we've permitted other items, of jewelry (such as pins, brooches, tie clasps, etc.). Is there a scriptural reason for these differences, or is the reason an arbitrary one?

• My parents wear wedding rings to symbolize their commitment to each other. Yet some members of our church accuse them of being too liberal. Hasn't the church decided that wedding rings are okay? Why do these members still keep causing trouble?

• Aren't expensive homes and cars just as bad (or worse) than jewelry? Are they "acceptable"?

[1] "Jewelry–A Clarification and Appeal" was published in the *Adventist Review*, December 4, 1986, 15; in *Ministry*, April, 1987, 25; and in *The Lake Union Herald*, January 27, 1987, 21.

Aren't expensive homes and cars just as bad (or worse) than jewelry?

Focusing the Discussion

Here are four perspectives on the jewelry issue that will assist you and your teens in coming to a decision on this issue.

• "What the Bible (Really) Says." Youth ministry professional Steve Case takes a careful look at the jewelry texts in Scripture, but from two very different perspectives. Which one do you follow, and which one is right?

Perhaps the entire jewelry debate is rooted in the way we approach our study of Scripture. What rules do you follow in studying what the Bible says? In other words, what is your "hermeneutic"?

Perhaps the entire jewelry debate has its roots in the way we approach our study of Scripture.

• "Looking at the Outward Experience." Pastor Gary Russell establishes four biblical principles to guide our decisions in this discussion. He reminds us that "standards are largely subjective" but challenges us not to ignore biblical principles.

Study these passages with your youth group and see how they read and apply the principles. Ask questions like, Why do different cultures treat modesty in different ways? What can we learn from these cultural differences? How is pride related to wearing jewelry? How do we improve our "inner beauty"?

• "Because We're Adventists." Stephen Chavez is an assistant editor of the *Adventist Review*. He shares with us a very personal reflection on the jewelry discussion and identifies three simple principles which guide him in this area.

Do you think it's dangerous to express the opinion that our church's stand on a particular topic is filled with contradictions? Or should reappraisals be encouraged within a faith community? Can we express criticism and love our church at the same time?

How do we improve our "inner beauty"?

• "Jewelry and the Spiritual Experience." Dick Duerksen is Vice President for Creative Ministries in the Columbia Union. He is also editor of the Columbia Union *Visitor*. He receives dozens of "letters to the editor" each month. Here he shares some of the letters received on the topic of jewelry.

Of special interest may be the two exercises at the end of the article: Read a Bible passage and list behaviors, and the second exercise ask to react to a story told at the beginning of the article.

Can we express criticism and love our church at the same time?

• "Suggested Additional Resources" is a bibliography on the topic of jewelry to provide you with additional perspectives and suggestions for discussion.

What the Bible (Really) Says

Steve Case

Rules of interpretation are called "hermeneutics."

How can people read the same Bible and come up with such different conclusions? Easily! The topic of jewelry is only one example. While it is admirable to begin one's defense with "The Bible says," perhaps one should ask, "Does the Bible really say that?"

Some say, "You can prove anything you want from the Bible." This is true if you select only certain passages from Scripture, but not if you follow sound rules for interpreting the Bible. These rules are called "hermeneutics."

For instance, when you read the Bible, what perspective do you take? Is the perspective of the writer *or* the perspective of the writer's intended audience more important? When you think of what the people of Corinth who received the "First letter to the Corinthians" were thinking, you're applying a simple rule of hermeneutics—ways of interpreting Scripture.

The "Key-Text" way of interpreting

The major hermeneutical approach of the Seventh-day Adventist Church has been the key-text method. The key-text approach identifies and compiles as many texts as possible on a given topic to arrive at "doctrinal truth." The more texts you collect, the stronger your position. The context is secondary.[1] While some people look down on this hermeneutical approach today, it is a legitimate approach for Bible study. We still use it, as did a number of biblical writers.[2]

A good example of the key-text hermeneutical approach is *Bible Readings for the Home*, published by the Review and Herald in 1914, with additional copyrights in 1935, 1942, 1958, and 1963. The format poses questions that receive answers from specific texts of Scripture. Sometimes added commentary strengthens the proposition. Let me stress again that this is legitimate hermeneutics (rules to understand the Bible).

Contextual Hermeneutics

Sometimes referred to as an exegetical (or explanatory) approach to understanding Scripture, a contextual

[1] Some have suggest that those opposed to the ordination of women at the General Conference session in 1995 utilized a key-text method for Scripture study.

[2] We often quote Paul (1 Corinthians 2:9 in the *King James Version* of the Bible) "Eye hath not seen, nor ear heard, neither have entered into the heart of man, the things which God hath prepared for them that love him" as proof that we have no idea how great heaven will be for us since God's plans far exceed anything we have seen, heard, or imagined. Yet the next verse states, "But God hath revealed them unto us by his Spirit." Yet Paul's quote of Isaiah 64:4 seems different than the context of Isaiah 64, where God stands apart from all pagan gods as the One who acts on behalf of his people. It appears Paul used Old Testament verses out of context on occasion as he wrote in the New Testament!

185

hermeneutic first seeks to understand Scripture in context. The verses before and after the one being studied must be considered. The entire chapter and the book must also be understood. The historical context colors the meaning and forms a backdrop for understanding a given text.

For example, Paul wrote that women should keep silent in the churches "for it is a shame for women to speak in the church." 1 Corinthians 14:34-35. When it comes to the role of women in the church and whether or not they should be ordained as pastors, these two verses make it clear that women should never utter a word inside a church.

But contextual hermeneutics calls for a deeper look.

But contextual hermeneutics calls for a deeper look. The historical context reveals that the men sat in the front of the synagogue and the women sat towards the back. It is the broad biblical principle of orderliness in worship which is carried out through the social customs of a given culture. And a study of the place of women in pagan worship shows that women took an active part in these rituals, often using their sexuality as offerings in worship. Obviously the Apostle Paul wants Christian worship to be different. Orderly worship continues today, based on the social customs of today. Thus, we apply a contextual hermeneutic to understand the text.

A good presentation of contextual hermeneutics is the book *A Symposium on Biblical Hermeneutics*, edited by Gordon Hyde and printed by the Review and Herald in 1974.[1] Most Adventists who received a college education at an Adventist institution since the 1970s will recognize this as the primary way to understand the Bible.

[1]See also Lee Gugliotto, *Handbook for Bible Study* (Hagerstown, MD: Review and Herald Publishing Association), 1995, and V. Bailey Gillespie, *To Make Us Wise* (Pacific Press Publishing Association), 1995.

While both approaches to hermeneutics are legitimate, different conclusions can result. Seventh-day Adventists need to use a consistent approach to hermeneutics. Otherwise, we will reach different conclusions as we study the same Bible.

Putting It Into Practice

Let's consider the most common texts we refer to in the jewelry discussions and interpret them first from the key-text hermeneutic (in regular type) and then from the contextual hermeneutic (*in italic type*).

1 Timothy 2:9-10

> I also want women to dress modestly, with decency and propriety, not with braided hair or gold or pearls or expensive clothes, but with good deeds, appropriate for women who profess to worship God. 1 Timothy 2:9-10.

Key-text hermeneutics: Women are to dress modestly. It's not the outward appearance that counts with God but what is inside. Jewelry tends to be a cover-up for something lacking inside. Truly beautiful women don't need to add anything extra to their attire. They can dress modestly and let their good deeds provide their beauty.

Examples of inappropriate jewelry are mentioned, such as gold and pearls, and drawing unnecessary attention to one's hair. Today we could simply mention jewelry and most would understand it to mean rings, necklaces,

While both approaches to hermeneutics are legitimate, different conclusions can result. Seventh-day Adventists need to use an approach to consistent hermeneutics. Otherwise, different conclusions from the same Bible will be reached.

It's not the outward appearance that counts with God, but what is inside.

earrings and bracelets. These usually are used to draw attention to one's self, leading people to "look on the outward appearance, while God looks on the heart."

Contextual hermeneutics: *The basic principle of modesty in dress receives full endorsement with a further explanation that it means "with decency and propriety." The specific application presents a contrast of dressing with good deeds rather than braided hair, gold, pearls, or expensive clothes.*

Jewelry is too narrow an application for the text, which refers to all dress. Perhaps we have difficulty identifying "expensive" clothes. Expensive according to whose standard?

The context is worship, with males called to lift up holy hands in prayer (verse 8 for males precedes modesty for females in verse 9).

Modesty comes from decency and propriety evidenced by good deeds, not merely omitting a few pieces of jewelry.

1 Peter 3:3-4

Your beauty should not come from outward adornment, such as braided hair and the wearing of gold jewelry and fine clothes. Instead, it should be that of your inner self, the unfading beauty of a gentle and quiet spirit, which is of great worth in God's sight. 1 Peter 3:3-4.

Key-text hermeneutics: The consistency of Scripture couldn't be clearer as Peter echoes Paul's admonition for women to focus on the inner person rather than outward adornment. And what do women use for outward adornment? Jewelry and other expensive ornaments. It's all for show when God says that a person's true beauty comes from inside. The biblical proof continues to mount regarding God's call for no jewelry while those in the world continue to pile on jewelry in an effort to cover up their emptiness.

Contextual hermeneutics: *While the context of 1 Timothy 2 is worship, the context of 1 Peter 3 is submission. Peter mentions Sarah as an exemplary biblical model for wives. The Bible gives no explicit record of Sarah wearing or not wearing jewelry. However, her husband provided a fair amount of jewelry and fine clothes when Eliezer went in search of a bride for Isaac (see Genesis 24).*

If one's inner beauty is to exceed one's outer beauty, in a sense only godly women should wear jewelry, for they would be the ones whose inner beauty would still outshine their outer beauty. Others would be providing false advertising by suggesting that their inner selves agree with what is seen on the outside.

Note that the context is submission of wives to husbands, not all females to all males. And lest this be perceived as a female issue, husbands are reminded to be considerate and respectful of their wives or else their own connection with God will be in jeopardy (see 1 Peter 3:7).

Isaiah 3

The Lord says, "The women of Zion are haughty, walking along with outstretched necks, flirting with their eyes, tripping along with mincing steps, with

Modesty comes from decency and propriety, evidenced by good deeds, not merely omitting a few pieces of jewelry.

The biblical proof continues to mount regarding God's call for no jewelry.

If one's inner beauty is to exceed one's outer beauty, in a sense only godly women should wear jewelry.

ornaments jingling on their ankles. Therefore the Lord will bring sores on the heads of the women of Zion; the Lord will make their scalps bald." In that day the Lord will snatch away their finery: the bangles *and headbands* and crescent necklaces, the earrings and bracelets *and veils, the headdresses* and ankle chains *and sashes, the perfume bottles* and charms, the signet rings and nose rings, *the fine robes and the capes and cloaks, the purses and mirrors, the linen garments and tiaras and shawls.* Isaiah 3:16-23 (italics supplied).

Key-text hermeneutics: The association basically tells the story. Notice the attitude of the women of Zion. They are haughty, and their attire gives them away. Notice that they not only wear jewelry but also lots of it. It's on their heads, necks, ears, wrists, fingers, and even their ankles. They can't seem to get enough of it.

Not surprisingly, God's judgment falls on these people. The same might be true at the last judgement where every secret is laid bare and nobody will be able to hide or cover up their insufficiency no matter how much jewelry they wear.

[Note: As far as the italicized words in the text are concerned, with key-text hermeneutics, even brief phrases may be dropped without losing the intent of the verse(s). Including them simply shows that what can be perfectly acceptable (sashes, purses, shawls, etc.) can become disdainful to God when combined with what God abhors (jewelry)].

Contextual hermeneutics: *The wider context (Isaiah 1-3) is one of judgment. But the sense of the text discusses perverting justice, oppressing the poor, rebelling against*

190

God, pride, self-sufficiency, paganism, and hypocrisy not wearing jewelry or other insignificant items.

The judgement results in not only headsores (Isaiah 3:17), but completely stripping the people, plus the removal of all food and water (see Isaiah 3:1).

God is asking for repentance that leads to a search for justice, encouragement of the oppressed, defending the cause of the fatherless and pleading the case of widows (see Isaiah 1:17) not removal of jewelry. God's call is far deeper and more comprehensive than jewelry.

Entering God's Presence

Some have stated that the Bible consistently shows, "When God's people come before Him in special consecration, He always asks them to take off their jewelry." Let's consider both of these passages.

So Jacob said to his household and to all who were with him, "Get rid of the foreign gods you have with you, and purify yourselves and change your clothes. Then come, let us go up to Bethel, where I will build an altar to God, who answered me in the day of my distress and who has been with me wherever I have gone." So they gave Jacob all the foreign gods they had and the rings in their ears, and Jacob buried them under the oak at Shechem. Genesis 35:2-4.

When the people heard these distressing words, they began to mourn and no one put on any ornaments. For the Lord had said to Moses, "Tell the Israelites, 'You are a stiffnecked people. If I were to go with you even for a moment, I might destroy you. Now take off

If the Lord will bring sores on the heads of the women, what will He do to the men?

With key-text hermeneutics, brief phrases can be dropped without losing the intent of the verse(s).

God's call is far deeper and more comprehensive than jewelry.

As Seventh-day Adventists, we believe we are living in the last days, a symbolic Day of Atonement. To symbolize to the world that this is a time of judgment many Adventists elect not to wear jewelry.

[1]Sigfried H. Horn, ed., *Seventh-day Adventist Bible Dictionary*, rev. (Washington DC: Review and Herald Publishing Association, 1979), 817.

your ornaments and I will decide what to do with you.'" So the Israelites stripped off their ornaments at Mount Horeb. Exodus 33:4-6.

Key-text hermeneutics: When God's people faced judgment and wanted to come especially close to their Creator, they took off their jewelry. As Seventh-day Adventists, we believe we are living in the anti-typical Day of Atonement. To symbolize this belief to the world, many Adventists don't wear jewelry in order to be close to God in the last days.

Contextual hermeneutics: *Jacob's call for his family to remove their earrings is linked to their separation from foreign gods. Because their earrings had cultic significance, wearing them as one approached God was like including a Satanic pentagram as part of one's church outfit.*

The Israelite custom of collecting jewelry came from plundering the Egyptians after departing from Egypt following 400 years of slavery (Exodus 12:35-36). While many throughout history have mourned in sackcloth and ashes, the Israelite culture at this time signified mourning by removing the jewelry they usually wore.[1]

If not wearing jewelry in the presence of God really mattered, why didn't God mention it to Moses or the Israelites in their specific preparations to face God when he spoke the Ten Commandments to them on Sinai (see Exodus 19:10-19)? Aaron fashioned the golden calf from the jewelry people were wearing (see Exodus 32:2-4). They still had plenty to create the tabernacle for God's presence (Exodus 25:1-9; compare Exodus 35:20-29) and they had a surplus for their own use (Exodus 36:2-7).

Summary

What hermeneutics do you use? What are your rules for interpreting Scripture? If you utilize key-text hermeneutics to study the issue of jewelry, you can develop a good biblical case against wearing it. If you employ contextual hermeneutics, the case against is less compelling.

If you're a Seventh-day Adventist, you probably hold the Bible as the final authority for truth. Some have suggested that if your training in Seventh-day Adventism pre-dates 1970, you're likely to prefer key-text hermeneutics. If your higher education dates after 1970, you probably prefer contextual hermeneutics.

When it comes to jewelry, it's not a matter of whether or not you follow the Bible; it's often more a matter of the way you use the Bible to establish your standards.

If you're a Seventh-day Adventist, you probably hold the Bible as the final authority for truth. Some have suggested that if your training in Seventh-day Adventism pre-dates 1970, you're likely to prefer key-text hermeneutics. If your higher education dates after 1970, you probably prefer contextual hermeneutics.

*Roger L. Dudley with V. Bailey Gillespie, *Valuegenesis: Faith in the Balance* (Riverside, CA: La Sierra University Press, 1992), 152.

Looking at the Outward Appearance

Gary Russell

In a sermon he entitled "Bangles," Chuck Scriven included the following story about his former colleague Jan Daffern:

Jan has told me about her experience some years back of taking classes at a Mennonite seminary in northern Indiana, near Andrews University. The Mennonites are very committed to simplicity and Jan remembers that the seminary women typically wore their hair either in a short blow-dry style or pinned up in a bun. When an acquaintance of hers among these Mennonite women decided that she should pin up her own long hair rather than let it hang conspicuously down her back, Jan made her a gift of some fancy barrettes and combs. But the gift missed the mark completely; to the Mennonite woman, those barrettes and combs were adornment when the whole point of the change in hairstyle was greater modesty.

Jan tells me that the women at the seminary took considerable offense at her own permed hair, not to mention her high-heeled shoes. To them these things seemed far removed from the ethos of Scripture. But they themselves, on the other hand, were entirely comfortable wearing wedding bands on their fingers and tiny studs in their ears.

It all seemed rather bizarre, this conflict between traditions, Adventist and Mennonite, which after all shared a common belief in simplicity.[1]

Between Truth and Culture

Inconsistencies are evident within the Adventist church as well, made more complex by the tremendous church growth outside of North America, which has forced us to make keener discriminations between truth and culture. One example is the debate regarding wedding rings. While Adventists in some cultures consider it imperative for married people to wear wedding rings, some, such as many North Americans, attach a meaning of pride, rebellion, extravagance, and/or conspicuousness to those who adorn themselves with this marriage symbol.

Cultural shifts take time. When church administrators voted at Annual Council that those wearing wedding rings "should be fully accepted in the fellowship and service of the church," they simply were acknowledging that a cultural shift had occurred. The data from *Valuegenesis* con-

> **"...these things seemed far removed from the ethos of Scripture."**

[1]Charles Scriven, *Bangles*, transcript from a sermon delivered at the Sligo Seventh-day Adventist Church, Takoma Park, MD, February 14, 1987.

firms this, showing that only 15 percent of young people, 35 percent of their parents, and less than half of the pastors consider the wedding ring inappropriate for Adventists.

While the principles of modesty and simplicity in dress have remained constant for Seventh-day Adventists, the application has changed to be relevant to the times. Those seeking baptism in the 1930s had to sign a set of baptismal vows that included:

> "refraining from the wearing of plumes, flowers, ornaments of gold, and from everything which could be classed as 'costly array.'"

By the 1970s that had changed to a point of no longer being part of the baptismal vows, but still having a part of the summary of doctrinal beliefs. This included:

> "The Christian is called unto sanctification, and his life should be characterized by carefulness in deportment and modesty and simplicity in dress."

The current baptismal certificate makes no mention of dress standards, but includes the following statement as part of the doctrine of Christian behavior:

> "While recognizing cultural differences, our dress is to be simple, modest, and neat, befitting those whose true beauty does not consist of outward adornment but in the imperishable ornament of a gentle and quiet spirit."

While the principles of modesty and simplicity in dress have remained constant... the application has changed to be relevant to the times.

Biblical Principles

But before accenting all your outfits with additional ornamentation, consider a few basic biblical themes that relate to this topic, realizing that God requires us to give him everything we have and are, an attitude possible only from a regenerate heart (see Romans 12:1-2).

Principle #1: Modesty

The principle of modesty rings clearly through this often-used passage regarding dress. Synonyms for modesty within the text include decency (reserve) and propriety (good judgment). Specific applications for Paul's day were braided hair, gold, pearls, or expensive clothes.

Applications are not necessarily timeless or cross cultural, although the principle of modesty is. It might be that the appropriate application of modesty to your situation today would prohibit the use of earrings, rings, necklaces, and bracelets. But don't necessarily limit yourself to such an application.

Keep in mind styles, colors of clothing, how you present yourself, and the content of your conversation. Modesty is far more encompassing than a plunging neckline or a finger ring.

The principle of modesty rings clearly through this often utilized passage.

1 Timothy 2:9-10

**Genesis 1:27,31;
1 Corinthians 6:19-20.**

Modesty is far more encompassing than a plunging neckline or a finger ring.

Decorating an object more than a person demonstrates a distortion of values.

**Isaiah 14:12-14;
Ezekiel 28:12-17;
Daniel 4:28-33,37.**

Principle #2: Humans Are Made in the Image of God

Something is out of sync when people decorate houses, cars, landscapes, art, and churches, but do not decorate the ultimate creation–humans. To be created in the image of God includes the identification of the human with the divine so that relating to humans is, in reality, relating to God (Matthew 25:40,45; 1 John 4:11-12; 2 Corinthians 5:18-21).

For those who would make holy pilgrimages or adorn a shrine or other physical element, Christ's words to the woman at the well (John 4:21-24) reveal that God zeroes in on the person having far more value than any location for something even as important as worship. Just as treating objects with greater importance than people demonstrates a distortion of values (1 Corinthians 3:16), decorating an object more than a person does the same (Hebrews 2:6-8).

To be in the image of God by creation and redemption places humans above all other earthly creations. People are not to be worshiped, but neither should they try to look inferior, thereby denying the image of God.

Principle #3: Pride is Part of Our Sinful Nature

This third principle needs to be held in balance with the second one. Because of our sinful nature, care should be taken in adorning the image of God lest individuals fall prey to the same temptation as Lucifer in fueling foolish pride.

This is not an admonition to purposely look slovenly. Perhaps you've known people who seem proud that they look so bad! Rather, it's good counsel to periodically take personal inventory and evaluate the level to which pride is fostered or discouraged in how one looks, acts, and is treated.

To label all wearing of jewelry as pride-based imposes a motive that may be entirely erroneous for some, and may even vary from one situation to another with the same person. But the problem of pride of adornment also includes other items such as influence, possessions, talents, status, etc.

Principle #4: A Stewardship of Simplicity

None of us should be comfortable in setting a specific monetary figure for what constitutes a simple lifestyle or an extravagant expenditure. How much is too much varies from one situation to the next; there's always someone who has more, which somehow seems to justify a larger expense account.

Instead of making a comparison to those who have more than you to determine if you're "poor," make your comparison to those who have less than you to determine if you're "rich." Our call is to live simply so that others may simply live. Those blessed with extra resources are in a position to give away more, which many wealthy people do. Some choose to live within a budgeted simple lifestyle and give away everything in excess of that.

Periodically take personal inventory and evaluate the level to which pride is fostered or discouraged in you.

Matthew 6:19-21,24,31-34; Luke 6:20; 8:14; 12:15-21; 18:22-27; James 2:15-17.

199

Our call is to live simply so that others may simply live.

Simplicity as a lifestyle also goes far beyond a few pieces of jewelry, especially costume jewelry. It also includes houses, cars, vacations, retirement packages, wardrobes, and more. When an adult requests a young person to give up jewelry, the youth might quickly retort that the adult should give up their expensive cars. Since most adults would not be willing to make that analogous commitment, they tend to function under a truce with the adolescent, which enables both young people and adults to deny or ignore the principle of a simple lifestyle.

Another element that complicates the determination of simplicity relates to how much a person has to begin with. For example, in North America, most Adventists are in the middle class in terms of socioeconomic status. It's easy to criticize people who drive automobiles beyond the budget of most in the middle class. Yet we fail to realize that the vast majority of people in the world don't own *any* car, much less two or more cars per family.

Apply the principle of a simple lifestyle to yourself rather than to others!

Before determining if one's lifestyle is simple, one usually asks, "Simple compared to what or whom?" Does a minister's salary guarantee a simple lifestyle? Does a heart surgeon's salary demand lavish materialism? Compared to someone in the upper class, do you spend a greater percentage of your income on an automobile? Is your lifestyle "simple" compared to half of the world's population that lives on a mere $100 a year? Apply the principle of a simple lifestyle to yourself rather than to others!

200

Principle #5: Inner Beauty to Exceed Outer Beauty

1 Peter 3:3-4; Proverbs 11:22; 31:30.

Making the outside appear more attractive than the inside presents a false, hypocritical image. However, selecting adornment appropriate to one's character development seems impossible to implement due to subjective variance. Also, one's outer beauty, to a certain extent, is beyond one's control. But character development beckons for participation with noticeable results. Also, outer beauty makes its greatest impact through first impressions in contrast to inner beauty whose impact increases over time.

A universal application of this principle is impossible. Like most principles, it will need to be applied personally and repeatedly. Identifying it provides a foundation for agreement and reasonable applications.

In a society that places a high premium on physical attractiveness, those whose outward beauty is considered "beautiful" in their given culture have to work much harder to develop their inner beauty since their outer beauty easily dominates their lives. Ironically, those not considered to be attractive have a tendency to develop their inner beauty since their appearance doesn't seem to provide many benefits.

Some have come up with the excuse "It's functional" to explain or defend their use of jewelry such as watches (bracelets), pendants (necklaces), and even watch rings (rings). While the Bible doesn't give a "functional makes it permissible" caveat, the simple beauties of nature reveal that God invented beauty, and it "functions" to inspire awe in the eye of the beholder.

Consider the beauty of a sunset and the blend of colors across a spring meadow. John likened the New Jerusalem to a bride adorned for her husband (Revelation 21:2). There's no need to use "functional" as an excuse to look nice. Beauty has a function all its own—to inspire the beholder to greater appreciation of what is seen and what stands behind it.

Aspiring to the Heights

What shall we do? Is jewelry acceptable or isn't it? Some implore, "Just give me the right answer, and I will/ might live by it." James Coffin offers this sage summary when he suggests that standards are largely subjective and somewhat arbitrary. He suggests that they may even change over time, and lend themselves to memorization rather than "thoughtful analysis." Another criticism he has is when we focus on standards, they lead us to the "bottom line" of acceptability rather than leading us to the heights which any Christian should seek. He urges us to think of the principles involved rather than the standards.[1]

Although some pass this off as a slippage towards perdition, it really is a more realistic, responsible, and encompassing view. Legislating the applications of modesty and simplicity in dress can be maintained only in a very small, closed system.

Beauty "functions" to inspire awe in the eye of the beholder.

[1]James Coffin, "The Standard Problem" in *Adventist Review* (June 8, 1988), 5.

To hold a rigid application is unrealistic and inappropriate—it's wrong! To throw away the biblical principles of dress and lifestyle is equally wrong. We need a reaffirmation of the biblical principles followed by discussion and personal application so Seventh-day Adventists are true to their Spirit-driven convictions as they live for God and others.

Outer beauty makes its greatest impact through first impressions in contrast to inner beauty whose impact increases over time.

*Roger L. Dudley with V. Bailey Gillespie, *Valuegenesis: Faith in the Balance* (Riverside, CA: La Sierra University Press, 1992), 155.

Being Adventist is not primarily about prohibitions. It's about living the truly abundant life that God intended us to live.

Because We're Adventists

Stephen Chavez

Because we're Adventists, that's why.

Growing up an Adventist, I suppose I heard that phrase a million times (900,000 times in Bible class alone).

Mention the word "standards" and certain images come immediately to mind: no smoking, no premarital sex, no caffeine, no meat, no jewelry, etc.

As I've gotten older, I've begun to understand that being an Adventist is not primarily about prohibitions. It's about living the truly abundant life that God intended us to live.

Understanding that helped me understand the church's position about smoking, drinking, and sex.

But what about jewelry? What's the difference between wearing a gold lapel pin (not jewelry) and a string of pearls (jewelry). What's the difference between a wedding band (not jewelry) and a bracelet (jewelry)? What about a necktie or scarf (not jewelry) and a gold chain or necklace (jewelry)?

It's clear that the church's stand on jewelry is a mass of contradictions. Any critical thinker is going to wonder just why jewelry is such a big deal to Adventists.

For years I defended the church's position on jewelry. I knew all the texts, but by themselves I thought they were a little weak. So I had to look beyond the texts to the principles behind them.

I found something broader than the church's position on jewelry. And I've come up with a philosophy about life that reflects what I understand about living a truly Christlike life. The church's standard on jewelry is no longer as important as my understanding of how Jesus would live if He were on earth. So my personal standard on jewelry can be summed up in three simple words: economy, simplicity, and modesty.

Economy

Some people have limited resources. I don't have the time or the money to track all the latest trends and pattern my life accordingly. I know I can get a ring, ankle bracelet, or gold chain for a few bucks. But why?

Why shop for things that don't make me a better person inside? It is said, "Beauty is only skin deep. But ugly goes clear to the bone." Jesus's emphasis on inner beauty makes

Any critical thinker is going to wonder just why jewelry is such a big deal to Adventists.

me want to spend most of my time and resources polishing up whatever characteristics will make me more like Him.

Besides, why be simply another "follower?"

Simplicity

I like things uncomplicated. I think Jesus does too. When He was on earth, He broke down religious traditions and conflicting standards into a simple, uncomplicated formula: Love God with all your heart, and love your neighbor as yourself.

When I go out, I shower, dress, comb my hair, and rush out the door.

To see some people in the mall, dressing must be a major operation: shower, dress, shave my head, put ring in ear, nose, navel. Ankle bracelets? Check. Pinky ring? Check. Necklace? Check. Bandanna? Check. Why would anyone willingly make their lives that complicated?

It seems to me that the "coolest" people—those most comfortable with who they are and what they are—don't need a lot of dangling accessories to make a statement. The simplicity of their appearance speaks volumes.

And I like to think that Jesus's life would be reflected best in clean, simple, uncomplicated clothes and accessories.

Modesty

Another word for modesty is "balance." Modesty isn't just refraining from wearing jewelry. It's a lifestyle of honoring Jesus.

To see some people in the mall, dressing must be a major operation.

I don't have a problem with people who wear jewelry. But sometimes it occurs to me that they're trying to get my attention with the jewelry they wear. When I see people wear nose rings, or half a dozen stud earrings (in each ear) it's like they're saying, "Notice me! I'm here! Pay attention to me!" "What I wear is more important than who I am!"

Christians shouldn't have to shout (literally or figuratively) to get people's attention. A consistent Christian's life, one that reflects Christ's character, is an ingenious way to attract attention, while at the same time lifting up Christ.

Modesty isn't just refraining from wearing jewelry. It's a lifestyle of honoring Jesus.

*Roger L. Dudley with V. Bailey Gillespie, *Valuegenesis: Faith in the Balance* (Riverside, CA: La Sierra University Press, 1992), 158.

Jewelry and Spiritual Experience

Dick Duerksen

I was the guest preacher at a church many miles from home. For my Sabbath sermon, I used texts from Romans and Galatians to describe how God is head-over-heels in love with us. I focused on God's unconditional grace and shared how God likes sinners so much that He offers them total acceptance and love and forgiveness and transformation. The congregation listened intently and seemed moved by the glory of God's grace. I met many new friends at the church door, shook a hundred hands, then followed the crowd to the fellowship hall.

The potluck was excellent. Two of the potato salad dishes were made without onions, there were two kinds of homemade dill pickles, and someone had even provided pecan pie for dessert.

During the meal, I sat across from a very happy young woman. I remember her smile, her earrings, and her story. I'm learning to look directly into eyes and purposefully ignore ear lobes, necklines and any jewelry that may be hanging there. But this time the jewelry was too beautiful and large to ignore. The earrings were turquoise and silver, obviously crafted by a talented artisan. In fact, the artist had taken a series of black lines in the stones and carried the design into the silver, creating a stylized picture of Kokopelli, the Navajo flute-player. They were exquisite!

"Do you have some Navajo friends?" I tried not to look at her ears. "Oh," her smile grew even brighter, "You noticed my earrings! Aren't they wonderful!" For the next 10 minutes we talked about her Navajo friends, her trips to the reservation, and the talented artist who had made the earrings especially for her. We also talked about her relationship with Christ.

"Last Sabbath was the happiest day of my life!" Her smile placed dozens of exclamation points around her words. "Last Sabbath I was baptized right here in the church. Now I'm a Seventh-day Adventist, and it's the best thing that has ever happened to me. Isn't it wonderful to be in love with Jesus!"

For a brief moment I wondered if her earrings had been baptized too. But I pushed that thought aside and continued the warm fellowship with my new friend.

As I was getting into my car for the trip home, the pastor's wife came walking slowly across the parking lot.

"Last Sabbath I was baptized right here in the church. Now I'm a Seventh-day Adventist, and it's the best thing that has ever happened to me. Isn't it wonderful to be in love with Jesus!"

209

I rolled down the window and told her how much I had enjoyed visiting their congregation. She leaned down, cleared her throat, frowned, and asked the question that had obviously been tormenting her all morning.

"Elder Duerksen, if I agree with what you said about God accepting sinners, about God liking people who are still doing sinful things, don't I have to throw out all of the Adventist standards?"

"What specifically concerns you?" I asked.

She leaned almost into the car and frowned even more deeply. Her next question was obviously genuine and filled with sincere hope for a useful answer. "How do I get the earrings off the new members?"

I imagined a confrontation between the pastor's wife and the joyful new member with the turquoise earrings. I saw hands reaching out to remove the offending objects. Then I stopped the mental film and asked, "Do you think it would improve her spiritual experience if the earrings came off?"

She hadn't thought of it that way before. I waited as her eyes looked up toward the sky, focused on an invisible cloud, and imagined the possibilities.

Her response was slow, thoughtful, and wonderfully honest. "No. I don't suppose removing them would improve her spiritual experience. But it would improve mine!"

Then her eyes locked on mine, and I could see the confusion and frustration welling up. "It was all so easy when everything was black-and-white. Now everything seems to be just shades of gray."

"Isn't it wonderful to be in love with Jesus!"

Angry and Joyful Jewelry Letters

Over the years I've collected quite a file of jewelry letters. They show a diversity that has once again renewed my confidence in the Seventh-day Adventist Church. We can have quite different opinions on some of these lifestyle issues and still be Adventists who are seeking to grow in the grace of Christ. I find that most encouraging.

Please read the letters carefully and notice the differing approaches to this issue.

"...if I agree with what you said about God accepting sinners... don't I have to throw out all of the Adventist standards?"

I personally don't wear jewelry, for a Biblical reason: "Now take off your ornaments and I will decide what to do with you." Exodus 33:5. When the Israelites were under judgment, God had them remove their ornaments. We have been under judgment since 1844 and, I believe, demonstrate that belief and its solemnity by refraining from ornamentation.

I do wear a wedding ring, again for Biblical reasons: "Abstain from all appearance of evil." 1 Thessalonians 5:22. Couples living together without wedding rings appear to be unmarried cohabitants. A pregnant woman without a wedding ring appears to be yet another "Murphy Brown."

I do not condemn or criticize those who do otherwise, again for a Biblical reason: "Do not judge, or you too will be judged." Matthew 7:1. We need to allow room for growth in this understanding and relationship with Jesus!

— *Ohio*

The Bible refers to jewelry as adornment. Does that strictly apply to earrings, bracelets, rings, and necklaces, or is there a broader meaning? Say I walk into church in a $40 dress wearing a $5 pair of earrings. Meanwhile, Mrs. Smith is wearing absolutely no jewelry. However she is sporting a $120 dress with $70 pumps. Mrs. Jones, on the other hand, appears quite fashionable in a $75 dress with a $20 silk scarf neatly held together by an "acceptable" $12 pin. "Ladies, you look lovely today. Who is that woman with the earrings?"

My concern is that many Adventists have become pro's at "straining gnats while swallowing camels." Please, let's all try to look at hearts as Christ does.

— *Ohio*

We can have quite different opinions on some of these lifestyle issues and still be Adventists who are seeking to grow in the grace of Christ.

As I have learned about the Adventist doctrine, I have embraced all aspects of it except this thing about jewelry. I cannot understand why I am not supposed to wear my earrings, and yet, I see men in the church wearing gold tie clasps with jewels. The whole absurdity of this came to me when I learned that it is "OK" for women to wear a pin, but necklaces and earrings are not appropriate.

I have read the scriptures on this issue and do not read them to say that jewelry is forbidden. To me, we are instructed to dress modestly and not to become obsessed with our appearance but instead to be concerned with our spiritual or "inner" character.

We must remind ourselves that salvation does not come from what we wear or don't wear, from what we eat or don't eat, or from what church we are members of. Salvation comes through grace!

—*Texas*

I am sure that God looks with great sorrow at the amount of time we spend worrying about who's wearing earrings this Sabbath or who's just bought the latest model of car, or "Where did she get that dress?!" I find that when I am focused on Jesus and what he has done for me, I see lots of happy, shining faces looking heavenward with me. What are they wearing? I honestly could not tell you. But their eyes are shining and Christ's love is plain to see.

— *Virginia*

We cannot afford to have two views on this subject. Pride and arrogance against a plain command is rebellion against God. There are many good reasons for this tenet of faith, and only eternity will lay it out fully for our view. Yet for now a plain "Thus says the Lord" should be enough for any of us.

—*Alberta, Canada*

A standard is not a specific behavior. A standard is like a ruler or yardstick that has many inches on it. It is a guide for behaviors in a specific category. Therefore, we must allow room for personal decisions as, with God's help, our friends find the mark they can function on.

—*Pennsylvania*

Modesty and simplicity in dress are Bible principles. For those who would make the Sabbath a holiday and not a holy day, recreation becomes wreck-reation. Dress is matter of opinion and not principle and diet is based on taste and not health. Music is primarily a feeling rather than an affirmation of faith. Such people systematically undermine the gospel. A change of heart always is attended by a clear conception of duty.

—*Virginia*

My concern is that many Adventists have become pro's at "straining gnats while swallowing camels."

I would like to know where in the Bible it says that we can't wear jewelry. I don't mean to overdo it, but just a simple chain, pin, or ring. I really would like to read it in the Bible.

— Maryland

I've discovered that the only way to make quality decisions about jewelry is to listen more to God than to the voices of neighbors and friends. Although that's often hard to do, I've found that the following six principles can serve as a simple guide for listening to His wisdom. Consider the first two as you look at the wide issue of lifestyle and then use the next four principles to evaluate your options regarding this specific decision.

These are decisions you can make!

Two Overarching Lifestyle Principles

1.   Romans 2:1-4 – *The Principle of Judgment*. It is not my responsibility to judge others. It is my responsibility to follow God into His radical lifestyle.
2.   1 Peter 2:16 – *The Principle of Freedom*. God has given me the gift of freedom. I am to use that gift to serve others in love.

Four Principles to Help Evaluate All Lifestyle Choices

1.   Hebrews 12:1 – *The Principle of Excess*. Could this slow me down spiritually?

There are many good reasons for this tenet of faith and only eternity will lay it out fully for our view.

214

2.   1 Corinthians 6:12a – *The Principle of Expedience*. Is this profitable and useful in my life plan?
3.   1 Corinthians 6:12b – *The Principle of Enslavement*. Can I be Spirit-controlled in this?
4.   Romans 14:13 – *The Principle of Example*. Does this allow me to be a Christlike model for others?

With these principles working to help you make some decisions in your life, God will work in you to feel consistent and obedient.

Some Exercises to Try

1.   Read Colossians 3:1-14. This passage describes what happens when a person has chosen to follow Christ. Paul lists a number of character traits and behaviors that "come off" and others that are "put on" as a person becomes a Christian. Make two columns on a sheet of paper. Title the first "Comes off," the second "Goes on." Under each column write a simple description of the contemporary behaviors and traits you believe are included in this text. When you are finished, write a one-sentence definition of "The Contemporary Christian Lifestyle."
2.   Reread the story at the beginning of this article about the pastor's wife's reaction to the new church member with earrings. Then ask the following questions:

I've discovered that the only way to make quality decisions about jewelry is to listen more to God than to the voices of neighbors and friends.

- Why did the pastor's wife feel she had to get the earrings off of the new member?
- Why would the removal of the earrings improve her spiritual experience?
- What is our Biblical responsibility for adjusting the behavior of others in the church?
- How does God expect us to influence the lifestyle of others?
- How do we know which "standards" are Biblically based and which are the result of our culture?

Suggested Additional Resources

Baram, Robert, ed., Spiritual Journeys: Toward the Fullness of Faith (Boston, MA: St. Paul's Books, 1987).

Campolo, Anthony, *Who Switched the Price Tags* (Waco, TX: Word), 1986.

Chilton, David, *Productive Christians in an Age of Guilt Manipulators* (Tyler, TX:Institute for Christian Economics, 1985).

Daily, Steve, *Adventism for a New Generation* (Portland, OR:Better Living Publishers, 1993).

Foster, Richard *Freedom of Simplicity* (San Francisco:HarperCollins, 1989).

Sider, Ronald, *Rich Christians in an Age of Hunger* (Downers Grove, IL: InterVarsity Press, 1984).

Smith, Michael W., "Picture Perfect" and "Cross of Gold" on *Change Your World* (Irving, TX:Reunion Records, 1992).

Shelton, Charles M., *Morality and the Adolescent* (New York, NY:Crossroad, 1989).

Tyner, Stuart and Gillespie, V. Bailey eds., *Walking On the Edge* (Lincoln, NB: Church Resources Distribution Center, 1996).

Section 6
Thinking About God's Will

Section 6
Thinking About God's Will

What's the Discussion About?

People don't debate it much, but most of us would love to get a straightforward answer to the question: What is God's will for my life?

Many within the church have grown up hearing the encouraging statements: "God loves you and has a wonderful plan for your life." The message is that we are very special to God, that He loves us individually, and He has a plan for our lives. What a boost to our self-esteem!

But when the "plan" seems vague, or prayers for direction seem unheard, we're left wondering if God really does have a plan for us. This may prompt the question:

"God loves you and has a wonderful plan for your life."

219

Does God really love us?

"Of course God loves us!" we tell ourselves. Is the problem with us? Is God trying to reveal His plan, but we simply can't hear it because we're so far from Him? Ironically, this self-esteem booster can backfire into a self-esteem crusher when we don't receive the expected map with our name on it.

If God does have a plan for our lives, how do we discover it and how do we know it's the right plan? If we don't find an obvious answer, are we on our own?

The Background of the Discussion

God told Adam and Eve what to eat and what to stay away from. He gave Noah specific plans for building the ark. He called Abram to leave Ur and move to an unknown country. Messages from God were received through prophets to His people. God spoke to King David through Samuel and Nathan; He spoke to his people through Jeremiah and Ezekiel; and He spoke directly through Jesus.

But it's been 2,000 years since Jesus spoke to us directly. Where is God's voice today? Do we hear it in the still, small voice as Elijah did? Should we rely on signs as Gideon did? Should we exercise our faith as did the priests who carried the ark across the Jordan River? Should we accept a religious leader's word as the voice of God, as the Israelites did with Samuel?

The self-esteem booster can backfire into a self-esteem crusher when we don't receive the expected map with our name on it.

We become more interested in God's will if we're faced with a major decision like, Where should I attend college? What should I major in? Should I marry this person? Should I accept that job offer?

In less complex societies, such questions are seldom asked. If you're male, you farm the land. If you're female, you care for the home and bear children. But increasingly complex societies lead to increasingly complicated issues to wrestle with.

There are those who testify of visions, dreams, or "the hand of God" that led them. But it's difficult to affirm these brushes with the supernatural when they don't happen to us or because we're unaware of when they occur.

We have focused on a few people with wonderful revelations of God's will for their lives, while the majority feel spiritually inferior because they don't have a clear indication of God's will for their lives. If God revealed His will to Abram, why not others in Ur (or in Abram's family)? What did Abram do all the years God didn't speak directly to him?

Perhaps the truism should be "God loves you and is very interested and involved in the choices you make in life."

Questions Youth Are Asking

- What is God's will for my life?
- Should I be a _____? (fill in the blank)

Where do we hear God's voice today?

221

If God has a specific will for us regarding our vocation, does he also have a specific person for us to marry?

- Should I marry _____?
- If I have two job offers, how will I know which one God wants me to take?
- What part do I play in this decision-making process?
- How can I decipher what "trusted counselors" tell me when their advice differs?
- Should I ask God for a sign?
- How can I hear God through the "still, small voice"?
- What's the difference between the "still, small voice" and my own conscious or subconscious thoughts?
- What's the difference between a "closed door" and God testing my persistence?
- What should I do if there aren't "open doors"?
- Does it make any difference what I do if there is more than one "open door"?
- What will happen to me if I miss God's guidance for me? Will I be lost or have a bad life then?

Focusing the Discussion

Here's a look at the chapters for this section regarding the will of God.

•"The Butcher, Baker, and Candlestick Maker." V. Bailey Gillespie, Professor of Theology and Christian Personality and Executive Director of the John Hancock Center for Youth Ministry at La Sierra University, takes us through familiar questions and experiences of wondering what is God's will for our lives in the area of vocation.

What indications have you had for your vocation? How much is up to you, and how much does God guide you? Have you ever felt "called" to a vocation? Do you know someone who was? How did they know? How did they respond?

•"One Step At A Time." Celeste Ryan, editor of *Adventist View,* shares her personal experience of choosing a vocation through the challenges of adolescence (and beyond). She writes of several steps she takes to discover God's will for her life. These steps may help you in focusing your own questions and answers about God's will and just how He impacts your reality.

How many of these steps do you take? Which ones work for you and which ones don't? Why? What other steps would you take to discover God's will if you didn't discover it by taking these steps?

• "God's Plan For You." V. Bailey Gillespie continues his exploration of finding God's will by giving four assumptions and six biblical principles for discovering God's will for your life. Careful study of these texts and principles may help you with the questions of this chapter.

To what extent do you use the Bible to discover God's will for your life? How many of these biblical principles do you follow? What would you need to do to implement

What did Abram do all the years God didn't speak to him?

223

To what extent do you use the Bible to discover God's will for your personal life?

all of them? What are the ways that God reveals Himself in your life? How certain are you of God's will for your life? How detailed does God get in giving you direction for your life? How specific is it?

The Butcher, Baker, and Candlestick Maker

V. Bailey Gillespie

The anxiety and excitement could be felt all over the auditorium where the evangelist was speaking. There was a certain sense of expectation in the air. You knew something was coming, something important. It must have been in the preacher's voice because at once it seemed to become serious, the lights lowered, and the choir repeated the same verse of that slow, thoughtful song, yet one more time. The preacher's voice rang clear, and somehow you knew in your inner soul it was directed right at you.

"Would you like to give your life to God?" came the voice cutting through the air, creating feelings of guilt and confusion. Now you knew he was talking especially to you. "Will you follow God's plan for your life?"

The preacher's voice rang clear, and somehow you knew in your inner soul it was directed right at you.

Church youth hear this kind of thing often, and there is always a sense in which hearing it again only brings those old feelings to the surface. Even though there would be tears in the most fragile souls, there was an atmosphere of "here we go again," and "let's hear it one more time, only this time I won't cry."

The preacher droned out his call for service. But still, even with these feelings, some youth moved forward, down to the altar of the church, and knelt with a sense of inner peace. Did they know God's plan for their lives? Did they understand the complexities of being "called" by God? Some of the youth at the meeting were not as kind to the preacher as others. These openly challenged the minister on his assumptions. After a meeting like that, one youth went up to the preacher and said, "Okay, how do you know you are doing what God wants you to do?"

Another said, "What sign have you had that you should be a minister?"

Yet the unspoken questions that had been raised by this event lingered in the minds of many teens for years.

"What if I never find out what God wants me to do?"

"What if I never feel moved to do something for God?"

"What if I have so many things I want to do with my life that I can't decide?"

These are questions asked hundreds of times by youth concerned about their future.

How do you know you are doing what God wants you to do?

Burn That Bush!

You probably have never had a "burning bush" experience. Moses, in the Old Testament, knew for sure that the voice calling him was from God. Once Moses asked to know the name of Reality so that he could say something to others, so he would know just who was calling him to talk to the Egyptians. He wanted a god like the pagans. They had a god with a name, so he asked God what his name was.

If I am going off to Egypt, he reckoned, I want to know what you are up to. And Yahweh answered, "Here's my name: I AM WHO I AM." But when we read those words today, we tend to think of things like "being." And Yahweh was not talking about being, but acting. God said, "I'm up to what I'm up to, and you are not going to tell me what to do. One of us is God, Moses, and it isn't you."

Moses saw this was time to change the subject. "Look, Yahweh," he said, "I'm not equipped to lead an exodus. Look at me, a simple shepherd."

And God answered Moses by saying, "What is that in your hand?"

"It's a rod, a simple shepherd's's stick," Moses responded.

"That's all you need. The rod is a symbol of the background and potential that you, Moses, bring to this moment. Remember your time in the palace and in school? You have been preparing for just such a time as this," God reminded Moses.

You probably have never had a "burning bush" experience.

Moses was feeling backed into a corner, but he thought of the perfect out. "You see, I have this BIG problem, God. When I get flustered, I stutter. Can you see me before the mighty Pharaoh saying, "Yea, Man, Yahweh s-s-s-says le-le-le-le-let m-m-m-m-my p-p-p-p-people g-g-g-g-g-go!?"

God's answer was Aaron. He told Moses that he was to write down the messages and Aaron would deliver them if Moses couldn't. He was unable to escape the call.

So Moses faced the same moment that has come to many people throughout history; that moment when you realize something has to be done, something has to be decided. You must put behind your own selfish desires and inabilities and step forward in faith. Moses had been called in a moment and there was no way out. He knew that he must work for God.

After hearing just such a story, we often wonder why it never seems to happen that way to us. God seldom breaks into our lives with fire and lightening to point out the direction we must go. And doubts about God's power and ability to touch our lives come into question again.

Balance these concerns with the opposite conclusion that can be drawn from the story of the call of Moses. These include thoughts that I am not important enough for God to bother telling me what I am to do. Is it any wonder that young people who are committed to Christ experience frustration and feelings of inadequacy? They want to be used by God, but they don't know how or when He will inform them of His plans.

We often wonder why it never seems to happen that way to us.

What Does History Teach Us?

One of the earliest discussions regarding vocation is found in the New Testament. The characters in the story are the disciples of Jesus, and the setting is just prior to the triumphal entry into Jerusalem. The ambitions of James and John are articulated by their mother. The woman asks Jesus for something.

"What do you want?" Jesus asked.

She said to Him, "Command that these two sons of mine may sit, one at your right hand and one at your left, in your kingdom."

But Jesus answered, "You do not know what you are asking. Are you able to drink the cup that I am to drink?"[1]

[1]Matthew 20:21-22.

God Calls Us To "Come and Die"

The disciples were not aware that to follow Christ in His vocation meant to be persecuted and eventually even die for the cause of the kingdom of God. Most people forget that the calling of God includes deep commitment and a sense of mission, often at the risk of personal loss. Vocation in the Bible often has meant learning to give oneself in service.

There have been situations like this throughout the history of Christianity in the United States. Since the earliest days of the circuit riding preachers on the East and Midwest, there have been people "called" by God to enlist, enroll, beg, cajole, and/or invite others to find their place

Young people want to be used by God, but they don't know how or when He will inform the of His plans.

Most people forget the calling of God includes deep commitment and a sense of mission, often at the risk of personal loss.

in the service of God. Seldom has the invitation been omitted in major youth rallies, convocations, weeks of prayer, and during moments of quiet retreats. Many workers in the cause of God can trace their first hunches that God wanted them in "the work" to such a series of meetings or a moving altar call at a youth conference in Mexico City, Atlantic City, or Zurich.

Words like "calling" and "vocation," "life work" and "career," "working for God" and "doing God's will" all conjure up ambivalent feelings of surety and anxiety among the followers of Christ. Just how do you know what you should do with your life? Just how do you know the job you finally elect to spend your waking moments performing will be what God wants you to be doing? And to even add a more complex question to this list, we might add, how do you know you are doing what God really wants you to do in the great cosmic plan that we often have heard we should fulfill?

And then on the other side of the question, what if I find I am not doing what I should be doing? What then? Am I lost forever and have to carry the guilt throughout my life knowing what I might have been or could have become? Do I have to go to sleep with the burden of the unsaved millions in faraway lands that have never heard the voice of the loving Savior? I am sure these questions and worries were not in the mind of the evangelist when he spoke with a tone of complete sincerity, "Don't you want to give your life to God?"

Crises in Identity

Let's add another dimension to this problem. Most people, as they grow older, go through times when they wonder what they will be doing for the rest of their lives. They go through moments of crises in identity. And, according to recent surveys, most adults change their profession at least three to seven times during their life. Just where did we first learn about our life dream?

The answers often come at an early age with ideas and dreams of being a fireman, policeman, housewife, mother, dancer, or movie star, butcher, baker, or candlestick maker. The answers to the questions of life work come when older people in society model the "good life" for us as we begin to grow and think for ourselves.

Later it seems we get more serious about our life calling. We find ourselves falling into some categories. Doctor, teacher, nurse, preacher, or housewife seemed at one time for many Adventists, the only possibilities. We are told that a life of service is the goal for Christians, and these life-work choices seem to be the only ones available. After all, look around you in the churches. Who are the leaders? Aren't they the physicians and teachers? Don't the preachers have a kind of "special" status in the church? And aren't all the girls supposed to learn to play the piano, become teachers or nurses, and marry ministers or physicians? Isn't that the way the story goes?

If it is not the American dream, it is at least an illusion promoted by some male's particular viewpoint about work-

What if I find I am not doing what I should be doing?

231

ing for God. Well, if you think this is the way it should be, you were living on another planet during the decade of the 80s, and the pace is even faster in the 90s. Obviously, a new look at what vocation really means must be explored. Both men and women need a sense of vocation.

Let's examine the problem of career and vocation and try to come to some understanding how to decide and choose what God really wants you to be and do.

A life of service is the goal for Christians.

What Is Vocation?

The easy answer to this question is to simply say it is your job, your work. It is the thing that fills the time between eight o'clock in the morning until the closing bell at five o'clock at night. This eight-hour day sets the parameter around the workaday world and marks off the hours when leisure time begins. Five o'clock is when we finally get to do what we have been longing to do all during the working day. This scenario is all too often played out in the routines of thousands of the workforce during any given day.

When we think of words like "vocation" and "calling," many images come to mind. We think of the myriad of individuals in days gone by, leaving their life work to pursue their vision for the sake of some greater cause. We are reminded of the Crusaders who followed their visions. Their calling must have been very clear for the Crusaders to nudge thousands to leave the comfort of their homes and set out to the Holy Land intending to free it from the infidel hordes. I have often wondered how clearly I would have to see my calling to follow people with names like Peter the Hermit and Walter the Penniless.[1]

Nevertheless, people throughout history have sensed, perceived, felt, been captured by, sent, directed, enlightened, and even shoved into directions that defy logical analyses and do not fit carefully designed models of psychological theory in order to accomplish what they thought they had been called to do.

Originally, the term "vocation" was translated from the Latin word *vocatio*. This word was used to describe "one's calling." To have a vocation was to be called by God to do something special. The professions during this time were limited. Clergy and professorial types dominated the choice of careers. Lawyers and churchmen were the only option for the well-educated class during this time.

Since the church was the interpreter of truth and the major social institution that interpreted life for individuals in the villages and townships in Europe, one's vocation often was interpreted by the church to mean professional ministry. Priest and lay priests were the highest calling of that time. It was not unusual for someone to feel impressed that God was calling him or her to do something in some special way for some special group of people. For some, it meant giving up all worldly possessions and walking to and fro on the earth seeking and begging an existence. For others it meant going to the university, writing a work of theology, or teaching in the seminary.

[1]Will Durant, *The Age of Faith* (New York: Simon and Schuster, 1950), 589.

Originally, the term "vocation" was translated from the Latin word *vocatio*.

In Adventist educational circles a parallel structure emerged from the early days of our church. This pattern was less organized than the Catholic vision of vocations but nevertheless had a subtle influence in the lives of early employees of the church. This attitude still prevails in many parts of the Adventist church where new schools are established and students see their first calling to be used in the church's work.

Individuals in the later 1800s chose education and training to become workers for the church rather than for the sake of learning or their enrichment and options it would provide them in society. Adventist education thrived in the early days because individuals felt called to work for God, and the place to be trained was in a Seventh-day Adventist environment. Thus, the SDA school system was begun.

There was an understanding when you graduated from an Adventist school there would be work in the church. This is no longer true even for graduating theology majors. Now the church is in the business of education for different reasons. We have not forgotten our original mission, but the mission has become cloudy with the reduction of jobs available in the church. This changes our view of vocation and forces us to take a new look at its true meaning.

Even though our denomination employs thousands of people around the world, it cannot absorb all of its graduates. In a workshop I conducted in Poona, India for 120 church workers, they told me how bitter classmates had become because the church could not hire all of the

To have a vocation was to be "called by God" to do something special.

ministers who graduated. People who had spent four years of their young lives in a church educational environment were frustrated when told to look for other employment when they graduated.

We face a similar problem in North America today. It is even more focused on the training of women for pastoral ministry in the church. Since the Adventist church does not ordain women to pastoral ministry at the time of this writing, how does one encourage this portion of the church population who have abilities and spiritual gifts and show real promise for ministry? This is a problem the church must resolve soon if it is to encourage a valuable part of the church population that feels "called" to service.

The same is true for youth ministry. Some who feel "called" to work specifically with young people get rammed into the pastoral preparation mold of conventional pastoral ministry. With only six-tenths of one percent of the churches in North America having a youth pastor, there aren't very many openings for those called to youth ministry.[1]

It would seem to really understand vocation, we must learn to use the broadest meaning of the term in order to make sense of our current situations. Vocation is something everyone can be committed to; it is not just reserved for the "safe" professions. Everyone must develop a sense of what God's calling is for them. Perhaps that is more important than deciding if one should be a "butcher, baker, or candlestick maker."

There was an unwritten guarantee that when you graduated from one of our schools there would be work in the church. This is no longer true.

[1] Steve Case, "Youth Ministry Report Card," in *Adventist Review* (April 9, 1992), 16. This estimate is based on approximately 25 full time youth pastors in the more than 4,400 churches in North America. Some "youth pastors" carry a large amount of other pastoral duties, but if they were added, the number of churches with youth pastors would "swell" to just over two percent of all churches in North America. Statistics from the annual *Youth Ministry Professional's Directory* published by the John Hancock Center for Youth Ministry note that in 1994 there were 142 individuals who claimed to be responsible for youth. The increase is encouraging, however slight.

"When I grow up, I'm going to be a doctor."

One Step At A Time

Celeste Ryan

"When I grow up, I'm going to be a doctor—a pediatrician," I proudly announced, leaving my parents ecstatic. In fact, as many proud parents often do, they began to spread the news to our relatives, their co-workers, friends, church members, and even the gas station attendant, the milk man, and the mail lady.

But a few years later, as an early teen, I changed my mind. I learned about the kind of commitment it would take to become a doctor and quickly realized that as much as I hated school and studying, I'd never make it. At first I thought it was too late because by this time my parents had already told everyone in the universe!

I didn't bother to explain to them that now I was going to be a singer—the next Whitney Houston. Every day when I got home from school, I'd close the living room blinds, pump up the stereo, whip out my hairbrush (microphone), and sing "The Greatest Love of All" over and over *and over* again.

After that brief period, I vaguely remember wanting to pursue careers as a professional softball player, an interior decorator, a saxophone jazz artist, and queen of the fashion design industry in New York, Paris, and Milan.

Before I knew it, I was a senior in academy. At that point I honestly didn't know what I'd do with my life. I remember that it was the beginning of second semester and everybody was talking about what they would study and where they had applied to attend college.

My English teacher, who had grown tired of my constant babbling about fashion and magazines, decided I should create a fashion magazine for my major English project. I did and enjoyed every minute of it. It was the greatest thing he ever did for me.

From that point on, I knew without a doubt that I was going to be the editor of a fashion magazine someday. Journalism was the reason God must have placed me on earth, and therefore, journalism was what I'd study in college.

A Purpose In Life

For the first time, it seemed to me that there was a reason for my existence. There was a reason for me to be on this earth—something I was supposed to be doing. It

What childhood fantasies did you have about what you would do when you would "grow up and get big"?

was as if God had finally acknowledged my presence and pointed me in a particular direction instead of allowing me to flounder from dream to dream.

Figuring out your purpose in life isn't an easy task. It's actually quite difficult. How can a young person know God's will for his or her life? How should we know what choices to make and whether or not we're on the right track?

In my short life I've learned to follow several steps when I'm needing some direction, some word from the Lord, some answers. Here they are.

Get To Know the Lord

We can do that by reading the Bible, God's letter to us. He intends for us to use it and learn about him through it. The Bible is the basis for our relationship with our Maker and Savior. We are told that, "In the beginning was the Word, and the Word was with God, and the Word was God."[1]

When asked why Jesus was called the Word, an eight-year-old girl replied, "Because Jesus is all God wanted to say to us."[2] As we read about Jesus' life in His Word, we get to know Him, his ways, how He spoke, how He handled different situations, how He made decisions, and how He related to people. And we can apply those situations to what we encounter in our lives today.

To establish a relationship with the Lord, start by finding a version of the Bible you can understand, not

Figuring out your purpose in life isn't an easy task.

[1] John 1:1 (NIV).

[2] *The New Student Bible* (Grand Rapids, MI: Zondervan), 945.

merely read! In my experience, until I got to know Him, the other steps were harder to follow.

Seek and You Will Find

One of my favorite texts is, "Ask and it will be given you; seek and you will find; knock and the door will be opened to you. For everyone who asks receives; he who seeks finds; and to him who knocks, the door will be opened."[1]

[1]Luke 11:9-10 (NIV).

Once you get to know the Lord by reading His Word, you've got to communicate with Him through prayer. When He becomes real in your life, talking to Him is like talking to your best friend—you never run out of things to say. You can share everything, not be ashamed of anything, ask questions, and look to him for guidance. Together you can explore your hopes and dreams, try out new talents you discover, and work on figuring out your niche.

My mother always tells me "Much prayer, much power; little prayer, little power." When I was younger, she frequently advised me to talk to the Lord about what was going on in my life. "Jesus longs to talk with you," she would say. "He's very interested in your life."

At that time it was so hard to comprehend what she was saying. How could someone I couldn't see, touch, or hear communicate with me? And why would He be interested in my life?

Today I know that He is interested. When you're

How could someone I couldn't see, touch, or hear communicate with me?

[1] John 10:4.

looking for answers and guidance, seek out your friend Jesus. He always has time to talk.

Listen

When you're trying to figure out what to do about a certain situation or decision, listening for God's answers is just as important as talking to Him. Sometimes you just have to wait to see what He's going to say.

When I told this to my friend Nancy, she asked, "But how do you discern His voice? How do you know when He's talking to you as opposed to someone else?"

According to Scripture,[1] sheep follow their shepherd because they know the shepherd's voice. If we are like sheep and Jesus is our shepherd, we'll follow Him because we recognize His voice.

For me, the stronger my relationship with God, the easier it is to hear his voice and the more I want to listen. I know that God has good things in store for me because He has my best interests at heart. I also consult with my parents and mentors. They also have my best interests at heart.

My mother says that on more than one occasion, "coincidence" has led her to believe she was hearing the voice of God. She says that after praying, she's had two or three people come to her and say the same thing; yet none of them consulted each other or knew the others had talked with her. They just felt impressed to tell her these things.

José Rojas, youth director for North America, says that sometimes he discovers God's will as a result of God's actions. "When God closes a door, He opens a window," he says. "And when one opportunity is suddenly withdrawn or falls through and another comes along, it's as if God is letting us know that the first choice wasn't the right one."

Believe and Act

Listening to God and discerning His voice takes time. But when you believe you know His will, act on it. Do what He says.

Sometimes you've got to take the long road. Sometimes He takes you in a different direction than you want to go. But be flexible and remember a true friend won't try to steer you wrong.

I recently took a job that I didn't want. It wasn't a job that required my communication or psychology degrees, and it certainly didn't call on my experience in journalism. I remember asking God what He was doing. "How is this job going to be a part of Your will for my life?" I asked him.

Yet it turned out to be a blessing. I learned more than I ever imagined I would, and it gave me more experience in journalism and several other fields.

When you believe you know God's will, act on it.

241

One Step At a Time

In my life, God seems to reveal his plans slowly.

That experience taught me the most valuable lesson on discovering and knowing God's will for my life—don't expect for Him to map it all out. You've got to be prepared for an adventure that changes one step and one day at a time.

When I entered college, I felt that journalism was the reason God put me on this planet. Now I realize that was only the beginning. I've learned that when I follow God's plan, I've got to be prepared to take some side trips and some different routes.

In my life, God seems to reveal His plans slowly when He believes I'm able to handle them—when He knows I'm ready. It's the most frustrating part of our relationship because I *always* think I'm ready, and it's only in retrospect that I see and agree with His reasons.

Realizing God's plans for my life one step at a time is exciting because I never know what's going to happen next. But because of my friendship with Him that started with establishing a Bible-based relationship, communicating and listening to him, and believing and acting on His promises; I'm not afraid.

I cling to that proverb, "Trust in the Lord with all your heart, and lean not on your own understanding. In all your ways acknowledge Him, and He will direct your paths."[1]

[1]Proverbs 3:5-6.

God's Plan For You

V. Bailey Gillespie

Finding God's will for one's life involves far more than merely selecting a good vocation or getting a prestigious job. Sometimes we're tempted to treat God like a genie, pulling him out of a bottle (or Bible) to get a piece of magic to help us on our way. But God is personally involved in our lives, not intermittently available for trouble spots. He's interested in a relationship with us, not an occasional brush with the divine. So how does this relate to our vocation?

Involved in the Passion of God

James Fowler suggested that in order to fully understand vocation today, we must understand a very important theological concept. One's vocation involves partnership

Sometimes we're tempted to treat God like a genie—to get a piece of magic to help us on our way.

243

with God the Creator, partnership with the governing action of God, which includes recognizing we cannot be selfish or greedy, and partnership in the redemptive action of God.

We are compassionate with those in bondage. We work for the release and the reclamation of those that are caught in oppression of all kinds. That means we work in our life calling to free those that are alienated, in economic oppression, or have spiritual problems. We, in our sense of vocation, are truly "co-workers" with God, as the New Testament suggests.[1]

Fowler suggests that we become one with the passion of God. Once we learn and catch this vision of our potential it will be the single most fruitful way of finding a principle to orchestrate our changing life.[2]

Finding God's Plan for Your Life

How do you find this sense of calling? How do you learn about the great plan that seems to exist in the universe for you? There are many ways to answer these questions. One way is simply to watch God open and close "doors," sometimes in a dramatic or miraculous manner. This, however, does not answer the question of how God leads us. It assumes that God is totally in charge and our choices do not count in deciding what is right for us. If this position really is true, discovering God's specific plan for our lives is crucial!

But what if we do not see him acting specifically in our

[1] 3 John 8. See also 2 Corinthians 6:1.

[2] James W. Fowler, *Becoming Adult, Becoming Christian: Adult Development and the Christian Faith* (New York: Harper and Row, 1984), 85.

lives? Should we assume that we are not right with God, that our Christian experience is weak? Could it be that we are not praying hard enough? Such outlooks demonstrate a subtle form of righteousness by works.

But there is another, more helpful way to view God's work and will in our lives. Picturing God as the cosmic doorkeeper places Him at the center of all action in this universe. But let's look at four assumptions that recognize our responsibility in the decision-making process while still allowing God to be in charge.

Assumptions

Assumption #1: God wants the very best for us. This is so obvious I hesitate to begin here at all. Whatever we choose that is good for us is the will of God. We do not have to speculate about God's plan for us if what we do is beneficial to us by helping us grow toward the kingdom of God and if it provides others the freedom to do the same. For example, we know that it is God's will to help those who do not have as much as we do. No need to fret about that one. We know God's will without waiting for some special sign, because God wants what benefits his kingdom.

Assumption #2: We have real freedom. God's plan for us is to be perfectly free to choose for ourselves. If we are puppets working God's will, looking for the moment when God gets us into the job or situation He wants, then we do not have real freedom at all, and our responses in life aren't true responses.

Assumption #1: God wants the very best for us.

Assumption #2: We have real freedom.

245

But if we are free to make choices, then God wants us to make choices that make a difference to us. When we choose, we are doing God's will too. By exercising our freedom of choice, we are proving God's loving nature and demonstrating His care for us. True love demands truly free choices! Learning to make choices that really are our own is important.

Assumption #3: We have many options.

Assumption #3: We have many options. There are many ways you can be used by and for God. Exceptionally talented people often have a number of equally acceptable options, not just one. Their job is to dedicate their talents to His work and to spend time learning how best to use them.

This assumption of options stands in contrast to some of the Bible prophets who were given a specific assignment by God, such as Jonah's call to preach in Nineveh or Jeremiah's call from the womb to be a prophet for God. If you experience such an unmistakable directive from God, DO IT. But realize that such Biblical examples were exceptional rather than the norm for most people.

God does not often break into our lives, but when we are committed to using our talents for his service he shows us more gifts. When we begin to use what we have for him we often discover other gifts we can use as well.

Assumption #4: God's work is never done.

Assumption #4: God's work is never done. There are many ways to be of use to God, and there are many ways to catch a vision of this passion we have been talking about. The student in school, the garage mechanic, the cook, the physician, the fast-food employee, all provide for others a model of God through their life witness. To believe that there is only one job in which God can use a person indicates a narrow view of God's ability to work through a variety of humans and situations. At the same time, to think that God needs only me to do his work is extremely egotistical.

Biblical Principles

With these assumptions in mind, let's consider how God's will really works in our lives.

Principle #1: God Wants People Ready To Include Him In Their Lives

Romans 8:29; Romans 12:1-2; Ephesians 1:11-12; Ephesians 2:10.

God desires people with renewed minds; people with new perspectives and new commitments. So by inviting God to be involved in our plans, God becomes included in our choices. And our choices, in effect, become His choices too. This process is like a quest. You make a mental frame of reference, like a search for something worthwhile. By including God in your planning and your search, you invite God's action in your life.

When the Bible speaks of predestination, it's in terms of becoming like Jesus. Many have made the mistake of considering predestination only in terms of being an automaton playing out God's fantasy in robot-like fashion. God has predestined us to become like Jesus in character, provided we choose to have Him come in and transform our lives in this fashion.

Matthew 25:14-29;
1 Corinthians 12;
1 Samuel 17:38-40.

When the Bible speaks of predestination, it's in terms of becoming like Jesus.

1 Samuel 16:1-3; Isaiah 8:20; Jeremiah 2:13.

Principle #2: Evaluate One's Abilities and Watch God Reveal Additional Ones

In the New Testament, Philip began with only limited use of his talents and gifts, but later he became an evangelist. At each stage of his commitment, God was able to use all of Philip's potential and abilities to do His will. For twenty years He worked in Caesarea in Palestine and nurtured the people there. As He grew in grace, his gifts increased. That is what happens to us too.

Principle #3: Make Choices That Are Consistent With God's Revealed Will In Scripture

We may need to explore what Christians are all about. We may even have to do some talking with others to find what the kingdom of God really is. Then we can use our God-given powers to choose and act for God, knowing that we are doing God's will and not simply experimenting in some mystical cosmic calling.

Also, along this vein, spend time examining what others think you should be doing. The Holy Spirit's whispered thought in your mind is not the only avenue through which God can reveal His will to you. God works in this world in other people's lives as well. They might have some insight into what you should do with your life. They have watched you grow up, have seen your life change, and they also pray. Perhaps God will use them to touch your curiosity or spark your interest in a profession that is of service. There are so many career options today. We do not have to be limited by a few traditional professions.

Principle #4: View Yourself As Part of God's Mission

Christ's work at the carpenter's bench was as much a part of His mission as the three years of active ministry. This concept is not an ego that cries, "Look at me! See what I am doing." Rather, it humbly requests, "Lord, please use me in your work." In this way we fulfill God's plan because we see the potential we have in working for God in any profession.

Principle #5: God Has Equipped Us To Make Decisions

Simply by choosing we participate in God's greatest gift to us—the freedom to make choices and accomplish them, knowing that our choices make a difference.

Waiting for God to make all choices for us denies the power of choice He gave us at Creation and restored with redemption. It leads some to neglect their God-given thinking processes, falsely assuming that their humanity has deteriorated to the point that God can't empower them to think or act.

The Holy Spirit's whispered thought in your mind is not the only avenue God can reveal his will to you.

Luke 2:51; Romans 12:3-8.

Deuteronomy 8:10-20; 1 Samuel 26:23-24; 1 Kings 12:13-16.

Acts 5:17-20; Acts 10:28;
Proverbs 3:5-6.

Cosmic calling is not a mystical, vague feeling we get when we happen to do God's will.

Principle #6: Watch for Indications of God's Providence

We must be involved in a very active process. I like to call this the action step. Begin to live with accomplishments. Expect the Holy Spirit to lead you. Ask for the Holy Spirit and watch Him work with you in clarifying His purpose. This may come in startling ways. When it arrives in a relatively mundane fashion, accept this, too, as God's working. God isn't limited to the spectacular!

Cosmic calling is not a mystical, vague feeling we get when we happen to do God's will. We choose; God teaches. We act; God nudges. We decide; God inspires us to do more for Him. We check what others think, and we explore the options of our potential through testing and interviews. We take responsibility to find the vocation that is our calling. God is excited about our freedom to choose. It is by encouraging us to exercise choice that He proves to this world He loves it.

Calling and vocational choices are key factors in the motivation to identify with causes beyond ourselves and to move otherwise stagnate and stable people toward some goal that is outside of their limited purview and conception. Having a sense of vocation provides direction and identification of God's plan.

We may never see the lightning or see the burning bush in order to know what we are supposed to do with our lives, but we feel assured that by expanding our choices and exploiting our potential we are doing God's will.

Suggested Additional
Resources

Campolo, Anthony, *Wake Up America* (New York: Harper Collins Publishers, 1991).

Campolo, Anthony, "Vocation" in *You Can Make a Difference* (Waco, TX: Word Incorporated, 1984).

Chamberlain, Gary L., *Fostering Faith: A Minister's Guide to Faith Development* (New York, NY: Paulist Press, 1988).

Fowler, James W. and Keen, Sam, *Life Maps* (Waco, TX: Word Book, 1978).

Fowler, James W., *Weaving the New Creation: Stages of Faith and the Public Church* (San Francisco, CA: Harper Collins, 1991).

Friesen, Garry, *Decision Making and the Will of God* (Portland: Multnomah Press, 1988).

Insight (Hagerstown, MD: Review and Herald Publishing Association, December 3, 1988).

Roof, Wade Clark, *A Generation of Seekers* (San Francisco, CA: Harper Collins, 1993).

Rushkoff, Douglas, *The Gen X Reader* (New York, NY: Balantine, Books, 1994).

Shelton, Charles M., *Adolescent Spirituality* (Chicago: Loyola University Press, 1983).

Venden, Morris L., *How to Know God's Will in Your Life* (Boise: Pacific Press Publishing Association, 1987).

Westerhoff, III, John H., *Bringing Up Children in the Christian Faith* (San Francisco, CA: Harper & Row, 1980).

Section 7

Thinking About Sabbath Keeping

Seventh-day Adventists claim a biblical position while other Christians, we suggest, are simply following tradition.

Section 7

Thinking About Sabbath Keeping

What's the Discussion About?

Seventh-day Adventists often surprise other Christians by introducing the seventh day as the Sabbath of the Bible. Such an issue frequently becomes a point of debate. It is because Seventh-day Adventists claim a biblical position while other Christians, we suggest, are simply following tradition.

Rarely do Seventh-day Adventists argue about whether or not the seventh day is the Sabbath of the Bible. Instead, the debate *within* the Seventh-day Adventist church focuses on *how to keep* the Sabbath holy.

Apart from the basic principle of rest (don't work), the Bible says very little regarding how to keep the Sabbath

254

holy. Yet Seventh-day Adventists have a well-established tradition of Sabbath DOs and DON'Ts. For example,

DO: go to Sabbath School
          attend church
          participate in a potluck
          take a nature walk
          sing at a convalescent hospital
          attend MV/AY (afternoon youth meeting)
          give Bible studies
          dress up (Sabbath clothes are your best)
          hand out literature
          visit inactive members

DON'T: work (medical & church work are okay)
          play (unless adapted with Bible names)
          go boating
          swim, snorkel or SCUBA
          talk about secular things (like sports)
          associate with non-SDAs
          eat at a restaurant
          pay admission (to parks, beaches, etc.)
          buy anything at a store (no shopping!)

Most of the DOs and DON'Ts (and this is only a small sampling) have their roots in very positive, biblical truth. But children are unable to make the linkage between

The debate *within* the Seventh-day Adventist church focuses on *how to keep* the Sabbath holy.

principles and applications. As a result, they memorize specific behaviors as either being proper or improper. Unfortunately, they often fail to also memorize the basis or foundation for the behaviors.

When the next generation comes of age, parents who know behaviors but not the basis for them aren't nearly as likely to pass on the memorized behaviors. What has been learned by rote is not internalized because it lacks a proper foundation for the proper behavior.

Converts to the Seventh-day Adventist faith often have a difficult time knowing exactly what is appropriate and what isn't. They are likely to make some embarrassing mistakes until they are fully socialized into the Seventh-day Adventist subculture. Nobody really needs to tell them exactly what is okay and what isn't. If they are truly spiritual, they will catch on soon enough!

In the *Valuegenesis* survey, young people scored nearly as high as adults when it came to belief in the principle of Sabbath observance. What wasn't evaluated was which specific behaviors were permissible and which ones weren't. It's quite probable that what young people think is an appropriate activity for Sabbath would be on the taboo list for many adults.

The Background of the Discussion

Seventh-day Adventists frequently point to excesses by the Jews when it came to their Sabbath observance. On one hand, their laxness and failure to keep the Sabbath holy

In the *Valuegenesis* survey, young people scored nearly as high as adults when it came to belief in the principle of Sabbath observance.

indicated their breaking of the covenant with God.[1] On the other hand, their intense fervor to not make the same mistake as their ancestors led to persecution of those who broke the Sabbath traditions.[2]

The more contemporary roots of the Seventh-day Adventist church can be found in mid-nineteenth century New England. While the great Advent Awakening, led by William Miller and others, focused attention on the return of Christ, Seventh-day Baptists, with roots in Puritanism, emphasized Saturday as the Bible Sabbath.

Use your imagination for a potential conversation between an Adventist Millerite (AM) and a Seventh-day Baptist (SDB).

AM: "Why all this fuss about worshiping on Saturday or Sunday. You'd better start looking for the coming of the Lord, because He will be here soon."

SDB: "You'd better hope that the Lord doesn't return soon, because if He does, you will be left behind since you're keeping the wrong day as the Sabbath."

When Christ didn't return towards the close of 1844 as the Adventists expected, several earnest seekers for biblical truth found the Advent of Christ *and* the Seventh-day Sabbath to be key tenets. The issue debated was which day—Saturday or Sunday—was the Bible Sabbath.

Once they settled the issue as Saturday being the Sabbath, they also accepted with it the Sabbath observance of the Seventh-day Baptists. In a very real sense, Sabbath observance for Seventh-day Adventists has its roots in nineteenth century Puritan New England.

[1] See Ezekiel 20:1-26.

[2] See Mark 2:23-3:6; Luke 13:10-17; John 9:1-41; Matthew 11:28-12:14.

Most of the DOs and DON'Ts have their roots in very positive, Biblical truth.

As long as Seventh-day Adventists remained an intact group during the Sabbath hours, norms for Sabbath observance could be easily maintained. But as those in the denomination moved to higher socioeconomic brackets, their greater independence and mobility led to a more privatized Sabbath experience. Group norms become much more difficult to maintain in such an environment. Couple this with a failure to transmit biblical principles for Sabbath observance and you have an erosion of what was once a "given" within the Seventh-day Adventist church—proper Sabbath observance.

Questions Youth Are Asking

- What's wrong with _____ (you supply the activity) on Sabbath?
- Why do adults want everything to be slow and sleepy on Sabbath and young people want to be active and on the go?
- What's wrong (and what's right) with eating out on Sabbath?
- Jesus was accused of breaking the Sabbath in His day, so why worry if we're accused of the same thing?
- What's the difference between doing something on Sabbath "as a group" versus "doing it by yourself"?
- Why is the Sabbath so boring?

Focusing the Discussion

The time seems ripe for a reawakening of the historical and biblical roots for Sabbath keeping. Those who throw out all Sabbath observance restrictions seem destined to also lose the Sabbath itself. Those who hold to the observance without a clear and biblically sound foundation are likely to misapply their misunderstanding of the Sabbath. This would be tragic both for them and for those they come in contact with concerning the Sabbath and its observance.

Acknowledging a rich cultural diversity necessary for keeping the Sabbath holy throughout the world, the articles in this section seek to give a necessary foundation for people to apply the truth of the Sabbath for their lives within their particular culture.

• "Examples of Sabbath Observance." Steve Daily, campus chaplain at La Sierra University gives a rich historical background to Sabbath observance. Which examples that he gives do you find amusing? Which ones cause discomfort or disagreement? And which ones can you identify with? To what extent do you find Sabbath observance to be challenging?

• "The Challenge of Sabbath Observance." If the Bible isn't as specific as we'd like, can we glean principles for Sabbath observance. Steve Daily identifies four such principles. Do you agree with these particular Sabbath obser-

Sabbath observance for Seventh-day Adventists has its roots in nineteenth-century Puritan New England.

Fill in the blank: What's wrong with doing _____ on Sabbath?

If Adventist young people are to find new excitement and meaning in the Sabbath, we need to challenge them to get involved in being active participants on Sabbath rather than passive observers.

Those who hold to Sabbath observance without a clear and biblically sound foundation are likely to misapply their misunderstanding of the Sabbath.

vance guidelines? Are they biblical? Are any left out? How does your current Sabbath observance compare with these biblical principles? How challenging is this for you?

• "A Sabbath Snapshot." Family Ministries Director Willie Oliver shares a quick overview of the principles he sees in one familiar Sabbath passage. Then he invites us to go through a process of discovering the guidelines we typically use and the source for these. These exercises take the participant beyond theoretical debates and one person's view against another. This calls for a realistic appraisal of where one is and to what extent they will follow the principles of Scripture and not merely tradition.

• "Now Try This." Steve Daily makes an appeal for implementing the four biblical principles of Sabbath observance he identified earlier. How would you apply these principles? Would they be different for a group than they are for an individual? What could you do when there is disagreement between people in a group when it comes to applying these principles?

• "Suggested Additional Resources." This section gives the reader some great possibilities for further study on this issue. Take this to heart for your personal study. You could also make it a group endeavor and have various people take different resources and report their findings back to the group for discussion.

Examples of
Sabbath Observance

Steve Daily

Valuegenesis Byte
Youth and Orthodoxy

The students in Adventist schools had greater percentages than students in public schools when it came to a definite belief in the Second Advent (91% to 84%), the state of Sabbath (91% to 86%), the state of the dead (89% to 76%). No significant differences were found between them on the ten commandments, creation, Ellen White, the true church, and the investigative judgment. We must be cautious in making interpretations here, however, since it is likely that the public school sample may represent "the cream of the crop."*

*Roger L. Dudley with
V. Bailey Gillespie, *Valuegenesis:
Faith in the Balance* (Riverside, CA:
La Sierra University Press, 1992), 87.

When teaching Freshman Bible classes on the life of Jesus at La Sierra University, it was my custom to draw a figure on the board on the first day of class which illustrates how differently we all view reality. It is a simple figure; five parallel horizontal lines intersected by five parallel vertical lines which result in a large square with several smaller squares enclosed (see figure 1). I then ask the students how many squares they see on the board. There are always several who immediately count four down and four across and respond by saying 16. After a pause others will say 17, 21, 24, 26 and on it goes. If there are students who cannot find at least 16 squares I know I'm in for a rough quarter. But the average student who looks at this configuration will answer somewhere in the range of 16 to 30.

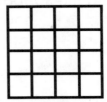

**How many squares
do you see?**

Figure 1

However, many individuals can stare at this figure for several minutes and never see more than 16 squares. "Sixteen-square" people tend to be more concrete thinkers who have rather inflexible personalities. And there is nothing wrong with that, providing they are not intolerant of those who see more than 16 squares. Unfortunately, rigidity and intolerance are personality traits that often go together. History has taught us that these traits are most dangerous when combined with an intense religious zeal for truth. Any doctrinal discussion can quickly be short-circuited by such a mentality, and the issue of Sabbath observance is no exception to this rule.

There is no better way to turn off Adventist young people than to rigidly define for them what activities are acceptable or not acceptable during the Sabbath hours. Such an approach is dangerous because not one of us is wise enough to adequately make such definitions. Any attempt to list appropriate or inappropriate Sabbath activities which are more specific than the general principles given in Scripture becomes vulnerable to numerous arguments which expose its inconsistencies.

Secondly, such an approach does more harm than good because it fails to teach young people to think for themselves and to establish principles that will govern their behavior. Sabbath keeping becomes a game of meeting the expectations of parents, teachers, or the church in general, rather than an experience which grows out of an internalized personal relationship with God that allows one to stand for principle like Daniel and his three young compan-

> There is no better way to turn off Adventist young people than to rigidly define for them what activities are acceptable or not acceptable during the Sabbath hours.

ions. In addition to these points, many young people have a natural aversion or resistance to authoritarian "sixteen-square" religion.

Jesus and the Sabbath

Jesus was neither rigid nor theoretical in his approach to religion. He did not get involved in doctrinal debates unless the doctrine in question was being misused to hurt human beings or as an excuse to avoid meeting human needs. He was intensely practical in his theology.

All of this is important background when we consider the issue of Sabbath keeping because, here again, Christ's primary concern was how Sabbath observance relates to the question of human need. Jesus engaged in doctrinal dialogue with the Jews over the issue of Sabbath keeping in Matthew 12 because of their restrictive ideas about how the Sabbath was to be kept, which evolved over several generations, had become harmful to human beings.

Before the Babylonian exile in 586 BC, God's prophets forcefully condemned Israel and Judah for habitual Sabbath breaking.

So when God's people were actually taken into captivity, to a great degree they attributed their misfortune to their lax Sabbath keeping and attempted to reform themselves. After they returned to Jerusalem, Sabbath keeping was emphasized so strongly that the Old Testament prohibitions were carefully enforced, and gradually a host of specific interpretations concerning these laws were formu-

Jesus was neither rigid nor theoretical in his approach to religion.

263

lated, which had become so detailed by Christ's day that the Sabbath had degenerated into an institution which exemplified Jewish legalism in its worst form.

There literally were thousands of rules forbidding various activities on the Sabbath[1] By plucking a few heads of wheat (Matt. 12:1) the disciples were guilty of breaking at least four Sabbath prohibitions: reaping, winnowing, threshing, and preparing a meal. Beyond this, by their actions they were condemned for carrying a burden on the Sabbath. A burden was defined as anything that weighed as much as two dried figs. A Jew could not even carry a handkerchief in his pocket, and use it to wipe his face, without violating the Sabbath. Therefore, it was common practice to sew a cloth into one's upper garment to wipe one's face. Once sewn into the garment it was considered part of one's clothing and did not constitute a burden.

On the Sabbath it was forbidden to light a fire or extinguish a lamp, to ride a beast of any kind or to travel more than a Sabbath day's journey, which was about two-thirds of a mile.

It was a sin to cut one's fingernails or pluck a hair. All healing was condemned except for life and death emergencies. Sexual intercourse was forbidden on the Sabbath. An egg laid on the Sabbath could not be eaten by a Jew. It was sinful to write more than two letters of the alphabet. It was forbidden to look in a mirror on the Sabbath, and it was even considered unlawful to spit on the ground lest thereby a blade of grass might be irrigated. Each of these things

[1] Two entire tractates of the Jewish Mishnah, tractate "Sabbath," and tractate "Erubin," are devoted entirely to the countless minute Sabbath regulations which had become a part of Jewish tradition by Christ's day.

Sabbath keeping becomes a game rather than a personal relationship with God.

constituted work, making it a violation of the Sabbath.[1] Even to contemplate work was wrong; therefore, it is not surprising that Jesus and his disciples were constantly being accused of Sabbath breaking.

When one reads through the Jewish Talmud and Mishnah, it is tempting at times to dismiss such restrictive regulations as ridiculous nonsense and to wonder how serious, intelligent people could have ever been so blinded and distorted by legalism that they actually attempted to enforce such bizarre notions. However, our approach to the question of Sabbath observance as Adventists, while avoiding the specific prohibitions mentioned above, has traditionally been very similar to that of the Jews. Too often we find ourselves thinking in legalistic categories.

My experience as a pastor, university chaplain, and teacher has been that young and old Adventists alike tend to approach the issue of Sabbath observance with questions about what specific activities are right or wrong. And a proof text or an Ellen White statement generally becomes the source from which answers to such questions are provided. But regardless of whether one's views are strict or permissive, such an approach still boils down to either legalism or gross externalism (attempting to define right and wrong in terms of outward behavior).

Contrary to popular thinking, strict Adventists do not have a monopoly on this kind of mentality. Adventists who are very permissive in their personal Sabbath observance and extremely accepting of what other Adventists may do on the Sabbath can still be guilty of creating their own

[1] *Ibid.* See also *Seventh-day Adventist Bible Dictionary* edited by F. D. Nichol (Washington, DC: Review and Herald Publishing Association, 1960), 936-937; and William Barclay's *The Gospel of Matthew, Vol. 2* (Philadelphia: Westminster Press, 1958), 25.

I have known Adventists who refused to work on the Sabbath or conduct major business on the Lord's day, but who might feel that activities such as watching TV, playing ball, swimming, skiing, sailing, shopping, etc., are generally not wrong activities in which to participate on the Sabbath.

"Adventist Mishnah." Their lists of "inappropriate Sabbath activities" would simply be shorter and more indiscriminate.

I have known Adventists who refused to work on the Sabbath or conduct major business on the Lord's day, but who might feel that activities such as watching TV, playing ball, swimming, skiing, sailing, shopping, etc., are generally not wrong activities in which to participate on the Sabbath. Others, who would never condone participation in such activities, might work at a Sabbath job on a regular basis because their particular profession or position happens to be one that does not raise too many eyebrows in the Adventist subculture.

Then there are those Adventists who are the most rigid and restrictive Sabbath keepers. They create an "Adventist Mishnah" which is much more comprehensive than their "permissive brothers and sisters." Their list of DON'Ts includes not only all forms of work, business, and pleasure but attempts to precisely specify how any given activity is to be labeled in regard to these categories.

For example, very strict Adventist homes arbitrarily might condemn bicycle riding, taking a shower, preparing any part of a meal, looking at a newspaper, throwing a Frisbee, doing the dishes, talking about any kind of "nonspiritual" subject matter, etc., on the Sabbath regardless of the circumstances. And there are highly influential leaders in the church who will advocate just such an approach to Sabbath observance.

The problem with this approach is that it arbitrarily defines Sabbath keeping in terms of outward behavior or specific activities. A religion of prescription can never be an adequate substitute for a religion of principle. The question that needs to be asked by both strict and permissive Adventist young people today is not "what is wrong with this particular activity on the Sabbath?" but "what is right about this activity under these specific circumstances based on the principles which I hold to be true?".

How do I determine my principles? By looking to Jesus and observing the way He answered His accusers with principles.

Jesus dealt with the specific accusation of Sabbath breaking in Matthew 12 by using three rather interesting illustrations that drive home one basic principle that justified the behavior of His disciples. The first illustration is found in verses three and four. Jesus referred to a specific violation of the Mosaic law from Leviticus 24, and then He condoned David's disobedience under the circumstances. The legalist will have great difficulty with this passage because Jesus clearly teaches that the principle of human need supersedes the principle of strict obedience to God's law.

The next two examples that Jesus cited reinforce this idea that to keep the Sabbath in a true spirit of righteousness, one must not allow the day to degenerate into a host of legalistic DOs and DON'Ts, but gain a vision of the opportunities that the Sabbath provides for service to other human beings. Jesus

might be on Finals.

A religion of prescription can never be an adequate substitute for a religion of principle.

said that the priests did all kinds of things that were considered unlawful on the Sabbath, but these actions were acceptable when done in a spirit of service. And He closed His arguments by quoting Hosea 6:6 (Matthew 12:7).

God desires Mercy, than sacrifice

If the Sabbath primarily has become a day of ritual and restriction or a day of self-centeredness and self-indulgence rather than a day of kindness and service to family and humanity, we have strayed from the Sabbath that Jesus kept.

In one of the first churches where I served as pastor there was a very conscientious, elderly woman who was extremely rigid in her Sabbath keeping. While she was at church one morning, a kind non-Adventist neighbor decided to mow her lawn and fix up her yard while she was gone. First, he did this because her yard needed help and she was unable to do it. Secondly, he did it because he wanted to do something nice for her as a gesture of friendship. But when she returned home that Sabbath she was shocked and angered by what had been done. She gave the neighbor a most severe tongue lashing, condemned him for his violation of the Sabbath, and warned him never to do such a terrible thing again. I wonder which of these people was really keeping the Sabbath in the spirit of Jesus that day.

Christ caused controversy because He purposely did things which were disturbing to many people. The powerful religious leaders were especially threatened by Jesus because they desperately wanted to maintain the status quo while Christ constantly attempted to broaden the narrow forms of religion which existed in His day.

> **If the Sabbath primarily has become a day of ritual and restriction or a day of self-centeredness and self-indulgence rather than a day of kindness and service to family and humanity, we have strayed from the Sabbath that Jesus kept.**

THINKING ABOUT THE SABBATH

After His confrontation with the Pharisees over His disciples' Sabbath keeping, Matthew says that Jesus left that place and went directly to the synagogue where He performed a miracle that was, from a political standpoint, like committing suicide. He purposely violated the Jewish law by healing a man with a withered hand, even though it certainly was not any kind of an emergency situation. Talk about being controversial!

The Bible does not speak of anyone who was more controversial than Christ. The record states that after Jesus committed this act on the Sabbath, the Pharisees left and made plans to put Him to death. In her commentary on this story, Ellen White says that false religion teaches its adherents to be careless of human needs, sufferings, and rights. It seeks to attack people and hurt them. It attempts to remove those who disagree with its particular understanding of truth and tends to be extremely condemning by its very nature.[1]

In contrast to the "liberal" Pharisees like Hillel, whose life was saved on the Sabbath and who believed it was good to serve others on the Sabbath, Jesus was confronted by "conservative" Pharisees on seven different occasions concerning Sabbath keeping. Five of these seven instances involved situations where Christ was condemned as a law breaker because he helped or healed various individuals who needed help. There was the man with the shriveled hand, a man with a bowed back, a blind man, an invalid, and a man with dropsy.

It is lawful to do good on the Sabbath.
*Matthew 12:8 (12)

Religious leaders accusing Jesus & disciples. "Jesus is Lord of Sabbath."

The powerful religious leaders were especially threatened because Jesus constantly attempted to broaden the narrow forms of religion which existed in His day.

[1]Ellen G. White, *The Desire of Ages* (Mountain View, CA: Pacific Press Publishing Association, 1940), 287.

To keep the Sabbath in a true spirit of righteousness, one must gain a vision of the opportunities that the Sabbath provides for service to other human beings.

For Jesus, the Sabbath was not a day to minimize or ignore one's social responsibility to humanity, but a day to magnify it.

In every case these were not emergency situations, but individuals that Christ could just as easily have helped on any other day of the week. Therefore, Jesus was condemned for doing "unnecessary" work on the Sabbath.

He chose to perform these acts of mercy on the Sabbath, not just to cause controversy, but because he wanted to demonstrate that true Sabbath keeping involves going out of one's way to meet human needs where those needs exist regardless of whether or not they happen to be emergency needs.

For Jesus, Sabbath observance and social ethics could not be separated. The Sabbath was not a day to minimize or ignore one's social responsibility to humanity, but a day to magnify it. Christ's own act of healing the man with the withered hand provides us with the best interpretation of his statement, "The Sabbath was made for man, and not man for the Sabbath" (Mark 2:27).

The Jews distorted the Sabbath into a day of enslaving, tyrannical regulations, and this was a serious sin. But their greater sin was in clinging so tenaciously and rigidly to their doctrinal traditions that they would kill a man or hurt a human being rather than change. How ironic that they could crucify the Son of God and then quickly remove him from the cross so that they could meticulously keep the Sabbath.

When Jesus identified his true followers with a single sign, he did not refer to the Sabbath but said, "By this shall all men know who my true disciples are, by their love for their fellow human beings" (John 13:35).

Adventist Sabbath Observance

The issue of Sabbath keeping is a timely topic in the Adventist Church today because, as always, the devil seeks to divide us by driving us to extremes that blind us to the essence of true religion. These extremes are not unique to Adventism, but have existed in nearly all Protestant churches. On the one hand, Protestantism began in this country with the Puritan Sabbath which was a very strict holy day.[1] The Puritans sat on hard wooden benches in uncomfortable temperatures and listened to sermons that lasted two to three hours each, and prayers which often exceeded one hour. They were switched with a stick if they fell asleep or failed to pay attention. All amusement, work, and worldly conversation were forbidden. One English poet wrote that he actually saw one Puritan perform the "hanging of a cat on Monday for the killing of a mouse on Sunday."[2] Another Puritan was arrested for kissing his wife at the gate of their home on Sunday after returning from a long trip at sea.

In the nineteenth century, many Protestants still observed Sunday as the Sabbath in such a strict fashion that it easily degenerated into a day of rituals and external regulations which led to a burdened religion of legalism.[3]

However, during the nineteenth century there were many other Protestants in America who adopted from Europe the "continental Sabbath," which was more of a holiday than a holy day. The Sabbath became a day of self-

[1] For a detailed description of the Puritan Sabbath and its relation to Adventist Sabbath observance, see Walter Douglas, "The Sabbath in Puritanism" in *The Sabbath in Scripture and History* edited by Kenneth Strand (Washington, DC: Review and Herald Publishing Association, 1982), 229-243.

[2] Douglas Bush, *English Literature in the Early Seventeenth Century* (Oxford: Clarendon Press, 1962), 47.

[1] See R. J. Bauckham, "Sabbath and Sunday in the Protestant Tradition," in *From Sabbath to Sunday* edited by D. A. Carson, (Grand Rapids, MI: Academic Books, 1982), 311-342.

gratification. Christians began to spend an hour in church on Sunday and then devote the rest of the day to amusement, recreation, shopping, work, and business as usual.

For most Protestants today, this extreme has become common practice. And, unfortunately, there are an increasing number of Adventists who are adopting a similar philosophy of Sabbath observance in reaction to the opposite legalistic extremes which have traditionally existed. This is particularly the case with young people in the church, who seem to be much more inclined towards the extreme of permissiveness, or treating the Sabbath as a holiday, than they are towards strict legalism.

Let's try a biblical approach!

Our history of Sabbath observance shows a variety of pitfalls and failures. Our current situation could be viewed as hopeless by some. But the time couldn't be more ripe for a new approach to Sabbath observance. Let's try a biblical approach!

The Challenge of Sabbath Observance

Steve Daily

I attended a Seventh-day Adventist pastors' meeting several years ago in which the speaker invited all 800 of us in attendance to stand up and take a position on an imaginary line running from the front to the back of the building based on the kind of Sabbath observance that we experienced growing up in our own homes. The great majority of us indicated that we grew up in a home that tended towards the extreme of what he defined as strict Sabbath keeping (showers taken and shoes shined before sundown, etc.). He then asked us to move to the position on the line which best indicated the kind of Sabbath observance that is being practiced in our homes today with our own children. It was interesting to see the obvious mass movement towards the

The great majority of us indicated that we grew up in a home that tended towards the extreme of strict Sabbath keeping.

273

Can we avoid the extremes of rigid legalism on the one hand, and careless permissiveness on the other hand?

These four principles are
1. **Worship**
2. **Fellowship**
3. **Rest**
4. **Service**

Exodus 20:8-11.

opposite end of the spectrum. In recent generations, Adventists have become much more permissive in their Sabbath observance, and this is most evident in the Sabbath keeping of our young people.

So, the practical question we all are faced with as Adventists today is, Can we avoid the extremes of rigid legalism on the one hand, and careless permissiveness on the other hand? To do so requires a clear identification of principles that will preserve the sacredness and promised blessings which accompany true Sabbath observance.

Biblical Principles

When we talk about Sabbath keeping, I believe that the key word is balance. There are four major principles which govern Sabbath observance in scripture and they are all equally important. These four principles are worship, fellowship, rest, and service. It is my belief that we can best evaluate any Sabbath activity by asking how it positively contributes to at least one of these four principles.

Principle #1: Worship

The Sabbath provides us with a special opportunity to remember the Creator and to spend time praising God for the gift of life and all that comes with it. This can be done in our moments alone with God; it can be done as a nuclear family; or it can be done as a church family. Hopefully, it will be done in all three contexts.

It is important that we learn to praise God and to worship him from Sabbath to Sabbath, in good times and bad times. You cannot read through the Psalms without being overwhelmed with David's capacity to praise God no matter what the circumstances. Too many Adventists are spiritually inhibited in their praise. Like Michal, we often are critical of those who have learned to dance before the Lord with all their might. We often are uncomfortable with new and innovative forms of worship.

We need to recognize that young people generally are open to new experiences, they have an enthusiasm that loves adventure and experimentation, they relate to different kinds of music than some of us who are over 30 do, and they are quite willing to listen when their peers are brave enough to stand up and humbly share what God means to them in their own experience.

I do not make these statements from a philosophical or speculative viewpoint. Rather, these observations are based on what I have seen on our campus when we experimented with a new worship service each week that was designed specifically to meet the needs of Adventist college students. In these services, I witnessed young people praising God with every form of musical instrument, from harp to synthesizer. The young people praised God through drama, religious dance, clapping, and many other forms of worship that I was not accustomed to seeing in Adventist church services. But what made this experiment most rewarding for me was to see Adventist young people going

It is important that we learn to praise God and to worship him from Sabbath to Sabbath, in good times and bad times.

to church with excitement, praising God with energy, and worshiping him with greater enthusiasm than I had ever witnessed.

Worship and praise are as necessary to true Sabbath observance as spectators are to the Rose Parade. The Sabbath loses a great deal of its meaning without worship and praise. If we are not going to teach our young people to dance before the Lord with all their might, then we must at least provide them with the opportunity to teach themselves to praise the Lord.

I am not suggesting that every church needs to have an alternative worship service for those who enjoy more youthful forms of praise, although this may not be a bad idea. But I am suggesting that we need to provide for greater freedom in our Sabbath worship. Part of every Sabbath should be spent in uninhibited praise to God, either alone with God at whatever place seems suitable, or by letting young people design and conduct family worship with the greatest possible freedom of expression, or in the context of the larger church service itself. Preferably it would occur in each setting. When we learn to truly worship, we've taken the first step in making the Sabbath a delight.

The Sabbath loses a great deal of its meaning without worship and praise.

Hebrews 10:25; Galatians 6:1-3.

Principle #2: Fellowship

The high school and college years generally are characterized by a growing independence from parents and an increasing tendency to be influenced by peer relationships.

276

Young people spend more and more time outside the home with friends as they attempt to establish their own identity. Here again, the Sabbath provides a unique opportunity to engage in activities with friends that can draw young people closer to God and to each other. More than any other day of the week, the Sabbath presents Adventist youth with the time to experience the kind of Biblical fellowship or close Christian friendship that the Bible describes as being absolutely essential for maturity in Christ.

It is idealistic to assume that the majority of Adventist young people will be inclined to create an atmosphere where this kind of fellowship can thrive on the Sabbath, even if they had a desire to do so. Therefore, structure and balance are particularly crucial to this principle. Parents or youth leaders who are willing to be part of a rotation that provides a home or adult supervision for outings on Sabbath afternoons can promote activities that have tremendous value for young people.

For those who do not like large social gatherings, emphasis should be placed on spending some time with one or two friends who are not turned off by discussing issues or concerns of substance or making a new friend or doing something together as a family that will provide particular time for listening to hurts or needs that might be expressed. The Sabbath often is an ideal time for a family council.

The important question when we consider fellowship is, "Does this activity maximize the opportunity for per-

More than any other day of the week, the Sabbath presents Adventist youth with the time to experience the kind of Biblical fellowship essential for maturity in Christ.

Genesis 2:2; Exodus 20:8-11; Isaiah 58:13-14; Hebrews 4:9-10.

Does this activity maximize the opportunity for personal sharing of individual joys, concerns, needs, and struggles of the Christian walk?

sonal sharing of individual joys, concerns, needs, and struggles of the Christian walk?" The more vulnerable and self-revealing we are as leaders in this regard, the more we will find young people opening up to us and becoming real people in the way they relate to each other.

Principle #3: Rest

One of the most crucial functions of true Sabbath observance is to ensure that we experience a mental, physical, social, and spiritual change of pace. Such a change rejuvenates the human mind, body, and spirit and thereby supplies a weekly balancing, stabilizing effect which promotes the greatest human health and happiness. When Scripture says that God "rested" on the seventh day it does not mean that God took a nap all afternoon. The Hebrew word translated as "rested" actually means to cease from one's regular activities. Therefore, the principle of rest is the broadest of the four principles that we will discuss.

Any activity in which we are involved on Sabbath should somehow overlap with this principle of rest. A conscious effort should be made to make the Sabbath different from every other day of the week in every possible way. Even people who do not believe in God can actually benefit greatly from observing this principle of rest.

Various studies dealing with the productivity of factory workers, for example, have shown that overall productivity definitely increased when workers were given a day off rather than being expected to work a seven day week.[1] By working fewer days and fewer hours, more was accomplished because human beings are not machines.

We all need to experience a mental, physical, social, and emotional change of pace on Sabbath which sets the day apart from the hectic schedules that most of us maintain during the week. The nature of this change of pace will differ from individual to individual just as weekly activities differ. Some may be in desperate need of physical rest on Sabbath while others may feel a need for a hike, bike ride, or some other form of physical exercise that they find difficult to fit into their weekly schedules. But even these activities are greatly enriched if they can be combined with meaningful fellowship or meditative worship.

Anything that can be done that makes the activities on Sabbath esteemed, especially to children, certainly fits under this category of rest. For this to be a reality, preparation must be undertaken before the day of rest arrives. When special Sabbath meals can be prepared which offer foods or desserts never served on other days of the week, or when family games or other activities that allow members of the family to spend meaningful quality time together can be planned that are not used on other days, this gives the Sabbath a distinctive flavor of its own that is not forgotten as children grow older. When they reach their high school and college years, they will find it easier to treat the Sabbath differently themselves.

[1]Degler, Carl *Out of Our Past* (New York: Harper and Row, 1970), 364ff.; Brownlee, E. W. *Women in the American Economy* (New Haven: Yale University Press, 1976), 186.

A conscious effort should be made to make the Sabbath different from every other day of the week in every possible way.

Preparation must be undertaken before the day of rest arrives.

[1]See Isaiah 58:14 and Hebrews 4:9-10.

Matthew 12:9-14; Mark 2:27-28; Luke 13:10-17; John 9:13-16.

In our efforts to avoid giving young people a negative "holier than thou" impression of our Sabbath keeping, it is easy to fall into the trap of talking about the same subject matter and doing the same kinds of things that we are inclined to do on any other day of the week. Here again, balance is the key. It may be appropriate to talk about sports or cars with young people who are absorbed with these topics on the Sabbath, but the youth leader should never come to the point where he or she is so comfortable with these kinds of topics that no effort is made to steer conversation to the more important areas of personal struggles and needs. As young people learn to more effectively make the Sabbath a day when their activity patterns are different, they will proportionally experience the tremendous "advantage" that is promised to all those who enter into Christ's Sabbath rest.[1]

Principle #4: Service

I have saved the principle of service to be dealt with last for two reasons. First, because I believe that this principle, more than any of the others, is emphasized in the New Testament relation to Christ's Sabbath keeping. And secondly, because I feel that this principle, more than any of the others, has not been properly observed by Adventists in spite of the fact that it may hold the greatest potential for making the Sabbath attractive and meaningful to non-Adventists.

Adventists generally make an effort to incorporate worship into their Sabbath activities at least through their participation in Sabbath services or church attendance. Most Adventists also attempt to engage in fellowship with other believers either by eating with other church members or getting together in some social context on Friday night or Sabbath afternoon. Adventists, more than most other Christians, also strive to treat their Sabbath as a distinct day in harmony with the principle of rest that we have discussed. But when it comes to the principle of service, it seems that Adventists, along with Christians in general, have lost the vision that Christ provided in regard to the Sabbath.

The Sabbath keeping of Jesus, as recorded in Scripture, focused on meeting human needs. If there is any aspect of Sabbath observance which provides a tremendous, untapped resource for Christians today, this is it. Jesus spent many Sabbath hours meeting the needs of human beings regardless of whether or not those needs were of an emergency nature (see Matthew 12:9-14; John 9:13-16; etc.). He demonstrated that one of the great purposes of the Sabbath was to benefit those who truly needed help. He felt so strongly about this that he subjected Himself to all kinds of condemnation and persecution to emphasize this point.

Therefore it follows that when God's people catch a vision of what it really means to keep the Sabbath, they will occasionally or regularly take part of a Sabbath day to bring joy into the life of a lonely or needy person by serving

The Sabbath keeping of Jesus, as recorded in Scripture, focused on meeting human needs. If there is any aspect of Sabbath observance which provides a tremendous, untapped resource for Christians today, this is it.

When God's people catch a vision of what it really means to keep the Sabbath, they will serve on Sabbath.

on Sabbath. The actual form of service may vary dramatically, such as visiting, helping, or voluntarily cleaning, or repairing, or doing whatever that person's particular needs call for. In this way the Sabbath becomes more than just a curiosity to those neighbors or individuals in one's community who benefit from these acts of service. It becomes a genuine testimony to God's love.

Admittedly, the idea of mowing a widow's lawn on the Sabbath is going to be controversial or even unthinkable for some Adventists. Traditionally, we have tended to condemn all nonemergency forms of work on the Sabbath, just as the Jews did.

For the last several years, students on our campus have been involved in various projects to meet the needs of the poor, elderly, and disabled in Riverside. Each year I have suggested that a larger number of students could participate in such activities if they were carried out on Sabbath afternoon as well as Sunday mornings and Friday afternoons.

As we moved closer to administrative approval, there was also increased resistance, sometimes quite forceful, from some in administrative positions. Change will often come slowly, but that should not discourage us from working for these changes if they are mandates from Christ.

Obviously, this principle of service needs to be kept in proper perspective. It would probably not be appropriate to spend every Sabbath doing yard work even for needy widows. There needs to be balance. However, in the past, our problem has generally not been that we have spent too many Sabbath hours in meaningful service, but too few, if any at all.

Guidelines are needed for such activities. Service activities on Sabbath should always be voluntary (not for pay). They generally should be directed to non-Adventists (even a needy Adventist might not feel comfortable having me mow his or her lawn on Sabbath). They should not overshadow the other important principles of Sabbath keeping. And they should be done in a spirit of joyful willingness, never out of guilt or obligation. When these guidelines are followed, I have seen the kind of fulfillment and happiness that this type of activity can bring to both the young people who serve and to those who are served.

Worship, Fellowship, Rest, and Service. These four principles make Sabbath keeping a blessing and a joy when they are all kept in proper balance. These four principles make the challenge of Sabbath observance a positive experience for young people rather than a frustrating or guilt-producing burden.

Worship. Fellowship. Rest. And Service. These four principles make Sabbath keeping a blessing and a joy when they are all kept in proper balance.

283

A Sabbath Snapshot

Willie Oliver

It's potentially dangerous and somewhat superficial to consider only one passage of Scripture when it comes to broad themes such as the Sabbath. However, it *can* be useful to take a quick look at one key portion of the Bible—a snapshot in the photo album of the Sabbath.

A familiar Sabbath text still needs to have principles deduced from it for the Christian to apply to personal living. Consider this exercise for Isaiah 58:13-14 (NIV).

If you keep your feet from breaking the Sabbath and from doing as you please on my holy day, if you call the Sabbath a delight and the Lord's holy day honorable, and if you honor it by not going your own way and not doing as you please or speaking idle words, then you will find your joy in the Lord, and I will cause you to ride on the heights of the land and to feast on the inheritance of your father Jacob. The mouth of the Lord has spoken.

The three significant principles that jump out at me in this passage can be summed up in the single words RESPECT, HONOR, and JOY.

Respect

To keep God's Sabbath day holy one must believe that God exists, He is the Creator of heaven and earth, and that He is worthy of our allegiance for no other reason than that He is Creator.

Ascribing sacredness to the Sabbath acknowledges our belief in God's sacredness and our acceptance of His dominion over the universe. Disregarding the sacredness of the Sabbath, in contrast, signals our lack of respect for God and a lack of awareness of His presence.

Honor

When we respect God and accept the sacredness of the Sabbath rest, we honor Him by communing with Him and spending that day in activities that draw us to God instead of to mundane things. Because He is a holy God and has declared His special day holy, we must accomplish holy endeavors during this time.

The three significant principles that jump out at me in this passage can be summed up in the single words:

- **RESPECT**
- **HONOR**
- **JOY**

As a break from the typical daily pursuits, the Sabbath provides a haven of time for focused communion with God. No wonder some speak of a special sensing of God's presence on this holy day.

Joy

Those who make the Sabbath what God intended it to be enter into a close fellowship with Him that others cannot know. Isaiah suggests that we will experience true joy in the Lord.

To be sure, nothing can equal the joy felt when one is at peace with God. And what can compare to the feeling of being enveloped in an intimate relationship with the Divine?

Your Turn

But don't just take this from someone else. Apply Scripture to your own life after you've synthesized the Sabbath principles you will follow. You'll also need to identify the source of these principles—are they based on Scripture, the writings of Ellen White, tradition, what your parents or other authority figures passed on to you, or is your source unknown? I'm hopeful you will find these exercises helpful!

As a break from the typical daily pursuits, the Sabbath provides a haven of time for focused communion with God.

Yes or No?

Please write a "yes" or a "no" beside each activity if you think it would be an appropriate activity for the Sabbath hours. The first column is for you individually. The second column is for a group (like your family/friends). Space is provided for you to give a reason for your choice.

Individual	Group	Activity
Y	Y	Eat a big Sabbath lunch
N	N	See a movie at the theater
N		Water-ski
Y		Feed the homeless
N		Do arts & crafts
N		Do homework
N		Paint a needy person's house
N		Work only if it's an emergency

Individual	Group	Activity
N	_____	Eat at a restaurant
N	_____	Go 4-wheeling
N	_____	Clean a needy person's house
N	_____	Clean a needy person's yard
Y/N	_____	Catch up on your sleep
Y	_____	Study the Bible
N	_____	Clean up a park
N	_____	Remove graffiti
N	_____	Play outdoor games with kids
Y	_____	Visit shut-ins
N	_____	Play volleyball
N	_____	Go shopping
Y	_____	Spend all day in a seminar

Applying Biblical Principles to Your Activities

1. List several activities in which SDAs might participate during Sabbath.

2. Then identify the principle that determines whether or not that particular activity is appropriate for Sabbath.

3. Name the source of the principle (such as a Bible text, Ellen White quotation, common sense, one's upbringing, tradition, what's been taught, etc.).

Activity	Principle	Source
1. _____	_____	_____
2. _____	_____	_____
3. _____	_____	_____
4. _____	_____	_____

Activity	Principle	Source
5. _____	_____	_____
6. _____	_____	_____
7. _____	_____	_____
8. _____	_____	_____
9. _____	_____	_____
10. _____	_____	_____

Now Try This

Steve Daily

What would happen if . . .

Here are a few radical, but practical, questions for your consideration.

1.   What would happen if we encouraged our Adventist young people to spend an occasional Sabbath afternoon fixing up the yards and homes of needy senior citizens or disabled people in their communities?

2.   What kind of witness would result if Adventist physicians refused to charge their patients for services rendered on the Sabbath, choosing simply to send them a note explaining the true meaning of the Sabbath instead of a bill.

3.   I wonder how differently we would be viewed as a people by non-Adventists in our community, if every

Sabbath provided a visible testimony that we are committed to meeting the practical needs of our fellow human beings?

4. Was this practice of meeting basic human needs a primary focus of Christ's Sabbath keeping, and if so, was it the aspect of Sabbath keeping that he most specifically referred to when he said, "Sabbath was made for man"?

What God Has Joined . . .

We have identified four harmonious Biblical principles of Sabbath observance (Worship, Fellowship, Rest and Service) which sound good and seem to be very practical. However good theology is not enough. We still need to ask how these principles can be implemented in our lives and in our churches.

It is easy to get excited about the great truths of God, to make lofty resolutions when we are convicted by a sermon or a book, or to get supercharged emotionally at inspirational retreats, but never convert these experiences into tangible actions that strike a blow at real life. Youth leaders have the most difficult challenge of trying to offer teenagers activities and programs that are more than just "baptized entertainment." To have a master plan that provides meaningful spiritual growth over a three- or four-year period and which also includes specific direction for how it can be implemented on a week-to-week basis takes tremendous commitment, creativity, and careful and sub-

We still need to ask how these principles of worship, fellowship, rest, and service can be implemented in our lives and in our churches.

stantial planning. In short, it takes a team of youth leaders with a vision.

Obviously, there is also a danger of becoming so directive and organized that we lose sight of individual needs and let programs come before people. This is the very problem the Jewish leaders had when they so structured the nature of Sabbath observance that they lost the spirit of the day and became blind to human need as a result.

The point is, we must not confuse a prescriptive or legalistic approach to Sabbath observance with the need for thoughtful planning, which is necessary if the principles we have discussed are to be observed with appropriate balance. Jesus was not bent on rigid organization, but neither did He send His disciples out without giving them specific instructions.

Plans without vision result in meaningless ritual. Vision without careful planning results in wasted energy and eventual burnout. Specific planning and creative vision are both essential, but we must first inspire young people with a vision before we expect them to get excited about becoming involved in long-range programs or projects.

Here again the method of Jesus has much to recommend. Jesus did not demonstrate the value of serving others and meeting human needs on the Sabbath by constantly preaching about it, writing books about it, or hosting a "Sabbath Jubilee Convocation." His method was much more effective and involved a set of simple, progressive steps.

Plans without vision result in meaningless ritual. Vision without careful planning results in wasted energy and eventual burnout.

293

It is easy to get excited about the great truths of God and never convert these into tangible actions.

Jesus first became aware of the most pressing human needs that existed in the community in which He ministered. This is the first challenge that faces a good youth leader. Unless you are living in some kind of sterile, artificial environment, you will be surrounded by human beings who are hurting and who need both physical and emotional help. These people can be found both inside and outside of the church, but they must be found. They can be found by talking to church members, visiting poor neighborhoods in your area, working with community resource groups like the United Way or other agencies that are listed in directories supplied by your city or county.

The needs are there. Once you compile a list of what you consider to be the most pressing human needs in your community you are ready to move to the second step.

Jesus began with a small group of quality people focusing on individual needs. In this age of media and marketing there is a tendency to glorify those who make a big splash by producing extravagant programs that attract public acclaim. This was not the method of Jesus, and this is not the kind of approach that attracts sincere young people who want to help others but not make a show of it.

Once you have a list of needs it is generally not difficult to find a few caring young people who will go with you on a Sabbath afternoon to help meet these needs. If this is not the case, you need to build some meaningful relationships with your youth. These young people can then humbly share with others the good feelings they received from participating in such activities, and they can also serve as a core planning group for Sabbath activities in general.

It becomes their job, with your creative input, to plan activities over a long period that will allow for the greatest balance between the four Sabbath observance principles of worship, fellowship, rest and service.

Go and Do Likewise

Jesus emphasized a practical religion that involved participation. Jesus was not content to leave His disciples with a religion of words. He challenged them to go out two by two and practice what He lived and preached.

If Adventist young people are to find new excitement and meaning in the Sabbath we need to challenge them to get involved in being active participants on Sabbath rather than passive observers. Obviously there will be a number of individuals who are not willing or able to do much more than observe. These should not be ignored or made to feel uncomfortable, but as opportunities for participation increase and the value of such experiences become highly visible, even the shy and apathetic can be encouraged to get involved.

In planning worship, a premium should be placed on praise, experimentation, freedom and participation. Young people should be encouraged to define their own forms of worship to experience the excitement of a firsthand faith.

If Adventist young people are to find new excitement and meaning in the Sabbath, we need to challenge them to get involved in being active participants on Sabbath rather than passive observers.

295

Fellowship plans for Sabbath should also maximize opportunities for participation. A number of youth ministry publishers can give any youth planning group more possibilities for such activities than they could ever exhaust. Ask Christian bookstores for catalogues of youth ministry programming ideas.

Even those activities which come under the principle of rest—providing a mental, physical, spiritual, social, and emotional change of pace—should focus on variety and participation. Don't plan the same kinds of activities every Sabbath, thereby leading Sabbath keepers into a rut.

Include some kind of service activity in your Sabbath. Being involved in service does not always mean going out and helping people. Sometimes young people need to be educated about the problems of poverty, injustice, etc., before they have a burden to help others. This can be done through skits, films or videos, and in many other ways. Education can work in tandem with well-planned activities that genuinely benefit people in need as well.

When the principles Jesus taught were internalized, Pentecost became a reality. Pentecost was the work of the Holy Spirit, not of human beings. When we put Jesus first, focus on individual needs rather than extravagant, highly publicized programs, and provide the opportunity for those who are humble and sincere to participate in ministry, miracles happen.

The Sabbath, more than any other Adventist belief or practice, provides the vehicle through which these steps

Unless you are living in a sterile, artificial environment, you will be surrounded by a multitude of human needs.

can be realized and God's miraculous works can become a reality in our lives.

Suggested Additional Resources

Andreasen, Niels-Erik, *The Christian Use of Time* (Nashville: Abingdon, 1978).

Bacchiocchi, Samuele, *Divine Rest for Human Restlessness* (Rome: Pontifical Gregorian University Press, 1980).

Brunt, John C., *A Day for Healing* (Washington, DC: Review and Herald Publishing Association, 1981).

Campolo, Anthony, *Ideas for Social Action* (El Cajon, CA: Youth Specialties, 1983).

Case, Steve and Cornforth, Fred, *Hands-On Service Ideas for Youth Groups* (Loveland, Co: Grop Publishing, 1995).

Chantry, Walter, *Call the Sabbath a Delight* (Carlisle, PA: The Banner of Truth Trust, 1991).

Davidson, Richard M., *A Love Song for the Sabbath* (Washington, DC: Review and Herald Publishing Association, 1988).

Heschel, Abraham, *The Sabbath: Its Meaning for Modern Man* (New York, 1951).

Mains, Karen Burton, *Making Sunday Special* (Waco, TX: Word Books, 1987).

Pate, Don, *52 Sabbath Activities for Teen Groups* (Hagerstown, MD: Review and Herald Publishing Association, 1995).

Solberg, Winton, *Redeem the Time* (Harvard University Press, 1977).

Strand, Kenneth, A., ed. *The Sabbath in Scripture and History* (Washington, DC: Review and Herald Publishing, 1982).

Have the young people plan Sabbath activities that will provide a balance between worship, fellowship, rest and service.

Section 8
Thinking About Alcohol

Section 8
Thinking About Alcohol

What's the Discussion About?

Few people question the biblical position that condemns drunkenness.[1] When the Book of Proverbs suggests, "Listen, my son, and be wise, and keep your heart on the right path. Do not join those who drink too much wine or gorge themselves on meat, for drunkards and gluttons become poor . . ." (Proverbs 23:19-21), we recognize the potential hazards that abound.

But what about moderate use of alcohol? Doesn't the Bible make a number of positive references to wine? And hasn't modern science pointed out that a moderate use of wine actually is healthier than a lifestyle that includes abstinence?

[1] For example see Deuteronomy 21:18-21; Proverbs 23:19-21; 26:9; Habakkuk 2:15; Matthew 24:45-51; Luke 12:42-46; 21:34-36; Romans 13:12-14; 1 Corinthians 5:11; 6:9-11; Galatians 5: 19-21; 1 Thessalonians 5:7-9.

299

The Background of the Discussion

Health issues became an element of interest and lifestyle practice for Seventh-day Adventists before the end of the 19th century. When the temperance movement in the United States called for the abolition of liquor, Adventists could give a hearty endorsement.

The debilitating effects of alcohol on individuals and society gave further support to an Adventist position of abstinence which was already based on the biblical principle of our bodies being the temple of the Holy Spirit. Although Seventh-day Adventist beliefs continue to include the position of total abstinence from alcohol, a decreasing percentage of members seem to put this belief into practice. A 1988 study of North American Adventists age 18 and older showed an inverse relationship between age and use of alcohol—an increase in the use of alcohol the younger a person is. While slightly more than 10 percent of the entire group used wine (at least monthly) in the previous year, the breakdown by age groups demonstrates the trend of increased usage by younger Adventist adults.

Over 65 years of age	1 in 20 used wine
44-65 years of age	1 in 10 used wine
30-43 years of age	1 in 5 used wine
18-29 years of age	1 in 4 used wine[1]

The *Valuegenesis* research project reported the following usage of beer, liquor, and wine.

> **Abstinence continues to be part of the fundamental statement of beliefs for Seventh-day Adventists and part of the vows for baptism.**

[1] Duane C. McBride, Patricia B. Mutch, Roger L. Dudley, April G. Julian, and Winton H. Beaven, "Adventists, Drugs, and a Changing Church" in *Adventist Review* (June 1, 1989), 12-15.

Practice	Experimental	Regular
Drink beer or liquor	14%	9%
Drink Wine	10%	6%

In the second set of questions about at-risk behaviors, the researchers asked how often youth engaged in the behaviors. They asked, "How may times, if ever, during the last 12 months did you do each of the following?" Seven choices ranged from 0 times to 40 or more times. The percentages below combine all the choices except 0 times. In other words they gave us the proportions of those who engaged in the practices, whatever the frequency. Here are the results regarding alcohol, beer, wine, or liquor. The statistics cause concern.

Drink alcohol (beer, wine, or liquor) while alone or with friends	(26%)
Go to a party where kids your age were drinking	(27%)
Have five drinks or more in a row (a drink is a glass of wine, a can of beer, a shot of liquor, or a mixed drink)	(13%)[1]

Part of the departmental structure of church leadership is a temperance department which promotes abstinence from alcohol. When these leadership positions are not filled or temperance duties are added to the responsibilities of people who fill other positions, a temperance emphasis often suffers.

[1] Roger L. Dudley with V. Bailey Gillespie, *Valuegeneisis: Faith in the Balance* (Riverside, CA: La Sierra University Press, 1992), 258-259.

The establishment of the Institute of Alcoholism and Drug Dependency at Andrews University demonstrates that Adventists acknowledge abuse of alcohol.

Other Discussions on the Subject

Seventh-day Adventists are not the only religious group opposed to the use of alcohol. Many people of other religious persuasions hold a position of abstinence from alcohol. Clearly not all Christians agree on how alcohol should be used, including whether or not to include it in the Communion service.

Perhaps one of the greatest barriers to a consensus within the Christian community is the fact that each person seems to have biblical grounds for their position. A person's presuppositions simply may be reinforced by a biased searching of Scripture. And it seems no matter what presuppositions you have regarding the use of alcohol, you can buttress them with Biblical support.

It seems that no matter what presuppositions you have regarding the use of alcohol, you can buttress them with Biblical support.

Questions Youth Are Asking

- Doesn't the Bible tell us to drink a little wine?
- What's the difference between having a glass of wine or taking Valium, muscle relaxants, cold medicine, or other (prescribed) drugs?
- If only 10 percent of people who drink become alcoholics, why should 100 percent abstain?

• Haven't medical studies proven that drinking alcohol is actually healthier than not drinking alcohol?

Focusing the Discussion

Sometimes it's difficult to be frank in a discussion with someone who is experimenting with alcohol. Frequently "pat answers" leave such a person thinking everything is okay. The purpose of these articles is to open discussion.

• "Mixing Alcohol, Abstinence, and the Bible." Steve Case looks beyond the wine texts for biblical principles that relate to moderate use alcohol.

Questions for you to ask include, What message do you think the "wine texts" in the Bible give? What principles in Scripture relate to the use of alcohol? What bias do you have about the debate before you discuss it? How has your life experience influenced your view of alcohol?

• "What Those Outside the Church Say." Quite apart from any basis in Scripture, an increasing number of people have a concern about alcohol abuse, and they're doing something about it. We'll also take a look at what the medical studies are and are not reporting.

Is the issue of alcohol something the Church should become involved with? Is it primarily a social or health issue rather than a faith issue? What questions do concerned citizens raise? What issues do they miss?

How has your life experience influenced your view of alcohol?

• "More Than 'Just Say No!'" Amber Murphy, one of the key leaders in the Adventist Youth-to-Youth movement shares her perspective on how to reach the heart of young people by understanding where they're coming from, what they're looking for, and what turns them off.

What position do you think you should take with young people? What about with adults? Isn't it up to each person to make their own choice? What can you really do about it? Why do you think people drink? Why do people choose not to drink?

Why do you think people drink?

• "Selected Additional Resources" contains more materials for the person who would like to give more study to this topic.

Mixing Alcohol, Abstinence, and the Bible

Steve Case

Valuegenesis Byte

Have you ever engaged in this practice during the last year?*

- Drink beer or liquor
  Experimental (14%)
  Regular use (9%)
- Drink wine
  Experimental (10%)
  Regular use (6%)

*SDA youth in SDA schools. Higher percentages for SDA youth in public education.

Acknowledging a bias towards the historic Adventist position of abstinence from alcohol, let's attempt an open search of Scripture regarding the use of alcohol.

Today, because the English word "wine" carries the meaning of fermented grape juice, we have a tendency to assume all biblical uses of "wine" mean fermented grape juice. Yet only a few decades ago "wine" referred to *both* fermented and unfermented juice of the grape.[1] But since the Bible wasn't written in English, it's better to consider the Hebrew and Greek words that have been translated into English as "wine."

The Hebrew word *yayin* and the Greek word *oinos* are used 212 times in the Bible. Both words mean the juice of the grape, either fermented or unfermented. One must

[1]Taken from the 1955 Funk & Wagnalls New Standard Dictionary of the English Language, quoted in Samuele Bacciocchi, *Wine in the Bible* (Berrien Springs, MI: Biblical Perspectives, 1989), 56.

consider the context to determine which meaning is intended.

Fermented Grape Juice

The first mention of wine in the Bible occurs in the story of Noah after the flood. According to Genesis 9:20-21, "Noah, a man of the soil, proceeded to plant a vineyard. When he drank some of its wine, he became drunk and lay uncovered inside his tent." It's not difficult to recognize that the wine Noah drank was fermented. For another clearly negative reference to wine, the familiar temperance verse, "Wine is a mocker, strong drink is raging: and whosoever is deceived thereby is not wise" (Proverbs 20:1, KJV) certainly fits the category of fermented grape juice.

Other Interpretations of "Wine"

But other verses seem to indicate the "wine" was unfermented.

But other verses seem to indicate the "wine" was unfermented. During the reign of Hezekiah, the Jewish Passover Feast was again celebrated. Following a special commemoration of the blessed event, Hezekiah made certain the priests and Levites continued their religious duties with remuneration coming from Israelite donations. According to 2 Chronicles 31:5,

> As soon as the order went out, the Israelites generously gave the firstfruits of their grain, new wine, oil, and honey and all that the fields produced. They brought a great amount, a tithe of everything.

Wine that is new and spoken of in a context of firstfruits hardly indicates fermentation. Yet this represents a number of "wine" texts in Scripture.

While some references to wine obviously classify it as a drink, other references place it as an acceptable offering to God. Numbers 15 records several instances of wine as a gift to the Lord.

> With each lamb for the burnt offering or the sacrifice, prepare a fourth of a *hin* of wine as a drink offering. (verse 5; a *"hin"* is about one quart or one liter). If a ram was offered, the giver was also to mix a third of a *hin* of wine as a drink offering. Offer it as an aroma pleasing to the Lord. (verse 7).

> According to verse 10, if the offering was a bull, "Also bring half a hin of wine as a drink offering. It will be an offering made by fire, an aroma pleasing to the Lord."

Still other uses of "wine" refer to the blessings of God. For example, for faithful covenant-keepers (Deuteronomy 11:14) says:

> God will send rain on your land in its season, both autumn and spring rains, so that you may gather in your grain, new wine and oil.

And in Joel 2:19 (KJV), God promises the following:

While some references to wine obviously classify it as a drink, other references place it in a category of an acceptable offering to God.

Sometimes wine refers to the blessings of God.

Behold, I will send you corn, and wine, and oil, and ye shall be satisfied therewith: and I will no more make you a reproach among the heathen."

Wine as Medicine

Scripture also contains examples of using wine for its medicinal properties. The passage frequently quoted for a pro-wine position indicates, "Stop drinking only water, and use a little wine because of your stomach and your frequent illnesses" (1 Timothy 5:23). The Good Samaritan also used wine in treating the robbed and wounded Jewish traveler left for dead along the road (Luke 10:34).

What is Your Interpretation?

Because wine texts vary so much in their meaning, a person's bias or learned interpretation will influence their understanding of wine texts that don't explicitly identify fermented or unfermented grape juice. When Jesus turned water into wine (John 2), the person with a bias in favor of fermented grape juice easily reasons that wedding feasts often include intoxicating drinks. The reader with a bias towards unfermented grape juice can't imagine Jesus utilizing His miraculous powers to create a drink that was in decay (fermented), and that would leave the drinkers out of control. The "best" drink would be the purest grape juice, which would be much more refreshing than the watered down version the guests probably had come to accept.

Three Categories

Biblical scholars also are divided by the fermented/unfermented controversy. Samuele Bacchiocchi classifies these scholars into three descriptive categories: The *moderationists* hold that the Bible condemns drunkenness but condones a moderate use of fermented wine. The *abstentionists* perceive Scripture as supporting a moderate use of alcohol, but find such an application imprudent, especially in many societies today. The *prohibitionists* maintain that fermented wine is bad, and all positive uses of wine in Scripture refer to unfermented alcohol, since God is opposed to the use of fermented wine even in "moderation."[1]

It's both comforting and frustrating to know that Christians lack a consensus regarding what Scripture teaches in the area of (fermented) wine. The comforting aspect is no matter what your position, you have "good" company. The frustrating element is, that in holding to your position, you cut yourself off from many others within the community of believers.

The Issue of Culture

In the United States, as many as 50 percent of high school students attend drinking parties at least once a month, and half of these teens get "bombed."[2] (The rate is lower among SDA teens, but we're not immune to these at-

On the Quiz !!!

[1]Bacchiocchi, *Wine in the Bible* (Berrien Springs, MI: Biblical Perspectives, 1989), 44-49. Bacchiocchi categorizes scholars of the moderationists view to include G. I. Williamson, Kenneth L. Gentry, and Norman L. Geisler. Scholars of the abstentionist persuasion include Billy Graham, Harold Lindsell, and Arnold B. Come. Scholars grouped in the prohibitionist camp include Robert P. Teachout, Stephen M. Reynold, Ernest Gordon, Frederic Richard Lees, Dawson Burns, Leon C. Field, William Patton, and Samuele Bacchiocchi.

[2]Dorothy Dusek Girdano and Daniel A. Girdano, *Drugs—A Factual Account* (Reading, MA: Addison-Wesley Publishing Company, n.d.) 49.

risk behaviors.) Are adult parties significantly different? Have bars become the gathering place in the United States? Is alcohol consumed with a meal, or is it more likely to be consumed before, during, and after the meal?

Based on these characteristics, *alcohol in the American culture today is abused*. Alcohol permeates all levels of society and in most social settings. Despite the work of organizations such as MADD and SADD and their change from promoting "don't drink and drive" to "don't drink," alcohol continues to drain American society even as this society embraces its use. God calls us to live to his glory (1 Corinthians 10:31).

Biblical Principles for Today

In contrast to those taken in by the miasma of an alcohol-abusing society, we are called to be examples of alcohol-free living rather than taking the chance of causing another susceptible person to fall (Romans 14:21).

Principle #1: God is for life, including the quality of life

With alcohol playing a pivotal role in 20 percent of all hospital care, 33 percent of mental health patients, 50 percent of auto accidents, 65 percent of boating injuries, 67 percent of those arrested for murder, and 80 percent of those in juvenile hall,[1] we are living in contradiction to the

---

Alcohol in the American culture today is abused.

Know the 4 Principles

Exodus 20:13; John 10:10; Ephesians 6:12-13.

[1]Seventh-day Adventist Church, *Twenty Reasons to Say "No" to Alcohol* (undated pamphlet available from the stewardship or temperance department of the North American Division of Seventh-day Adventists).

commandment not to kill and in refusal of God's offer of "abundant living." This involves more than capitalism, big business and free trade. Alcohol is a killer that is used by the principalities and powers of darkness, unseen except for its pernicious effects.

Principle #2: God offers His Spirit in contrast to spirits

Ephesians 5:18; Acts 2:15-18; Matthew 5:13-16.

Paul admonished the Ephesian believers to be filled with the Spirit rather than with wine. One reason presented for the moderate use of alcohol is that it releases a person's inhibitions. But is it wise to have one's inhibitions released? It depends on what is being inhibited and who will be in control when they are released. Admittedly, people may have some inhibitions from which they should be freed.

Why not be free with a security and steadfastness rather than a physical and moral weakening? Like the disciples on the Day of Pentecost, we may be accused of being drunk because our self-conscious inhibitions have been released by the Holy Spirit in contrast to those who must guard their reputations and position in life. By receiving the positive benefits of the Spirit without the negative side effects of the spirits, we can truly be salt and light to the world.

3 John 2;
1 Corinthians 6:15,19-20.

[1]See E.H. Siemann and L. Creasy, "Concentrationg of the Phytoalexin Resverastrol in Wine" in *American Journal of Enology and Viticulture* (Vol 43. No. 1, 1992).

Romans 12;
1 Corinthians 12;
Ephesians 4:7-16.

Principle #3: Our physical health is not dependent on wine

The medicinal qualities of alcohol are not necessary today because of society's high priority to improve water purification and waste management. The "benefits" associated with moderate drinking have received lopsided emphasis in the popular press, which has neglected to report the harmful physical results of even moderate use of alcohol. While good health is important to God and related to holistic living, the minor benefits possible with wine are available with unfermented grape juice.[1]

Principle #4: God speaks in the present to His people through an active spirit of prophecy

God reveals himself through the ministry of the Holy Spirit, giving gifts to build up the Body of Christ. If God's message to a culture is not clear in Scripture, God will send a specific message to that people for that time. While Scripture is adequate for our rules of faith and practice, God is not limited by Scripture in speaking to his people in the present (Revelation 12:17, cf. Revelation 19:10). Such messages must be tested in the light of Scripture even if expressed in modern language appropriate for a given time and location. Adventists have historically seen the counsel of Ellen G. White as aiding the discussion of religious issues, based on her rich spiritual experience and consistency with biblical expression. While her writings on alcoholism were written during an active temperance movement in North American culture, we believe the principles contained in these writings pertain to building a balanced health-related lifestyle.

And Finally . . .

A person's bias heavily influences that person's conclusions. Those with a bias for moderate use of alcohol, receive supportive for evidence from both Scripture and modern science. But there is ample support for abstinence, too.

Rather than just being satisfied with the support of either position, this chapter attempts to look beyond the obvious "wine texts" in the Bible and consider other Scriptural principles that would have a bearing on the moderate use of alcohol today, especially in North America.

Based on the four principles listed above, the abstinence bias stated at the beginning of the chapter continues, although with additional support. It is therefore recommended that the Seventh-day Adventist Church hold to an abstinence position on alcohol and seek to correct the negative results of alcohol abuse throughout our society.

For Christians, sometimes it's useful to temporarily put aside biblical passages and simply consider what those speaking outside the church have to say on a given matter. Listening to a different voice can give a new perspective of Scripture. For this reason we will now turn to what people outside the community of faith say about alcohol. While some may be Christians, they do not speak for Christians.

Adventists have historically seen the counsel of Ellen G. White as aiding the discussion of religious issues based on her rich spiritual experience and consistency with biblical expression.

A large number of people have been affected adversely by alcohol due to its negative impact through a relative or close friend.

[1]Duane C. McBride, Patricia B. Mutch, Roger L. Dudley, April G. Julian, and Winton H. Beaven, "Adventists, Drugs, and a Changing Church" in Adventist Review (June 1, 1989) 13.
[2]Hales, Dianne, and Robert E. Hales, M.D., "Alcohol: Better than We Thought?" in American Health (December, 1986), 39.

What Those Outside the Church Say

Steve Case

A large number of people have been adversely affected by alcohol due to its negative impact on a relative or friend. For some it may be a parent, for others a child or lifetime friend. Within the Adventist Church, about 20 percent claim to have been in a painful family situation because of alcohol and drug use by family members.[1] This number doesn't reflect the impact of alcohol abuse by friends or by drunk drivers whose alcohol use affects others.

In the United States, two-thirds of adults drink alcohol. Of these, 10 percent are known to be alcoholics.[2] This seems to suggest that alcohol is a problem for a small minority. However, the American culture camouflages all but the late stages of alcoholism. The estimated economic cost of alcoholism through reduced productivity, absenteeism, and treatment is $117 billion a year.[1] In addition, the major cause of death for 15- to 24- year-olds is alcohol-related accidents. Every 20 minutes a person is killed from drunk driving. This adds up to 100,000 lives lost each year in the United States (25 times more than deaths from all illegal drugs combined). An additional 650,000 are injured each year because of drunk drivers.[2] And we permit the sale of alcohol at 7-elevens and gas stations!

Part of the reason for such widespread use and abuse is the fact that the alcohol industry spends $2 billion a year on advertising using humor, adventure, or role models to promote their products. It is estimated that children will see 100,000 beer commercials before they are legally old enough to drink a beer.[3]

The surgeon general's recommendations at the 1988 Conference on Alcohol included: not advertising alcohol at colleges and universities, not using celebrities or portraying of high-adventure activities in alcohol ads, and not sponsoring sports events by the alcohol industry. These recommendations have gone largely unheeded.

Public Policies and Principles

In 1987, the National Association for Public Health Policy offered four guiding principles for public policies on alcohol use:

[1] "Americans for Substance Abuse Prevention" quoted in Twenty Reasons to Say "No" to Alcohol. (Washington DC, n.d.) 4.

[2] American Journal of Public Health (February 1986) 144-149, quoted in Twenty Reasons to Say "No" to Alcohol. (Washington DC, n.d.) 4.

[3] Donald Bowman, Newsletter for the California Council on Alcohol Problems (Spring, 1989) 2.

God is not limited by Scripture to speak to his people in the present.

1. Abstention is acceptable in all circumstances.
2. Alcohol consumption in high-risk settings is discouraged.
3. Heavy consumption is discouraged.
4. Moderate consumption in low-risk situations is acceptable.

These principles were to be manifested in the following rights which are considered fundamental to all Americans:

1. The right to know (accurate information about alcohol).
2. The right to safe roadways and communities.
3. The right to health-enhancing alcohol taxation (tax rates adequate to cover the total cost of alcohol-related problems).
4. The right to protect our teens (proper education, prevention of advertising directed to teens).
5. The right to safe workplaces (employee assistance programs for alcoholism, end government subsidies of alcohol in the military).
6. The right to health services (to alleviate the suffering associated with alcohol-related problems).

Americans, though refusing to take a prohibitionist position in the early 1900s by ratifying the 21st Amendment, have taken steps to prevent and heal the detrimental effects of alcohol abuse. Some wonder if the use of alcohol is more analogous to the use of guns (only their misuse is bad) or to the use of tobacco (any use is bad). Minimum ages govern permitted use of guns, tobacco and alcohol, but the use of guns has more restrictions than does the use of tobacco. How ironic that tobacco, recognized as a killer, is permitted because it is part of the American culture. Could the same be said of alcohol?

Proposed Medical Benefits of Alcohol

Alcohol is a depressant drug. For centuries it has been used medicinally for such purposes. Personal use of the substance comes into question because of its abuse and the concomitant results. But the proponents for alcohol argue it is a matter of saying, "No more," rather than an all-out "No." They suggest that 2-3 drinks per day is okay. In fact, it may be healthier than a nonalcoholic diet.

The American Heart Association (AHA) now includes alcohol levels in its list of nutritional guidelines—no more than 1.7 ounces of pure alcohol (3 beers, 3 glasses of wine, or 2 shots of whiskey or liquor) per day OR no more than 15 percent of one's caloric intake. The average American diet of 2,000 calories per day would have 15 percent of its caloric intake met by just 2 beers. The AHA recognizes current evidence that alcohol consumption is linked to reduced incidence of heart disease but does not see sufficient evidence to recommend using alcohol to prevent heart attacks, so the inclusion of alcohol levels in the AHA guidelines should not be misconstrued to imply a recommendation to drink.[1]

Those who favor a moderate use of alcohol point out that individuals should be aware of their personal drinking limit, determined by the blood alcohol level (BAL). This

How ironic that tobacco, recognized as a killer, is permitted because it is part of the American culture. Could the same be said of alcohol?

[1] Hales and Hales, 40.

317

Those who favor a moderate use of alcohol point out that individuals should be aware of their personal drinking limit.

[1]*Ibid.*

[2]Dr. Yano, et. al., responding to reports of their 1977 *New England Journal of Medicine* article stated, "Reports of our work in the lay press have, unfortunately, implied that judicious tipping is a good preventive health measure. This distortion of our conclusions is not justified by the data." reported by Harold Shryock in "Is Moderate Drinking Good for You?" in the undated special temperance issue of *Adventist Review*), 8.

varies due to weight (increased weight has an increased water volume which dilutes the alcohol); types of alcohol used (on an empty stomach water and juices slow alcohol absorption, so alcohol in vodka would be absorbed faster than alcohol in beer, wine, or wine coolers), food already ingested (slows absorption); how quickly alcohol is consumed (liver processes half an ounce each hour); gender (females generally have less body water to dilute alcohol); and age (older people have less body water to dilute alcohol).

A BAL of .05 is the level in which people describe the positive effects of relaxation, euphoria and a sense of well-being. As the BAL goes beyond .05, it becomes increasingly negative, going from being drunk to passing out to a coma to death.[1]

Reporting on research has been more polemic than the actual research.[2] For example, Michael Criqui's 1987 report supposedly endorsed moderate alcohol consumption. Yet he began his report with this cautionary emphasis.

"Before beginning a discussion of the roles of alcohol in cardiovascular disease (CVD), I think it is wise to consider the question of the overall effect of alcohol. Heavy alcohol consumption is positively associated with nearly every non-cardiovascular cause of mortality. For instance, in the Honolulu Heart Study consumption of alcohol above 40 ml (roughly two drinks) per day was associated with elevated mortality rates from cirrhosis, cancer, other non-cardiovascular disease, and all causes including CVD."[1]

The study included the presentation of up to two drinks per day resulting in an increase of positive HDL cholesterol and a decrease of negative LDL cholesterol. This finding grabbed the headlines rather than the concluding statement that "public health policy should continue to discourage the drinking of alcohol, especially non-moderate consumption."[2]

A flurry of studies provided adequate research to support people's biases,[3] enabling them to buttress their desired conclusions with scientific studies the same way they have used Scripture. Some argue that positive HDL (#2) increases with exercise, not alcohol which provides the negative HDL (#3). Stanford University researchers claim it's not HDL at all, but apolipoprotein A-1, a protein attached to HDL molecules that helps clear cholesterol out of the blood stream. Still others purport that apolipoprotein A-1 rises when people drink alcohol but drops when they don't.

Now researchers are considering what elements in alcohol activate the positive coronary reactions. Resveratrol, a phytoalexin, has received the initial nod. It's found in wine, with different quantities based on the type of wine and the climatic conditions in which the grapes were grown. Resveratrol is also found in purple grape juice (unfermented). The researchers aren't prepared to prescribe this as medication for reducing the risk of heart disease, but grape juice appears to be as effective as wine

[1] Michael H. Criqui, M.D., MPH, "The Roles of Alcohol in the Epidemiology of Cardiovascular Diseases" in *Acta Med Scand* (Supplement 717, 1987) 73-85.

[2] *Ibid.*

[5] See Galen C. Bosley, *Adventist Review* (May 1, 1986) 12-14.

against heart disease without the negative side effects of wine.[1]

While the debate continues on the possible physiological benefits of wine or grape juice in reducing heart disease, there is little debate on the deleterious physiological effects of alcohol. According to the National Academy of Science, "excessive alcohol increases risk of heart disease, high blood pressure, liver diseases, cancer, neurological disorders, and nutritional deficiencies. Moderate drinking carries risk of impaired neuromotor coordination and judgment. Small amounts can lead to dependence."[2] Is it really comforting to know that a loved one who is dead from cirrhosis of the liver or a drunk driving accident had low cholesterol?

While some physiological effects have a direct bearing on the drinker, some do not. Drunk driving is an obvious example, but another is fetal alcohol syndrome (FAS). 3,000-5,000 such births occur in the United States each year. The cause is a pregnant woman's intake of alcohol and its direct flow into the fetus from the mother's blood. Commonly the results are mental and motor retardation, distortion of physical features, and problems with major organs. The greatest damage is done early in the pregnancy, even before the female is aware she is pregnant. To prevent FAS, females must abstain from alcohol immediately prior to and during pregnancy.[3] This has serious ramifications because of promiscuity often associated with drinking.

[1] See E. H. Siemann and L. Creasy, "Concentration of the Phytoalexin Resveratrol in Wine," in American Journal of Enology and Viticulture (Vol 43, No. 1, 1992). See also the "Health Front" report in Working Mother (January 1993) 12.

[2] The National Academy of Science, Report on Diet and Health in Proctor, "What'll It Be?" (n.d.) 14.

[3] Elizabeth Sterndale, "Alcohol and the Pregnant Woman," in Ministry (March 1987) 25-26.

Summary

The alcohol industry will continue to promote the healthfulness of its product, especially since alcohol consumption continues to be in vogue.

12-step programs are "in," and advocacy groups, who are tired of alcohol abuse and its results, are organizing everywhere. Evidence continues to mount against the deleterious effects of alcohol on our culture. The question now posed is, "Will it be Christians or society as a whole who deal with the problem of alcohol?" People must recognize that the impact of alcohol abuse permeates our culture. All too often we get in discussions that fail to clarify what the principles are. There is no question that the use of alcohol has become a problem in today's society and even more dramatically, in the lives of hundreds of teenagers. Finding solutions to these problems is the challenge. Youth today can become a powerful influence for change in the area of abuse of any kind.

Nearly all teens recognize that crack and cocaine are very dangerous substances. The Gallup Youth Survey in recent years has found only about 1 percent or less of the teen population who report they are current users of either substance. However, far fewer teens consider either alcohol or tobacco to be very dangerous, although most recognize the substances can be at least somewhat dangerous. And as teens grow older, opinion that marijuana, alcohol, and tobacco products are dangerous substances often decreases.

People must recognize that the impact of alcohol abuse permeates our culture. All too often we get in discussions that fail to clarify what the principles are.

The "benefits" associated with moderate drinking have received a lopsided emphasis.

What is tragic, however, is that clearly alcohol has become the drug of choice of the youth of America. According to the findings a recent survey, teen drinking and substance abuse now are more likely to occur in affluent white suburbs than in minority neighborhoods of the inner city. In 1992, nearly one teen in five reported drinking alcoholic beverages at least once during the past month. By comparison, only 4 percent reported using marijuana. And, tragically, alcohol has been termed a "gateway drug" because it can lead users to try more dangerous drugs.[1]

[1]Robert Bezilla, Editor, *America's Youth in the 1990s* (Princeton, NJ: The George H. Gallup International Institute, 1993), 178-179.

More Than "Just Say No!"

Amber Murphy

Ask most teenagers on the street if they know drugs and alcohol are bad for them, and they will answer "Yes." Very few would venture to argue that addiction to alcohol is healthy or good. Yet the statistics show that many kids in America are still using. Why?

It's imperative that we look at this problem from a teenager's perspective if we are to ever understand. That means from *their* perspective, not the perspective of our own teenage years.

The teenage years can be very turbulent where, as Erikson proposes, kids are searching for their own identity. Peers play a large role and acceptance is everything. Teens tend to be hypercritical of themselves. Their hair is gross, their clothes

It's imperative that we look at this problem from a teenager's perspective if we are to ever understand. That means from *their* current perspective, not the perspective of our own teenage years.

are uncool, and they are fat. They are not sure they like themselves or their bodies, so why should doing a little damage matter? They see today, not the results twenty years from today. We are trying to sell kids on sobriety based on the ill effects of the future when they are dealing solely with the immediacy of today.

Scare Tactics

Scare tactics are even less effective, in my opinion. First of all, citing statistics out of context, for the purpose of instilling fear is detrimental. Statistics are rather nebulous to the teenage mind anyway. These are "other" people at "other" places and do little to dent the rather egocentric cushion teenagers seem to place around themselves. They thrive on excitement and thrills, not on safety and security.

Scare tactics can also be detrimental in that they can be misleading in the teenager's mind. They hear of people dying from drug use. They give in to pressures and smoke some marijuana and nothing happens. This only reinforces this behavior and builds ammunition against prevention tactics. Kids should be well informed and educated about the effects of alcohol use, but scare tactics are short-lived and can eventually do more to harm than to help.

Adventists At Risk

If the typical prevention avenues appear to be ineffective, what should we do? Where do we go from here? Should we

We are trying to sell kids on sobriety based on the ill effects of the future when they are dealing solely with the immediacy of today.

forget it and let our kids do whatever? Absolutely not! Unfortunately that's what we've done for too long. We think that alcohol use doesn't affect our kids. They are Adventists! This issue doesn't affect them— but it does. Our kids face the same insecurities and fears that all teenagers face. The difference, hopefully, is that they have a meaningful relationship with the Lord to which they can turn in working this out. We must get our kids to take a stand so when or if they are faced with this issue they have already made the decision, rather than just beginning to look at their options as the beer is handed to them.

It is naive to believe that our kids, solely because they are Adventists, will never be faced with the alcohol issue. They watch TV don't they? They go out in public don't they? And some day they may possibly go to non-Adventist colleges or get jobs in public settings. It is inevitable. At some point we must mix and mingle with the general public. We cannot hide our children in cocoons for life. We must prepare them for the challenges they will face rather than deny that they are there. "Because it's bad for you" just isn't a good enough reason anymore.

Now as much as I'd like to believe that our kids are only confronted with the alcohol issue from the outside, I know this isn't true. Our kids face this issue among their Adventist peers. And even this isn't the heart of the problem. Teachers, pastors, parents—the real issue is on the inside. Drinking is a symptom of a greater problem.

"Because it's bad for you" just isn't a good enough reason anymore.

325

What's the Problem

No one asked, "Why?"

I can hear people saying, "No! It can't be! Fix the drinking and the problem is gone, right?" Unfortunately, this is the way we have tended to deal with it. Drinking is the problem, friends are the problem, bad influences are the problem. But I want to propose that the real issue, the real battle is going on inside.

A friend of mine was expelled from one of our academies for drinking. As is the scenario in most of our schools, this student had to face the ad council regarding this behavior. In recounting the events of that day, my friend told me that upon his entrance to the room he was simply asked if he had been drinking. He answered honestly, yes. That was it. The end. No more questions. The student was expelled, the problem eliminated. Yet this same student, several years later, in recounting this event to me made this interesting observation. "The ad council only asked if I had done it, no one asked Why?" Why?

We look for the alcohol, see the problem, but do we ever stop to ask, "Why?" This particular student believes that it would have made all the difference in the world. This kid was reaching out for help. Things were out of control. The alcohol use was a desperate cry. Instead of asking why and seeing the alcohol as a symptom, we accepted it willingly as the problem, when in reality it wasn't the problem, just an indication of one.

I can't tell you how many times I've had kids say to me, "I just wanted someplace to fit in. I had an emptiness and it was filled through these associations. I was looking for something, and it was there." From coast to coast, I've heard the same thing over and over. Different faces, different stories but the same thought is conveyed. "I was reaching out for something and this is what I found. I found acceptance, understanding, love, and admiration from others when drinking. In other areas of my life—school, home, church I only found condemnation."

How sad. We have very high expectations from our kids, and when they fall short, what happens? When they are less than perfect, when they make bad choices, when they don't live up to what we want from them, what happens?

Christ calls upon us to love one another, not to judge one another. Yet it seems that often with adolescents, we are afraid of their exploring and coming up with answers we don't like. We become critical and judgmental of anything in their lives that doesn't align with what we think is right, and we expel them from the very place they need to be.

It saddens me to think of our kids feeling lost and alone, reaching out for loving arms and support and the only place they can find it is from Busch, Michelob or Miller Lite. Where are we? Quoting Bible verses, shaking our fingers or voting to eliminate them because "one bad apple spoils the bunch." What they really need is our love, acceptance, and support. When they reach out, it needs to be *our* hands they can hold on to, *our* shoulder they can cry on, and *our* ears they know will hear them, even if they've made a mistake.

> "I found acceptance, understanding, love and admiration from others when drinking. In other areas of my life—school, home, church I only found condemnation."

327

Alcohol doesn't discriminate. Can a church say the same?

Awhile back I read a statement that gave me a new perspective in dealing with kids who are "using." "Bad actions don't make a bad person and good actions don't make a good person." I couldn't agree more. Our kids are going to make poor choices. The question is, When they fall, who is going to be the one to reach down and pick them up?

Who will love them back? Alcohol doesn't discriminate. It will embrace any age, race, color. Tall, short, fat, beautiful, unattractive, charming, stupid, or awkward. Can we as a church say the same? Are we as accepting as Bartles & Jaymes?

In most cases, our kids are experimentally using. There is a big difference between addiction and experimental use. We must begin to differentiate between the two. Sadly, we treat kids who are experimentally using as if they were addicts, which only perpetuates that behavior. In other words, we encourage the addictive process when we have the opportunity to help kids make that change.

We must separate the action from the individual.

I do not mean to convey that usage is acceptable. It is not. However, we must separate the action from the individual. Alcohol drinking does not make the person ingesting it bad. It simply means that he or she is making a poor choice.

Suggested Additional Resources

Bacchiocchi, Samuele, *Wine in the Bible* (Berrien Springs, MI: Biblical Perspectives), 1989.

Coffin, James, "Does the Bible Condemn "Moderate" Drinking?" in *Adventist Review* (undated special temperance issue), 4-6.

Girdano, Dorothy Dusek and Daniel A. Girdano, *Drugs—A Factual Account* (Reading, MA: Addison-Wesley Publishing Company, n.d.), especially 32-60.

Proctor, Stoy, *What'll It Be?* The Christian and Alcohol (undated pamphlet available from The Health Connection 1-800-548-8700).

Scriven, Charles, "Booze," a sermon presented at Sligo Seventh-day Adventist Church (Takoma Park, MD: November 8, 1986), available in written form from the church.

Seventh-day Adventist Church, *Twenty Reasons to Say "No" to Alcohol* (undated pamphlet available from the stewardship or temperance department of the North American Division 301-680-6000).

Spickard, Anderson and Barbara Thompson, *Dying for a Drink* (Waco, TX: Word), 1985.

Stein, Robert H., "Wine Drinking in New Testament Times" in *Christianity Today* (June 20, 1975), 9-11.

Section 9

Thinking About Movies

"An Adventist is someone who doesn't attend movies."

[1] See *Valuegenesis* research about Adventist youth and standards. Roger Dudley and V. Bailey Gillespie, *Valuegenesis: Faith in the Balance* (Riverside, CA: La Sierra University Press, 1992).

Section 9
Thinking About Movies

What's the Discussion About?

In focus groups with Adventist young people around the North American Division, we often ask teens to define a Seventh-day Adventist church member. Invariably, their answers center on behavior issues, and almost always one of those behaviors has to do with watching movies. "An Adventist is someone who doesn't attend movies," they say. When faced with the difference between their own behavior (more than 90% of North American Adventist youth watch movies regularly[1]) and this antimovie definition, teens are perplexed. They don't know how to harmonize the conflict. Neither do older adults in the church.

While the prohibition of watching movies was once an accurate description of Adventist behavior, that accuracy began to fall apart with the arrival of technology by which we could bring movies home to view in our own living rooms. Technological development and cable movie networks (HBO, Cinemax, etc.), have encouraged us to focus our discussions on the *content* of the movies we view instead of the *places* we view the movie.

The Background of the Discussion

Adventists have long maintained an official position against movie theater attendance.

• In early days, this position was usually stated by drawing attention to the evils of the theater itself. The position might sound like this:

> Every institution has its own atmosphere. The church has the atmosphere of prayer. We find ourselves in a certain mood while within the influence of that atmosphere. A business office has another certain atmosphere. Likewise a moving-picture house has its own clearly defined atmosphere. The atmosphere of the theater hangs heavy with evil. The atmosphere produces its effect on ones who frequent such a place.
>
> For this reason, if no other, I think an Adventist presents a weak and worthless argument when he declares that he wishes to go to a moving-picture house only occasionally to see a good movie. Doubtlessly, I might secure at a saloon a glass of pure water to quench my thirst, but I would rather find a good drink else-

Technological development has encouraged us to focus our discussions on the *content* of the movies we view instead of the *places* we view the movie.

333

where. I don't like the atmosphere of a saloon. If I went in there, I might even be tempted to drink something else besides water. Adam and Eve found out long ago that the tree of the knowledge of good and evil was a bad tree to visit.

"The atmosphere of the theater hangs heavy with evil."

• In 1937 *Ministry* magazine published a series of guidelines for selecting a movie. A summary of the guidelines included this statement:

> "Films of a theatrical nature (i.e., not real life depictions) are an evil influence because they confuse the Adventist attitude towards theater, novel reading, and opera; create an appetite for further viewing; and play upon the emotions unnecessarily."[1]

The article lists unacceptable types of films, including those which portray Christ, the act of smoking, romantic lovemaking, scenes of violence, or comedy that degraded ministers or police.

[1]Report of the Minority Committee by the Standing Committee on Visual Education, "Principles and Standards in the Use of Motion Pictures: A Pronouncement and An Appeal From the General Conference Committee," in *Ministry*, May, 1937, 1-3.

• In 1971 *Ministry* raised the question of movies again by means of an interview with Richard Jewett, an academy pastor and Bible teacher. Jewett expressed reservation about movie theater attendance because it could become habit-forming and lead in the wrong direction. He admitted that there were "good" movies, but stated that total abstinence was the safest course to pursue as a goal.[2]

[2]Richard Jewett, "Interview With an Academy Bible Teacher About Movies" in *Ministry,* February, 1971, 36-37.

• Throughout the years of its publication, the *SDA Church Manual* has expressed this prohibition in terms of a warning, and in doing so, has come closer to discussing content issues:

"We earnestly warn against the subtle and sinister influence of the moving-picture theater, which is no place for the Christian. Dramatized films that graphically present by portrayal and by suggestion the sins and crimes of humanity–murder, adultery, robbery, and kindred evils–are in no small degree responsible for the present breakdown of morality. We appeal to parents, children, and youth to shun those places of amusement and those theatrical films that glorify professional acting and actors. If we will find delight in God's great world of nature and in the romance of human agencies and divine workings, we shall not be attracted by the puerile portrayals of the theater."[1]

• Today, while the church maintains its official stance against movies, the fact is that most Adventists watch movies regularly, in theaters and in their homes. You could accurately describe going to movies as the "default" Saturday night entertainment for Adventist youth. In fact some people surmise that not only do Adventist youth *go* to movies, they actually go to *more* movies than do their secular teenage counterparts.

Questions Youth Are Asking

• Since most are going to movies, isn't it now *okay* to go?
• What's the difference between watching a movie in your home, in the academy gym, or in a theater?
• Why do people keep referring to the bad atmosphere

You could accurately describe going to movies as the "default" Saturday night entertainment for Adventist youth.

[1]*Seventh-day Adventist Church Manual* (Washington, DC: General Conference of Seventh-day Adventists, 1990 edition), 146.

Since most are going to movies, isn't it now *okay* to go?

in a theater when the rules there have changed (you can't smoke or drink in theaters, it's quiet and comfortable)? It seems like the atmosphere is a lot worse at a baseball game.

• Why can't we just accept the idea that watching movies is a harmless and relatively inexpensive form of entertainment?

• What does entertainment have to do with your Christian experience?

• Since we know it's all fantasy, and that none of those people are really getting killed, why can't we just relax and enjoy the special effects?

Focusing the Discussion

Here are four perspectives on the movies issue that will assist you and your youth in coming to a decision about this pervasive standards issue.

• "A Moving Experience." Youth pastor Delwin Finch examines four biblical passages in search of basic and timeless principles we can apply to this facet of the entertainment issue.

Study these passages with your youth group, and see how they would read and apply the principles. Ask questions like these: How much conformity is inevitable by living in this world? How can entertainment activities be an "act of worship"? Make a list of events or people you think are admirable and praiseworthy.

• "And the Winner Is…" Stuart Tyner, Director of the

What does entertainment have to do with your Christian experience?

John Hancock Center for Youth Ministry at La Sierra University, lists "a few great movies" which "have made the hearts of believers soar." Unfortunately, the author observes, those great ones are few and far between. He then challenges us with three options for choosing the movies we watch or don't watch.

What movies would your youth group add to the list of "great ones"? Ask your youth to discuss the strengths and weaknesses of each of the three options. How would they apply the advice to "never watch a movie unintentionally"?

• "Movies: Where or What?" In this honest reporting of personal and family decisions, Fred Crowell reveals the process behind his entertainment decisions. In his study, Crowell asks some pointed questions that have helped him make decisions about particular movies.

How can we keep from being "desensitized" to the suffering and immorality in the world? Divide your youth group into small groups, ask them this question, then have them report to the larger group.

• "Selected Additional Reading" presents a bibliography on the topic of movies that provides youth leaders with more perspectives on the subject and additional suggestions for discussion and valuing activities.

Study these passages with your youth group, and see how they would read and apply the principles.

Is the Bible still the source for Christian principles in the 21st century?

A Moving Experience

Delwin Finch

Of course, the word "movie" cannot be found in a Bible concordance. The word "theater" does appear twice —in Acts 19, verses 29 and 31. Paul wanted to enter the theater, but his friends wouldn't let him. Paul wasn't trying to catch the latest flick on the silver screen. The theater in Ephesus was simply the town meeting place. It seated nearly 25,000. With a city in a riot about Paul's teachings, it's little wonder Paul wanted to speak to the crowd.

Is the Bible still the source for Christian principles in the 21st century? Yes, and these principles remain applicable throughout time. Just what are these basic and timeless principles? Consider these four when dealing with the issue of movies (and other forms of entertainment, for that matter).

Principle #1: We Have a World View to be Shaped

Romans 12:1-2.

"Therefore, I urge you, brothers, in view of God's mercy, to offer your bodies as living sacrifices, holy and pleasing to God—this is your spiritual act of worship. Do not conform any longer to the pattern of this world, but be transformed by the renewing of your mind. Then you will be able to test and approve what God's will is - his good, pleasing, and perfect will."

This passage is the immediate response to Paul's theology of salvation. Chapter 12 of Romans begins a section of the book which explores the application of salvation. Having developed in the previous chapters the idea that salvation comes through grace as a gift from God, Paul points out that Christians are to live out their lives in light of this wonderful gift of salvation by offering their bodies as living sacrifices. The action of giving oneself to God is *not for the purpose of salvation, but as a response to what God has already done.* Thus, our behavior, including the decision to view movies or avoid them, can never be an act of gaining merit in God's eyes.

One key principle found in this text is in the second verse: "Do not conform any longer to the pattern of this world, but be transformed. . ." The Christian no longer can go along with the ways of the world "in view of God's mercy." Repeatedly we experience the adage, "By beholding we become changed."

In one sense, movies give a reflection of our times by showing what touches the soul. From a business perspec-

The decision to view movies or avoid them can never be an act of gaining merit in God's eyes.

[1]See Fred Crowell, "Movies: Where or What?" later in this section.

Real life can seem quite mundane and boring in contrast to life on the silver screen.

tive alone, moviemakers cater to the demands of society. Economics seem to drive the movie industry more than a sinister desire to break up the family or concern for society's betterment.[1] Movies provide identification for the viewers. For some, movies provide an escape from reality; for others, a dream that nourishes hope to face reality. In this sense, movies give a reflection of our culture and society.

On the other hand, movies are incredibly unrealistic. Time becomes so condensed that a biography of a 70-year-old can be edited into two hours of intensity. Real life can seem quite mundane and boring in contrast to life on the silver screen. Only part of the story gets told in the film. For example, sexual promiscuity rarely gets fully exposed, showing bed scenes and eliminating the reality of dealing with unwanted pregnancies, sexually transmitted diseases, and psychological and spiritual consequences. Much of what movies portray today is a reflection of a particular world view and attitude towards society.

The pattern of contemporary American life is an increasing focus on "me" rather than on "others," possessions over service, and the pleasures of this moment. Movies reflect this in the depiction of sex and wealth as the ultimate source of satisfaction. It stands to reason that a continual diet of such an attitude will affect the viewer.

The solution offered in Romans to conforming to the world is a transforming renewal of the mind. What this transformation involves is not completely spelled out here by Paul, but it includes a nonconformity with the patterns of the world. The fact that this is to be a "transforming" change indicates that one should not simply avoid the patterns of the world, but turn these patterns around. Instead of being caught up in the world's standards, Christian's are to demonstrate in their lives that the world has no controlling power. Thus, in the area of movies, this principle leads to the following questions:

- What values are advocated in this movie, and do I agree with them?
- What has this movie done (or will it do) to aid in the renewing of my mind?
- What changes have occurred over the past year regarding my world view?
- What am I doing to positively influence my world view?

Principle #2: Garbage In - Garbage Out; Christlikeness In—Christlikeness Out

"Finally, brothers, whatever is true, whatever is noble, whatever is right, whatever is pure, whatever is lovely, whatever is admirable—if anything is excellent or praiseworthy—think about such things."

This verse comes near the end of Paul's letter to the Philippian church. After a series of exhortations to rejoice in Christ, pray, not worry, and trust in God, Paul concluded with a final word of encouragement to "think on these things."

Instead of being caught up in the world's standards, Christian's are to demonstrate in their lives that the world has no controlling power.

Philippians 4:8.

The list given seems incredibly positive.

[1]John Horn, "Parents and Kids Line Up for Feel-Good Films" in *The Sacramento Bee* (March 16, 1993), D1. See also Zillman, Dolf, Jennings Bryant and Aletha C. Huston, *Media, Children, and the Family Social Scientific, Psychodynamic, and Clinical Perspectives* (Hillsdale, NJ: Lawrence Erlbaum Associates, Publishers, 1994), 10-13.

[2]For example, Joshua 6:20-21, Judges 19, 1 Kings 11:1-5, Esther 2:12-17, Job 1:13-19, Song of Solomon, Isaiah 1-3, Hosea 1-3, Acts 5:1-11; 40-41, 2 Corinthians 11:24-29.

The list given seems incredibly positive. In a world full of lying and cheating, we are to look for truth and right. In our impure and often drab surroundings, we are to see the pure and the lovely. In fact, whatever is praiseworthy and excellent—this is to occupy our thoughts. How can we do this?

The answer is found in verses five and seven. We are to rejoice because the second coming is near and we are to have the peace of God "which transcends all understanding." The person who relies on God and presents all concerns to Him is able to have peace, a peace that guards one's heart and mind. By coming to God with our requests, we learn to rely on Him for everything. Once again, the emphasis is on the mind and the changes that take place as a result of being united with God.

The simple equation of "garbage in = garbage out" may be true for computers, but it should be questioned for humans. Can we use our minds to process the experiences, reacting and registering negative responses to what we disagree with and giving greater weight to deeper issues woven into the fabric of our complicated lives? Our desire to live in an untainted world is unrealistic on our planet.[1]

To be free of exposure to immortality, violence, and degradation, one would have to refrain from reading many portions of Scripture.[2] Movie lecturer Geoffrey Hill stated this problem humorously:

> One of the most common questions I get when I do film workshops and I show movies is, "Why do you

pick films with so much sex and violence in them?"
My answer is that I happen to like religious films.[1]

Evaluating a movie requires more than ears that count a few swear words or eyes that spot someone drinking an alcoholic beverage. The theme and overall message must be identified in order to put the specific pieces into proper perspective. The difference is the mind-set or world view that accompanies such presentations. Most movies depict life completely void of God. Whatever religious references are made usually come in the form of a caricature, such as simplistic stupidity or swindling crookedness. Scripture doesn't hide from the realities of terrible events, but it presents them within the framework of God as sovereign and personally involved in our lives.

What is spoken of in verse eight is another example of how important the mind is to God. In the first principle found in Romans 12, the emphasis was on the renewing of our minds. Now we are encouraged to fill our minds with good thoughts. There is a subjective element to this choosing. We are to decide what is lovely, noble, right, etc., and then we should think on these things. We are not told *what* to choose, but the *criteria* to use in choosing.

The biblical admonition to think on such things raises further questions about movies, questions that include:
- How is life portrayed by this movie?
- Is this portrayal realistic or desirable?
- Am I compromising my own standards by viewing this?

[1]"Geoffrey Hill Interview" in *The Door,* March/April, 1993, 21.

343

Most movies depict life completely void of God.

1 Corinthians 10:31-32.

We are not told what to choose, but the criteria to use in choosing.

- What is the environment?
- What is the content (message) of this movie?
- What does this movie tell me about my society?
- What is lovely, noble, right, admirable and praise-worthy about this movie?

Principle #3: Act to Glorify God, Not to Cause Others to Stumble

"So whether you eat or drink or whatever you do, do it all for the glory of God. Do not cause anyone to stumble..."

This passage comes at the end of a discussion about how Christians should act with the new freedom that they have in Christ. Paul wrote that we are not to abuse this freedom nor should we ignore our fellow believers. Since not everyone will agree on all issues, care must be exercised to not needlessly offend a brother or sister in Christ. Whatever we do should be to God's glory, and for the promotion of unity in the Church.

So the Christian should be concerned for the feelings of others. The issue is not so much diet (eating or drinking), but concern for a fellow believer. And this principle applies to the topic of movies. Suppose you feel that a particular movie has positive value. Will your choice of a particular movie affect a friend? If this movie would offend someone, could you do without it? Or are you a "participating mature Christian" who chooses a lifestyle evangelism that goes to where people are rather than living a disinfectant-style of holiness by distant example?

But the concern we are to have for others extends beyond our immediate circle of friends to the world around us. We are to do "all" to the glory of God. Not only is the amount of money spent on seeing a movie something for the Christian to think about, but the hours that are spent in front of a movie or TV screen. Somehow our entire lives should reflect the glory of God. The money and time spent on entertainment are not necessarily "evil" or "wasted" (even the most faithful Christian needs to relax sometime). Yet Paul is clearly calling for a lifestyle that reflects God in everything, including entertainment. Once we say yes to entertainment, we enter decision-making for specific choices based on larger principles.

This raises more questions.

- Is God being glorified by what I see?
- What am I trying to convey to another by attending this movie with them? (More commonly termed "witnessing")
- Does this form of entertainment reflect my priorities as a Christian?
- How is this portion of my integrated lifestyle showing Jesus to others?

Principle #4: We Live Our Lives from God's Perspective (The Soon Return of Jesus)

"Since everything will be destroyed in this way, what kind of people ought you to be? You ought to live holy

Since not everyone will agree on all issues, care must be exercised to not needlessly offend a brother or sister in Christ.

2 Peter 3:11-12.

and godly lives as you look forward to the day God comes and speed His coming."

Peter, in this passage, looks forward to the end of the earth and the coming of the Lord. He has written to the Christian Church about false teachers that were teaching heresy about the Second Coming of Christ. Peter strongly attacks these people and then concludes the epistle with a description of what the Second Coming will be like. He focuses on the judgment and destruction that will take place, followed by a call for holy living because of these final events. According to Peter, we ought to be living a certain way in light of the Second Coming.

This principle is a challenge to examine our lives in the light of eternity. Let us look beyond what we see and know now. A focus on the end of this world ought to influence how we live. Our choice of movies as entertainment can be a reflection of what we believe and the priorities in our lives. It can become the focus of much of our time and energy to keep up with the latest in movies, whether they are on TV, in the theater, or on video.

Yet people whose lifestyle is holy and godly need to interact with the rest of the world. The incarnation needs to continue for Christ to reach the world through us. Perhaps we need to give greater focus to maintaining our Christian connection as we live on the battlefield of this world and support each other in our attempts to do so, especially in the light of Christ's soon return.

Paul is clearly calling for a lifestyle that reflects God in everything, including entertainment.

Our choice of movies as entertainment can be a reflection of what we believe and the priorities in our lives.

This end-time perspective leads to several questions.

• Am I willing to let the Second Coming affect my priorities? How does it affect my choice of movies to view.
• Is this movie a part of "godly" life?
• Am I a lone Christian, going undercover into the world, or am I clearly for Christ and supported by fellow Christians?
• How do I live a godly life in these last days?

Can You Live This Way?

It was so much easier simply to stay out of a building which happens to be a theater. But this convenient rule has been stripped of it's sufficiency, by technological advances alone. It's time we deal with personal guidelines for what we watch and identify biblical principles for entertainment in general. Hopefully, this chapter will provide input to assist people to live for Christ in our media-saturated society.

It was so much easier to stay out of a building.

And the Winner Is...

Stuart Tyner

Raise your hand if you've ever seen a movie.

Raise your hand if you've ever seen a movie.

Go ahead. If you're reading this chapter in a meeting, the speaker will just think you're seconding a point. If you're sitting in your home by yourself, no one will ever know. It doesn't matter whether you saw the movie in a theater or at home on your VCR or on a movie network on your cable system or in a Saturday night fund-raiser in your academy gym. If you've *ever* seen one *anywhere*, raise you hand.

Now think of that moment when a movie has just finished its concluding scene. The characters fade into the background. The music gets louder. The credits roll. And you stand up and say, "Boy, that was good!" or "What a wonderful ending" or "That was really stupid."

Fix in your mind that moment when the movie's over. Think about what you'd say after a really great movie. Now let me ask you a couple of questions.

Wouldn't it be fantastic if *Christians* had come up with the whole movie idea in the first place? Wouldn't it be unbelievably exciting if every day millions of people actually paid money to see movies about the advancement of the kingdom of God? To cheer the triumph of good over evil? To thrill at the love that motivates Christians? To come to a deeper understanding of the challenges of the spiritual life?

Wouldn't it be incredible if every movie left us saying, "Wow, God is good!" or "What a powerful witness that was!" or "I want to be just like those Christians!

A Few Great Movies

Actually, a few great movies like that have been scattered throughout the short history of film, an occasional triumph that made the hearts of believers soar. Some have even been notable for their excellence. The 1966 Academy Award winner *A Man For All Seasons* told the story of the courageous Christian leader Thomas Moore who refused to violate his conscience, even in the face of the death penalty. *Ben Hur,* the 1959 Oscar winning portrayal of a first-century Roman whose life was changed by the crucifixion of Jesus, continues to inspire people. *Chariots of Fire*, the story of Eric Liddell a determined

Wouldn't it be fantastic if *Christians* had come up with the whole movie idea in the first place?

...the most "viewed in the academy gym for a Saturday night program" movie of all time...

Christian athlete who held his commitment to God above his duty to his country and refused to take part in the Olympics on his Sabbath, won the 1981 Academy Award winner for best picture (and in the process may have become the most "viewed in the academy gym for a Saturday night program" movie of all time). Adventists were highly curious about the movie *A Cry in the Dark*, the story of the mysterious death of Adventists Michael and Lindy Chamberlain's child. And we shouldn't leave out the 1965 multiple-Oscar winner about the loving influence of a young Christian girl on a large family in Nazi-occupied Austria, *The Sound of Music,* a universal favorite.

Other movies throughout the years have made us think about the triumph of good over evil, including the epic *Gandhi*, the brutally honest yet uplifting *Schindler's List*,the riveting *Dead Man Walking,* and even the Disney animated megahit *The Lion King*.

Still other movies have brought us face-to-face with issues of importance to Christians who are trying to win people to Jesus. There was the portrayal of the awesome, transforming power of the little phrase "thank you" and the overwhelming realization of true love so eloquently pictured in *Sense and Sensibility*. And many were moved by the stunning depiction of forgiveness in the early scenes of *The Mission*, portrayed by native South American Indians graciously cutting the burden from the back of Mendoza, a mercenary slave trader. *Amadeus* raised the question of whether we serve God for His glory or for our own advancement. Racism was explored with gentle under-standing in *Driving Miss Daisy*. The power of grace to overcome the challenges of a dying religious community was beautifully addressed in *Babette's Feast*.

A few movies have been positive in their portrayal of Christianity. *Sister Act II* was a warm illustration of effec-tive youth ministry, acted out in the arena of sacred music, with a wonderful rendition of "His Eye is on the Sparrow" and a happy, contemporary performance of "Joyful, Joyful We Adore Thee." *Shadowlands* was full of the Christian insights and the awakened love of C. S. Lewis.

And has there ever been a more powerful reminder of how we need to be ready to heal the hurts of our neighbors or a more motivating illustration of why we need to understand the true nature of prayer than when little Jenny knelt in the corn field with Forrest Gump and asked God to make her a bird so she could fly away from her abusive father?

Not Much To Get Excited About

But there's another side of the coin. Each year about *450* movies are produced and distributed in the United States alone. Many of these graphically and often *sympa-thetically* depict all the grunge and horror and evil of this world in naked, blood-soaked, desensitizing realism. In comparison to the overwhelming list of movies that *fail* to honor God, the list of notable movies with uplifting and

A few movies have been positive in their portrayal of Christianity.

351

inspiring Christian themes really isn't a very big one, is it? Even when you add in several almost-accurate biblical epics, a handful of stunning nature films, a dozen or so delightful old musicals, a few fairly decent family films and a group of documentaries, historical movies, and films of social relevance—even then, you still don't have a long list of movies that Christians can really get excited about.

Christians *didn't* come up with the idea for this successful communications vehicle. It isn't Christians who are doing the bulk of movie communication today. Finding an uplifting movie with positive Christian themes can be a difficult undertaking.

A Different Set of Values

And that's why there is – or at least why there should be—a continuing concern about movies. The stark fact is that the great majority of movies (90 percent? 95 percent? 98 percent?) are paid for, written by, produced and directed by, acted in, and marketed and distributed by people who don't share your Christian values. Screenwriter Paul Schrader, who several years ago adapted the controversial *The Last Temptation of Christ* for the screen, calls the entertainment industry "an empty, soulless empire."[1]

Let me give you an example. It's been widely observed that almost all the sexual activity depicted or suggested in movies and on television takes place between people who are *not* married to each other. And of the small percentage

It isn't Christians who are doing the bulk of movie communication today.

[1]*Time*, June 12, 1995.

that happens *within* marriage, most of that activity is negative, often accompanied by violence and usually devoid of selfless, giving love. What message about marriage is conveyed, for example, by Fox TV's *Married With Children*? Movies that depict sexual activity among teenagers are generally mindless, sophomoric, and tasteless. Roger Ebert, the film critic, calls the entire genre of teenage sex comedies "a libel against a whole generation."[1]

There's another thing being libeled here: the Christian position on the rightful place of sexual activity. The biblical ideal of a loving, satisfying sexual relationship experienced in the commitment and security of a marriage is almost totally absent from the mass media.

Violence is another illustration of the work of a different set of values. When violence is depicted as evil (as in *Schindler's List*, the *Star Wars* movies, or even *Aladdin*), it can be a clarifying illustration in a discussion about the government of God. But that's *not* the way violence is usually portrayed in movies. The fact is violence is most often glorified, justified, and glamorized. It's done by the *good* guys, not just the bad ones. Think of the majority of the characters played by Schwartzenegger and Stalone, Bruce Willis and Mel Gibson and the martial arts heroes. Think about the war movies, the cowboy movies, and the movies about the inner city jungles. Violence is accepted as a way of life. It may be unfortunate, but it's necessary, they tell us.

But people are beginning to question those values.

[1] Andrea Midgett, "Reviews and Refuse: An Interview with 'At The Movies' Film Critic Roger Ebert," *Insight* (November 8, 1986), 12.

The biblical ideal of a loving, satisfying sexual relationship experienced in the commitment and security of a marriage is almost totally absent from the mass media.

Violence is most often glorified, justified, glamorized. It's done by the *good* guys, not just the bad ones.

[1] Caroline Miller, editorial, *Lears*, October, 1993.

[2] Speech in Los Angeles, CA, May 31, 1995.

[3] *Time*, June 12, 1995.

[4] Caroline Miller, Editorial, *Lears*, October 1993.

[5] Reginald Dodrill, *Violence, Values and the Media* (Sacramento, CA: Foundation for Change, 1993), 46.

Why should the behavior we denounce for our children be glorified by our biggest role models and brightest stars?

"Hollywood has gotten a whole generation of teenagers addicted to the exhilaration of violence," points out Caroline Miller in a magazine editorial.[1]

Republican Senator Bob Dole charges the American entertainment industry with "the mainstreaming of deviancy" and "the debasing of America."[2] Democratic Senator Paul Simon talks about our nation's "crisis of glamorized violence." And Bill Bradley, Democratic Senator from New Jersey, points out that the level of violence to which our youth are exposed "creates a sense of unreality about the finality, pain, suffering, and inhumanity of brutal violence."[3]

"Along with the adrenaline rush, the kids get slick, seductive lessons in cynicism and hostility. These pictures are blatantly bad for us, and Hollywood is pretending not to know it, just as the tobacco industry is still denying that smoking can be lethal."[4]

"Why should the behavior we denounce for our children," asks Reginald Dodrill, "be glorified by our biggest role models and brightest stars?"[5] Where is the positive portrayal of a person who follows the beatitude for peacemaking or who attempts to obey Christ's command to love our enemies?

Faced With Three Options

So what choices do we have about movies? Let's get practical about the subject. What decision are we going to make when we're planning a Saturday night social activity? What options do Christians have for an evening date with someone who wants to know what movie we'd like to see? It seems to me that we can go one of three directions:

- a. We can watch virtually anything.
- b. We can totally eliminate movies.
- c. We can be discriminating in what we see.

Option One: Watch Virtually Anything

To choose the first option and watch virtually anything, we would have to accept the argument that what we see and hear and concentrate on has little or no effect on our spiritual life. To accept that argument means to turn our back on biblical wisdom and good sense. It would surprise me if a practicing Christian would seriously propose choosing this option.

Paul reminds us that the life of the Spirit and the ways of the world "are in conflict with each other," Galatians 5:17 (NIV), and then lists the results of the conflict. The *Message Bible* paraphrases that list like this:

> "Repetitive, loveless, cheap sex; a stinking accumulation of mental and emotional garbage; frenzied and joyless grabs for happiness; trinket gods; magic-show religion; paranoid loneliness; cutthroat competition; all-consuming-yet-never-satisfied wants; a brutal temper; an impotence to love or be loved; divided homes and divided lives; small-minded and lopsided pursuits; the vicious habit of depersonalizing everyone into a rival; uncontrolled and uncontrollable addictions; ugly parodies of community. I could go on."[1]

It would surprise me if a practicing Christian would seriously propose choosing this option.

[1] Eugene H. Peterson, *The Message* (Colorado Springs, CO: NavPress, 1993), 398.

"Recovering alcoholics don't spend a lot of time in bars. Dieters don't eat breakfast at Dunkin' Donuts."

[1]Duffy Robbins, *The Big Screen* (Elgin, IL: David C. Cook Publishing, 1994), 11.

If that sounds to you like a description of contemporary movie scripts, then the conclusion has to be that those contemporary movies are at war with the Christ-like ideal we are striving to reach.

Youth ministry educator Duffy Robbins puts it this way:

"Recovering alcoholics don't spend a lot of time in bars. Dieters don't eat breakfast at Dunkin' Donuts. It's just not smart. In the same way, knowing what we know about the power of sight and the open doorway it provides for temptation, we must caution kids about the kinds of movies and videos they watch. The eye of the couch potato is an open door to temptation." [1]

Option Two: Don't Watch Anything

To choose the second option and not watch movies at all, not only means cutting out going to the theater, it also means not renting videos to watch at home, not watching movies on cable TV, not watching regularly scheduled network movies, and even refusing to see movies sponsored by our church or school. The *place* where you watch the movie is no longer the focus of this discussion (and frankly, it never was a good argument); it's the *content* of a movie that makes the difference. And this option suggests that the content of *all* movies is inappropriate for Christians.

Incidentally, a number of people choose this option and are perfectly happy about it. Not all people who *don't* watch movies can be characterized as religious fanatics or ultraconservatives or old people. Many have found this route full of the joy of extra time for family and friends, for reading and conversing, for playing, exercising, working, and studying.

This choice does seem to me, however, to be mired in an antitechnology bias that severely confuses the medium and the message. If we can appreciate the way Jesus often made His point by telling parables, if we can choose to *read* only the best stories in print, then surely we cannot suggest that because a parable or a story is now captured on film or videotape instead of on paper, it suddenly becomes inappropriate for Christians. Such a position is as untenable as suggesting that going to church on Sabbath morning in *a car* is less holy than making the trip in a horse-drawn carriage.

Option Three: Make Good Choices

To choose the third option and become discriminating viewers means making some serious commitments. This is the most difficult option, much more difficult to maintain than just choosing not to see anything. It's a choice made even more dangerous by our very real tendency to allow our standards to slip and watch today what we wouldn't have allowed ourselves to watch yesterday.

For a Christian to choose this option means raising a high standard and sticking to it, regardless of what friends

Not all people who *don't* watch movies can be characterized as religious fanatics or ultraconservatives or old people.

are watching on Saturday night. That's a challenging choice to make. But it's an achievable goal, similar to what we achieve when we choose the best reading material, and eat the foods that are the most nutritious. As David Adams reminds us, we primarily need "to learn how to make intelligent decisions and avoid movies with negative or destructive messages."[1]

Let's examine a few principles of action for the discriminating Christian viewer.

What Are Your Long-range Goals?

What is it that you want out of life? What do you dream of doing? Of becoming? Do your plans include being a growing Christian? Do you want your relationships with other people more and more to reflect the attitudes and values of Jesus?

If your goal is to be more Christlike, then make choices that will contribute to the fulfillment of that goal. Don't spend time in pursuits that lead you away from your established objectives, that encourage you, directly or indirectly, to abandon those goals, or that lead you to adopt someone else's goals for your life. Don't get bound into a relationship, even an entertaining one, with any world view that's dangerous to the good health of your Christian experience.

If a movie has a strong element of the occult, for example, or a fascination with the dark side, refuse to see

[1]David Adams, *Movies, Music, TV & Me* (Loveland, CO: Group Publishing, 1991), 22.

To become discriminating viewers means making some serious commitments. This is the most difficult option.

If your goal is to be more Christlike, then make choices that will contribute to the fulfillment of that goal.

it. If it contains graphic and glorified violence, stay away from it. If it portrays substance abuse as attractive and acceptable, avoid it. If it glamorizes promiscuity, give it a thumbs down. If it makes you less sensitive to suffering, run away from it. If it makes it easier to stereotype men or women, races or religions, rich or poor, Christians or nonbelievers, get up and walk out. If the profanity makes you less careful with your own language, just say no.

Christians evaluate all their activities, even their movies, in the light that shines from the face of Jesus.

Don't Be an Accidental Viewer

Never watch a movie unintentionally. If an advertisement or article about a new movie captures your attention, don't rush to the box office. That's what ads are supposed to do! Don't rent the first video whose sexy cover reaches out and grabs you. Don't flip through the channels of your TV and watch whatever happens to be on. Always conduct some research before you view.

Check the Ratings

The MPAA (Motion Picture Association of America) isn't a card-carrying member of the Christian community. But when they rate a movie R, there's a pretty good reason. Listen to this MPAA explanation of how the rating system came to be.

Don't get bound into a relationship, even an entertaining one, with any world view that's dangerous to the good health of your Christian experience.

Never watch a movie unintentionally.

359

"The emergence of the voluntary rating system [meant] the movie industry would no longer 'approve or disapprove' the content of a film, but we would now see our primary task as giving advance cautionary warnings to parents so that parents could make the decision about the movie going of their young children. That decision is solely the responsibility of parents...

The MPAA explanation goes on to describe exactly what each rating means:

"G: General Audiences – All ages admitted...

"Some snippets of language may go beyond polite conversation but they are common everyday expressions. No stronger words are present in G-rated films. The violence is at a minimum. Nudity and sex scenes are not present; nor is there any drug-use content.

"PG: Parental Guidance Suggested...

"The theme of a PG-rated film may itself call for parental guidance. There may be some profanity in these films. There may be some violence or brief nudity. But these elements are not deemed so intense as to require that parents be strongly cautioned beyond the suggestion of parental guidance. There is *no* drug use content in a PG-rated film...The PG rating... is thus an alert for examination of a film by parents before deciding on its viewing by their children.

"PG-13: Parents strongly cautioned. Some material may be inappropriate for children under 13...

"Any drug use content will initially require at least a PG-13 rating...If nudity is sexually oriented, the film

"...we would now see our primary task as giving advance cautionary warnings to parents..."

will generally not be found in the PG-13 category. If violence is too rough or persistent, the film goes into the R (restricted) rating. A film's single use of one of the harsher sexually derived words, though only as an expletive, shall initially require the Rating Board to issue that film at least a PG-13 rating. More than one such expletive must lead the Rating Board to issue a film an R rating, as must even one of these words used in a sexual context.

"R: Restricted, under 17 requires accompanying parent or adult guardian...

"An R-rated film may include hard language, or tough violence, or nudity within sensual scenes, or drug abuse or other elements, or a combination of some of the above, so that parents are counseled in advance to take this advisory rating very seriously. Parents must find out more about an R-rated movie before they allow their teenagers to view it.

"NC-17: No children under 17 admitted...

"The reasons for the application of an NC-17 rating can be violence or sex or aberrational behavior or drug abuse or any other elements which, when present, most parents would consider too strong and therefore off-limits for viewing by their children." [1]

[1] Jack Valenti, *The Voluntary Movie Rating System* (Motion Picture Association of America, 1994), 3-8.

Also get to know the National Coalition on Television Violence. In their newsletter they take apart a movie act by violent act. They'll also tell you the number of instances of smoking, drinking, and drug use in a movie. Write for their newsletter; their address is in the margin to the right.

Another helpful source is the United States Catholic Conference which publishes reviews based on moral and

National Coalition on Television Violence PO Box 2157 Champaign, IL 61820.

[1] See *The Family Guide to Movies and Video*, edited by Henry Herx and Tony Zaza (NY, NY: Crossroad Publishing, 1988).

Read in-depth reviews in newspapers and magazines that aren't published by the movie industry. Get acquainted with Siskel and Ebert or with any of the hundreds of movie critics around the country. Practically every local newspaper has a movie critic.

entertainment values and attaches their own rating system to every film they review.[1]

Of course, no rating system is perfect. You'll have to exercise your own judgment in the end. But getting all the information you can will help you make a better decision.

Get Acquainted with Siskel and Ebert

Read in-depth reviews in newspapers and magazines that aren't published by the movie industry. Get acquainted with Siskel and Ebert or with any of the hundreds of movie critics around the country. Practically every local newspaper has a movie critic. Critics broadcast on almost every local TV channel. And they contribute to regular columns in all types of magazines. Many, like Roger Ebert, (*Movie Home Companion*, published by Andrews and McMeel) publish collections of their reviews.

Find one or two critics with whom you consistently agree. Check their reactions to the movies you've found helpful to your Christian experience. Then look at what they have to say about a new movie you're interested in.

Unfortunately, from time to time even your favorite critic may endorse a new movie that will stomp all over your spiritual values. Always look for hints of this danger in his or her descriptions.

And the Winner Is . . .

In the end there should be a better reason to avoid movies than not going to a place where movies are shown. And there should be a better reason to watch a movie than there's nothing else to do on Saturday night.

If we had long ago recognized that *content*, not *place*, was the defining argument for good movies, no doubt we would have learned by now how to make good choices. If we knew how to make good choices, probably we'd do two things differently. First of all, we'd realize how few really good movies there are and we'd watch a lot less. And secondly, we'd appreciate and sincerely celebrate the few excellent ones.

In both instances, Christians would be the winners.

If we had long ago recognized that *content*, not *place*, was the defining argument for good movies, no doubt we would have learned by now how to make good choices.

363

Surely the church shouldn't show this type of movie!

Movies: Where or What?

Fred E. Crowell

It's our first Sabbath visiting in a church we will call home for the next few years. We slide into the pew, hoping to go unnoticed so we can see what's going on in our new congregation. Opening the bulletin, we find an insert advertisement for a movie tonight in the youth chapel. That's good, because we don't have any plans for the evening.

But wait a minute! This must be a misprint! It says here they are going to show *Honey, I Shrunk the Kids*. Wasn't that at the theaters recently? Surely the church shouldn't be showing this type of movie!

My thoughts race. We have two teenage daughters whom we wouldn't allow inside a theater to see this movie.

Now here it is in our youth chapel. Maybe this church shouldn't be our new home!

Finding other activities that night, we chose *not* to watch the movie.

Two months later, after settling into this conservative Midwestern university town, we rented *Honey, I Shrunk the Kids* for home viewing. We were pleasantly surprised. It did not have bad language, gross violence, or immorality. We felt a bit guilty about misjudging the film before having seen it or reviewing a critic's comments.

What's more, I felt compelled to reevaluate my position on movies. As a pastor, what should I tell my members? Some still strictly follow our *Church Manual*'s guidelines. Others have revised their standards to a more open position.

I realize that many Adventists would never see a movie at the theater; others select carefully and feel comfortable in the theater watching a "good movie." A growing number of church members are willing to see anything that comes across the silver screen.

How can we as pastors deal with this confusing situation? I examined an article in an issue of *Insight/Out* (see *And the Winner Is...* earlier in this section) which explores the three options available: (1) watch anything and everything; (2) totally eliminate all movies; and (3) be a discriminating viewer. Let's ponder each of these options in turn.

I felt compelled to reevaluate my position on movies.

Option One – Anything Goes

Option number 1–watching anything and everything–would fill the mind with profanity, immorality, and violence. This transgresses the counsel given in Philippians 4:8:

> "Finally, brethren, whatever things are true, whatever things are noble, whatever things are just, whatever things are pure, whatever things are lovely, whatever things are of good report, if there is any virtue and if there is anything praiseworthy–meditate on these things."

Obviously we must rule out the majority of offerings from the motion picture industry.

Michael Shaugnessy, writing on pornography, human mutilation, and psychological dysfunction, reports that the popular "slasher" films rely heavily on desensitization so that people exposed to NC17- and R-rated movies tend to moderate their attitudes toward women and violence. What justification should there be to watch *Rambo* movies, the *Nightmare on Elm Street* series, or movies such as *Henry and June*?

Perhaps the following advice from Ellen White about reading material could also apply to the standard we set for movies:

> "Avoid reading and seeing things which will suggest impure thoughts. Cultivate the moral and intellectual powers. Let not these noble powers become enfeebled and perverted by much reading of even storybooks."[1]

Obviously we must rule out the majority of offerings from the motion picture industry.

[1]Ellen G. White, *Testimonies for the Church,* vol. 2. (1870), 410.

Now, what about the less offensive PG or PG-13 movies, which are targeted especially toward teens? While the sex in these "innocent" films may not be as explicit, the language as strong, or the violence as flagrant, inherent problems remain.

Lynn Minton, who features a column in *McCall's* magazine entitled "Movie Guide for Puzzled Parents," had suggested when interviewed about teen movies, that with some films, it's not so terrible that a young person sees them. What's terrible is when certain values go unchallenged.

Referring to the current wave of movies portraying sexually active, happy-go-lucky adolescents, Minton concludes that he does find some of these movies upsetting because of the image they project. Everyone's jumping in and out of bed casually, and hardly anyone's left out or emotionally upset by the encounter. He says that this is not real life. In real life, people sometimes get hurt. What's more, a young person who isn't interested in casual sex could well get from these movies the idea that something was wrong with her or him.

We have here a principle for judging movies that goes much deeper than simply how much sex, violence, or bad language is used.

Option Two – Total Abstinence

For me personally, the *second option* – eliminating movie watching totally—would be ideal. There are just not

"What's terrible is when certain values go unchallenged."

many good films available, and a zero-tolerance approach would remove the burden of determining which are OK and which are not. Time spent watching movies could be more profitably invested with the Bible or enjoying a Christian book, or in family activities. This approach, however, would also ban Christian films shown at vespers and Saturday night socials.

The old arguments were clear: (1) Movie theaters are bad places, the atmosphere is evil, your angels won't go there;[1] (2) Movies, like books of fiction, with their professional actors, harm the mind and the soul.

Unfortunately, while these arguments may support the ideal standard, for the great majority of people, they don't provide a practical or realistic rebuttal to the movie-going dilemma.

• First, theaters themselves are obviously not bad places. The church even holds evangelistic meetings in them occasionally.

• Second, all pictures and professional actors aren't bad. What about Faith for Today's productions?

• Third, most people have televisions, and VCRs, so movies aren't limited to theaters.

• Fourth, should we protect our children from reality to the point that they will find themselves confused, bewildered, and unprepared to avoid drowning in its muck?

• Fifth, the "absolutely no movies" approach isn't helpful or realistic in the nineties. Most Adventists watch movies and aren't going to stop because of renewed church pressure.

[1] The myth that your angel will stay outside a theater if you choose to enter supposedly is based on a quotation from Ellen White. However in a letter dated February 2, 1944, Arthur White, Secretary of the Ellen White Publications, wrote a response to an inquiry about angels leaving us when we enter a theater. "Many of our workers are of the opinion that there is such a statement, but are unable to turn to it, and we have never been able to find it."

The Third Option: A Workable Answer

We are left with the *third* option: being selective about what we watch. Since many members, young and old, view movies at least at home, I suggest offering some criteria by which they can evaluate their video menu.

Consider the concept of movies from a Christian perspective. All of life can be regarded as a continuum, with the devil and total depravity on one end and Christ and complete perfection on the other. To start with, all of us need to evaluate where our lives stand on that continuum. Having honestly done that, we can ask ourselves some questions about entertainment questions that go deeper than such matters as immorality, violence, nudity, and profanity. We must concern ourselves with broader principles, such as these:

1. What is the difference between a Christian's view of the film and a secular person's concept?
2. Does this movie enhance or detract from my system of values?
3. How does the movie make me feel and why?
4. What is the main point of the movie?
5. Is the theme Christian or anti-Christian?
6. How does this movie affect my relationships with Christ, my family, and my everyday associates?

Consider the concept of movies from a Christian perspective.

369

Putting into Practice

Using the above questions, one Saturday night I led our church youth group in an experiment on critical movie evaluation. First we went to a video store, where I asked them to select a movie, PG-13, PG, or G. They spent at least 45 minutes looking, picking up movies, and putting them back. In the end they decided on one called *Three Fugitives*.

The main stars were Nick Nolte and Martin Short. It was about a father robbing a bank for money to keep his little girl in a special school. Since the death of her mother, the little girl hadn't spoken a word. As Short's character was robbing the bank, Nolte, having just gotten out of prison for robbing banks, was there depositing the money he had earned while in prison. Short took Nolte hostage. The police, however, accused the ex-con with masterminding the holdup.

The rest of the movie showed the physical and emotional struggle between Nolte, Short, and his daughter. The hostage was torn between his own desire for survival and his interest in helping Short escape to Canada, where he could live in peace with his daughter. It was Nolte who finally got the little girl to talk again when he threatened to abandon the father and daughter to fend for themselves. In the end both men were arrested, but Nolte was freed and helped care for the little girl.

The youth and their leaders enjoyed the movie. It was very touching despite a fair amount of profanity and some

> ...one Saturday night I led our church youth group in an experiment on critical movie evaluation.

violence. We evaluated it from the standpoint of my six questions, which I had discussed with them earlier.

In answer to the first question, they felt that secular people and Christians would view the film in much the same way – as an entertaining comedy. They felt the Christian, however, would be more sensitive to the bad language. For some, the swearing did attack their sense of values. Others, however, said they heard such language all the time so it didn't really bother them.

Despite the swearing and a lack of realism in some of its portrayals (such as the bank holdup scene), the youth judged the movie in general to be good. They endorsed what they considered its main point and overall theme, helping others. Nolte, for example, was willing to forget about himself to risk helping Short and his daughter. One person said it reminded her of the good Samaritan story in the Bible.

Because assisting others with life's problems harmonizes with Christian principles, the youth concluded that watching the movie enhanced their relationship with Christ. They did, however, express a concern that continual viewing of films with profanity, violence, or immorality might desensitize them and leave them less resistant to these things in their own lives. They felt this would happen to them even if the movie came out OK in the evaluating criteria. They acknowledged that prolonged exposure to negative ideas and themes would make them weaker as Christians and jeopardize their stand for God.

They endorsed what they considered its main point and overall theme, helping others.

371

They acknowledged that prolonged exposure to negative ideas and themes would make them weaker as Christians and jeopardize their stand for God.

In Summary

As a pastor I am concerned when my members watch a lot of movies, including those on television. There's no way I can compete with the entertainment industry when I step up to the pulpit. The razzle and dazzle of Hollywood can make church services seem dull and hard to sit through.

The situation would improve if we parents and church leaders took stock of what we and our young people watch. I trust that the guidelines suggested here will help toward that end.

Suggested Additional Resources

Adams, David, *Movies, Music, TV & Me* (Loveland, CO: Group Publishing, 1991).

Dodrill, Reginald, *Violence, Values, & the Media* (Sacramento, CA: Foundation For Change, 1993).

Evans, John, ed., *Preview Movie Morality Guide* (Richardson, TX) Semimonthly newsletter with Christian evaluations of recent PG and PG-13 rated movies. (214-234-0195).

Insight (special issue on entertainment) especially "Patrolling the Do-Not-Go Line" by Rick Moyers (November 8), 1986.

Hill, Geoffrey, *Illuminating Shadows: The Mythic Power of Film* (Boston: Shambhala Press), 1992.

Medved, Michael, *Hollywood vs. America: Popular Culture and the War on Traditional Values* (San Francisco:Harper Collins/ Zondervan), 1992. Also see interviews with Medved in the July 7, 1994 issue of *Adventist Review* and the Fall '94 issue of *Giraffe News.*

Media Update Newsletter by Al Menconi Ministries, PO Box 5008, San Marcos, CA 92069-1050. Phone 619-591-4696.

Movieguide: A Biblical Guide to Movies and Entertainment (Atlanta: Good News Communications) semimonthly newsletter with Christian evaluations of recent movies rated R and up. (404-237-0326).

Postman, Neal, *Amusing Ourselves to Death: Public Discourse in the Age of Show Business* (New York:Penguin Books), 1986.

Robbins, Duffy, and Duckworth, John, *The Big Screen, Reviewing Your Viewing of Videos and Movies* (Elgin, IL:David C. Cook Publishing, 1994).

Schultze, Auentin, J., *Redeeming Television* (Downers Grove, IL: InterVarsity Press), 1992.

Veerman, David, *Video Movies Worth Watching: A Guide for Teens* (Grand Rapids, MI:Baker Books), 1992.

Youthworker, Fall 1991. A Youth Specialties publication. The theme of this issue is "The Media," and two articles are especially helpful: "Christian Culture, Christian Media, and Your Students," by Brian Lang; and the "Youthworker Roundtable: Teaching an Entertained Generation."

Youthworker, Fall 1992. A Youth Specialties publication. The theme of the issue is "Culture." There are several helpful articles with good background information.

Zillmann, Dolf, Bryant, Jennings, and Huston, Alteha C., *Media, Children, and the Family: Social Scientific, Psychodynamic, and Clinical Perspectives* (Hillsdale, NJ:Lawrence Erlbaum Associates, Publishers), 1994.

Section 10
Thinking It Over

Section 10

Thinking It Over

Steve Case

At first glance, the easy answer to the question, How shall I live as a Christian when it comes to lifestyle issues? is "Do what Jesus would do." But that becomes more difficult when we are pressed to explain exactly what Jesus would do.

The tendency is to label our own inclinations, habits, or cultural conditioning as "what Jesus would do." Without realizing it, we create Jesus in our own image instead of being recreated in His. Although the Holy Spirit is active in the believer's life, it is dangerous to rely solely on a subjective experience for truth.

A more objective approach takes an authority outside oneself. For the believer, the Bible stands as an ideal source

Without realizing it, we create Jesus in our own image instead of being recreated in His.

of authority. Admittedly, even our understanding of Scripture gets colored by our cultural conditioning. But it certainly has greater potential for being objective than each person claiming to have a personal revelation from on High!

While God continues to reveal Himself through the Holy Spirit to others, He already has revealed Himself in the past in Scripture.[1] It's not an "either/or" proposition, but a "both/and" opportunity. It's not EITHER the Holy Spirit speaks to me OR I find it in Scripture. It's BOTH the Holy Spirit speaks to me AND I find it in Scripture.

The Body of Christ provides another check and balance for discovering truth. An individual might read into an understanding of the Bible a bias which is already present and identified as a personal message from the Holy Spirit. But God continues to work through His Body, the Church, including the identification and acceptance of truth. "Lone Ranger Christians" will die without a connection to the vine, which includes contact and blending with the rest of the attached branches.

The rich diversity of ethnicity and culture within the Seventh-day Adventist Church provides a golden opportunity to separate one's cultural biases from one's identification of principles from Scripture. But we must engage in dialogue with those whose perceptions differ from our own to reap these potential benefits. We must challenge one another to identify biblical principles and explore various applications of those principles for our given time and culture. Once again, the activity of the Holy Spirit is critical.

[1] Hebrews 1:1-2.

The rich diversity of ethnicity and culture within the Seventh-day Adventist Church provides a golden opportunity.

376

A Matter of Identity?

In the past, many loyal Adventists have felt threatened by challenges to traditional interpretations of lifestyle issues. Perhaps some, after reading all or part of this book, will experience the same feelings. You may be asking, "If you take away our peculiar lifestyle standards, what makes us Adventists?" Such a question demonstrates a potential identity crisis.

Adventist lifestyle provides observable differences from other religions. At times it is convenient to single out an Adventist from the crowd because "they look like an Adventist." The segregation of Adventists from others has kept us in a neat sociological group. This lifestyle has shaped the environment for those who grew up in the church.

As the tidy isolated bastion faced rapid technological advances, and tremendous growth outside North America, lifestyle questions naturally surfaced. Some have maintained their Adventist traditions, especially in Adventist institutions.

The negative result of perpetuating an outwardly Adventist lifestyle has been the tendency to become spiritually complacent. It has become the Adventist identity. If this identity is based on lifestyle rather than Jesus Christ, we are guilty of idolatry, clinging to an anti-Christ rather than Jesus Christ. For those seeking outward signs of who a true follower of Jesus is, Christ's words, "by this shall all

The potential identity crisis: "If you take away our peculiar lifestyle standards, what makes us Adventists?"

377

[1]John 13:35; see also verse 34.

[2]See Roger Dudley, *Passing On the Torch* (Hagerstown, MD: Review and Herald Publishing, 1986), 66.

If our identity is based on these lifestyle issues rather than on Jesus Christ, then we are guilty of idolatry, clinging to an anti-Christ in place of Jesus Christ.

[3]Hebrews 11:1.

[1]See Ellen White, *Steps to Christ* (Mountain View, CA: Pacific Press, n.d.), 105.

know you are my disciples, if you love one another," provides an answer.[1]

Some wish we would accept what has been handed down rather than ask "Why?" But our culture provides opportunities for questioning, and Adventists promote education which fosters it. Because formal operational thinking creates the need for fresh questioning and dialogue, we must not only allow but also promote and encourage questions.[2]

Developing Faith

In fact, questioning does not reflect a loss of faith, but it is an indication of developing faith. When a person does not question, it may be an indication of childish or nonexistent faith. The obvious or observable requires no faith. The fact that the sun rises (and the earth rotates each day) requires no faith. But believing God is behind the certainty of that fact does require faith. At some point, a person needs to take a "leap of faith" based on adequate evidence but not beyond questioning, for "faith is the substance of things hoped for, the evidence of things not seen."[3] While God gives sufficient evidence upon which to base our faith, He also leaves room for doubt.[4] A good dose of questioning enhances faith and refines the evidence for trust in God. Restricting or inhibiting questions does not promote trust.

Some might be concerned by what others may think if we accept people's lifestyle which diverge from agreed-upon principles. It's a logical question. *What will others think?* What if they begin to think that we accept others?

378

What if we get accused of eating with tax collectors and sinners? If we do, we're in great company.[1]

The Freedom of Life In Christ

To close, please take to heart the following paraphrased passage from Galatians 5:

> Christ has made us free. Now make sure that you stay free and don't get all tied up again in the chains of slavery to Adventist dos and don'ts. Listen to me, for this is serious: if you are counting on Adventist dos and don'ts to make you right with God, then Christ cannot save you.
>
> Christ is useless to you if you are counting on clearing your debt to God by holding to these lifestyle issues; you are lost from God's grace.
>
> But we by the help of the Holy Spirit are counting on Christ's death to clear away our sins and make us right with God. And we to whom Christ has given eternal life don't need to worry about whether or not we are politically correct in our adherence to the SDA lifestyle traditions; for all we need is faith working through love.
>
> You were getting along so well. Who has held you back from following the truth? It certainly wasn't God, for he is the one who called you to freedom in Christ. But it only takes one wrong person among you to infect all others.

[1]See Luke 7:29-47, especially verse 34.

Questioning is not a loss of faith, but an indication that one's faith is developing.

379

Christ is useless to you if you are counting on clearing your debt to God by holding to these lifestyle issues; you are lost from God's grace.

When you are guided by the Holy Spirit you need no longer force yourself to obey Adventist lifestyle issues.

[1] Based on Galatians 5:1-2,4-9,13-18,24-26.

Dear brothers and sisters, you have been given freedom: not freedom to do wrong, but freedom to love and serve each other. For the whole Law can be summed up in this one command: "Love others as you love yourself." But if instead of showing love among yourselves you are always critical and intolerant, watch out! Beware of ruining each other.

I advise you to obey only the Holy Spirit's instructions. He will tell you where to go and what to do, and then you won't always be doing the wrong things your evil nature wants you to do. For we naturally love to do evil things that are just the opposite from the things the Holy Spirit tells us to do; and the good things we want to do when the Spirit has his way with us are just the opposite of our natural desires.

These two forces within us are constantly fighting each other to win control over us, and our wishes are never free from their pressures. When you are guided by the Holy Spirit, you need no longer force yourself to obey Adventist lifestyle issues.

Those who belong to Christ have nailed their natural evil desires to his cross and crucified them there. If we are living now by the Holy Spirit's power, let us follow the Holy Spirit's leading in every part of our lives.[1]

Appendix A
Christian Freedom

Some activities clearly are forbidden by God in the Bible. Jesus elaborated on several such major commands in the Sermon on the Mount. But where is the text that says movies are okay or not okay? What text deals with whether or not one should/can chew gum? We are responsible for understanding and applying biblical principles for specific behaviors. Here is an exercise that focuses on application of biblical principles. See what you think is, or is not permissible based on your reading of Scripture. Mark the following activities according to their proper classification: (+) for permissible and (-) for not permissible.

____Attending a play

____Speaking in tongues

____Buying insurance

____Wearing a necklace

____Mixed swimming

____Privately watching a video

____Listening to "Christian rock"

____Listening to jazz

____Using wine in cooking

____Eating pork

____Eating vegeburgers

____Eating fish

____Bicycling on Sabbath

____Boating on Sabbath

____Listening to rock music

____Wearing a wedding ring

____Wearing an engagement ring

____Attending a theater

____Wearing a two-piece swimsuit

____Wearing an expensive watch

____Drinking wine in moderation

____Going to a psychiatrist

____Playing a guitar in church

____Eating beef

____Playing football on Sabbath

____Taking a walk on Sabbath

____Playing frisbee on Sabbath

____Waterskiing on Sabbath

____Buying a lottery ticket   ____Ballroom dancing

____Aerobic dancing   ____Disco dancing

Questions:

• What do you base your decision upon?

• Do other Christians view it the same way as you do?

• How do you explain that sincere Christians disagree on some of these issues?

Appendix B

Summary of Biblical Principles for SDA Lifestyle Issues

Discussing Standards

1. The way of God and the way of the world are opposites. 1 John 2:15-17.

2. The spirit of the law exceeds the letter of the law. Matthew 5.

3. Don't purposefully offend others; and quit tripping over every little thing. 1 Corinthians 8:9-13; Matthew 15:12-14; 1 Peter 2:6-8.

4. Be accepting and tolerant, especially to those weak in faith. Romans 14:1-4.

Thinking about standards.

Dance

1. Dance is a component of divine worship. 2 Samuel 6:14; 1 Chronicles 15:29; Psalm 149:3; Psalm 150:4.

2. Dance is an appropriate expression of community joy. Judges 11:34; 1 Samuel 18:6; Matthew 11:17; Luke 7:32; Luke 15:25.

3. Dance should praise no other god but God/Yahweh/ the LORD. Exodus 32:19.

4. Dance should not promote inappropriate sexual arousal. 1 Corinthians 10:7-8; Matthew 14:6 and Numbers 25:3 by implication.

5. Appropriate dance is dance in which God is invited as a witness and participant. 1 Corinthians 10:31.

Thinking About Dancing.

Music

1. Intention. 1 Samuel 16:7; Psalm 150; Romans 14:1-4.

2. Music creates and/or expresses a presence that must be evaluated. 1 John 4:1-3; Philippians 1:15-18.

3. The lyrics communicate a message. Philippians 4:8.

4. Music communicates a message. It affects and/or expresses one's mood/feelings. 1 Samuel 16:23; 2 Chronicles 20:13-22.

Thinking About Music.

Sex

1. Commitment. 1Thessalonians 4:3; 1 Corinthians 6:12-13,19-20.

Thinking About Sexuality.

2. Control. Galatians 5:13; 1 Thessalonians 4:4.

3. Contrast. Romans 6:12; 1 Thessalonians 4:4-5; 1 John 2:15-17.

4. Consideration. 1 Corinthians 6:16; 1 Thessalonians 4:6a.

5. Consequences. 1 Corinthians 6:18; Galatians 5:13; 1 Thessalonians 4:6; James 1:13-15.

6. Capability. 2 Samuel 11:2-4; Proverbs 5; 1 Thessalonians 4:7-8; James 1:13-15.

Jewelry

1. Modesty. 1 Timothy 2:9-10.

2. Humans are made in the Image of God. Genesis 1:27,31; 1 Corinthians 6:19-20; Matthew 25:40,45; 1 John 4:11-12; 2 Corinthians 5:18-21; John 4:21-24; 1 Corinthians 3:16; Hebrews 2:6-8.

3. Pride is part of our sinful nature. Isaiah 14:12-14; Ezekiel 28:12-17; Daniel 4:28-33,37.

4. A stewardship of simplicity. Matthew 6:19-21,24,31-34; Luke 6:20; 8:14; 12:15-21; 18:22-27; James 2:15-17.

Thinking About Jewelry.

5. Inner beauty to exceed outer beauty. 1 Peter 3:3-4; Proverbs 11:22; 31:30.

Sabbath

1. Worship. The Sabbath provides a special opportunity to remember the Creator and to spend time praising

God for the gift of life and all that comes with it. Exodus 20:8-11; Hebrews 4:9-10.

2. Fellowship. The Sabbath presents Adventists with the time to experience the kind of Biblical fellowship or close Christian friendship that the Bible describes as being absolutely essential for maturity in Christ - Galatians 6:1-3; Hebrews 10:25.

3. Rest - Literally, to cease from one's regular activities—a mental, physical, social, and spiritual change of pace which supplies a weekly balancing, stabilizing effect that promotes the greatest human health and happiness. Exodus 20:8-11; Genesis 2:2; Isaiah 58:13-14; Hebrews 4:9-10.

4. Service. One of the great purposes of the Sabbath is to benefit those who truly need help; so Sabbath keeping should focus on meeting human needs. Matthew 12:9-14; Mark 2:27-28; John 9:13-16; John 5:1-18.

Thinking About The Sabbath.

Will of God

1. God wants people willing to include him in their lives. Romans 8:29; Romans 12:1-2; Ephesians 1:11-12; Ephesians 2:10.

2. Evaluate one's abilities and watch God reveal additional ones to us. Matthew 25:14-29; 1 Corinthians 12; 1 Samuel 17:38-40.

3. Make choices that are consistent with God's re-

**Thinking About
God's Will**

vealed will in Scripture. 1 Samuel 16:1-3; Isaiah 8:20; Jeremiah 2:13.

4. View yourself as part of God's mission. Luke 2:51; Romans 12:3-8.

5. God has equipped us to make decisions. Deuteronomy 8:10-20; 1 Samuel 26:23-24; 1 Kings 12:13-16.

6. Watch for indications of God's providence. Acts 5:17-20; Acts 10:28; Proverbs 3:5-6.

Alcohol

1. God is for life, including the quality of life. Alcohol is a major killer in our industrialized, hi-tech society in contrast to the agrarian society of the biblical era. Exodus 20:13; John 10:10; Ephesians 6:12-13.

2. God offers his Spirit in contrast to spirits. God desires positive benefits for us. Be filled with His Spirit which offers security and steadfastness without physical and moral side effects. Matthew 5:13-16; Ephesians 5:18; Acts 2:15-18.

Thinking about Alcohol

3. Our physical health does not depend on wine. Any medicinal benefits have been replaced by knowledge of health and hygiene. The "benefits" associated with moderate drinking are either lopsided or reproducible with unfermented grape juice (resveratrol). 3 John 2, 1 Corinthians 6:15,19-20.

4. God presently speaks to his people through an active Spirit of prophecy. Joel 2:28-29; Acts 2:14-21; Romans 12; 1 Corinthians 12; Ephesians 4:7-16; Revelation 12:17 cf. Revelation 19:10.

Movies

1. By beholding we are changed. Christians are transformed into Christlikeness through the renewing of their minds in contrast to being conformed to this world. 2 Corinthians 3:18, Romans 12:1-2.

2. Garbage in, garbage out; Christlikeness in, Christlikeness out. Philippians 4:8, 2 Peter 1:2-8.

3. Act to glorify God, not to cause others to stumble. The freedom Christ gives enables us to choose for the glory of God in all we do. 1 Corinthians 10:31-32.

4. We live our lives from God's perspective. The reality of Christ's imminent return affects our priorities. 2 Peter 3:11-12, 1 John 3:1-3.

Thinking About Movies.

For those who listen!

Cassette tape series of *Shall We Dance: Rediscovering Christ-Centered Standards* by Steve Case is available for $29. (Postage included)

Write to:
Piece of the Pie Ministries 3732 California Ave., Carmichael, CA 95608.

Scripture Index

Index

Shall We Dance

Rediscovering Christ-Centered Standards

C

D

Drug(s), 317; 322-324
  use, 314
Drunk, 306; 311
  drivers, 315
  driving, 315; 320
Drunkenness, 299; 309

E

Education, 348; 378
Eliezer, 189
Elijah, 220
Entertainment, 59; 7374; 82; 180; 335-336; 345-347; 352
  decisions, 337
Environment, 234-235; 258
Ephesian(s), 311
Ethic(s), 155; 165
Evangelist(s), 68; 120; 225; 230; 248
Eve, 146; 220; 334
Evil(s), 333; 349; 350; 380
  influence, 334

F

Faith, 220; 228; 303; 378
Feel (ings), 228; 344; 385
Fellowship, 274; 276; 279; 281; 286; 292; 295-296; 387
Female(s), 145; 1480149; 172; 188-189; 221; 318; 3209
Fermentation, 307
Fermented, 305-306; 308-309
  grape, 305
  grape juice, 305-306; 312
  wine, 309
Fetal Alcohol Syndrome (FAS); 320
Film(s), 120; 335; 3340-341; 352-353
  critic, 353
First fruits, 306-307

G

H

L

M

V

W

Y